GLASGOW:
GOING FOR A SONG

City Cultures

Series Editor: Tony Lane

As attention shifts away from Europe's old nation states and towards its cities and regions, this innovative new series explores the social and cultural character of Europe's great cities. A well informed grasp of the astonishing variety of urban cultures is vital for an understanding of the emerging new Europe. Before we can look forward to the transformation of our nation states we need a better understanding than is currently available of the undiminished potency of ideas of nation and national identity. A challenging approach to this problem can be found in an unravelling of the forces that have created the richly varied cultural characters of Europe's cities, cities which inspire intense loyalties among their peoples.

Already published:

Tony Lane, *Liverpool: Gateway of Empire*

Forthcoming:

Maurice Goldring, *Belfast: From Loyalty to Rebellion*

Glasgow:
Going for a Song

Seán Damer

LAWRENCE & WISHART
LONDON

Lawrence & Wishart Limited
144a Old South Lambeth Road
London SW8 1XX

First published 1990

Photoset in North Wales by
Derek Doyle & Associates, Mold, Clwyd.
Printed and bound in Great Britain by
Billings & Sons Ltd, Worcester.

Contents

'It is men who make the city, and not walls or ships with no men inside them.'

Thucydides: *History of the Peloponnesian War*, Penguin Classics, (trans. Rex Warner), 1972, p. 530.

For my gallus daughters,
Mairi, Anna and Jane

Preface

Glasgow has inspired a massive literature of both fact and fiction and shows every sign of continuing to do so, I am happy to say. Its inhabitants are ferociously proud of their city, yet amazingly warm and open to any outsider who is making a serious effort to understand it. I have benefited over the years from innumerable discussions, conversations and heated arguments about the place from my first encounters with my original sponsor, Emmet Price, an unbeatable guide, to my continuing dialogue with George Hunter about Glasgow in fiction.

There cannot be any other city in Britain, indeed Europe, with such a talented cast of poets, novelists and dramatists. Glasgow is well served by its writers. But my opinion has always been that the non-fiction books about Glasgow are badly wanting. Many of these are written by academics and are prone to a recital of the same antiquarian details from the same secondary sources. Many of them don't even bother to discuss the Glasgow working class, none of them get anywhere near doing justice to that remarkable group of people, and some of them are downright patronising. So my intention in this book was to write explicitly about working-class life, work, culture and politics, for these experiences are what made this city unique. This book then, is a contribution to what has come to be called 'People's History', that is, history from the bottom up. This is not to deny that Glasgow's middle class had a hand in its history; it did. Nor is this middle class absent from these pages. My point is that in the making of Glasgow its working class was much more important than its middle class, which has had far more than its fair share of attention in the previous literature. Apart from anything else, the intelligence and wit of Glasgow's working people are simply without parallel.

Many people have read all or part of this book, or otherwise offered me assistance. My thanks to George Hunter, Tony Fallick, Elspeth King, Bill Hughes, Gerry Mooney, Charlie Johnstone, Irene Sweeney, Ian Russell, Kenneth MacDonald, Gerry Finn, Iain Fraser, Fiona Byrne-Sutton, Andrew Jackson, Keith Burgess, Brian Martin and Chris Harvey. They are not responsible for the opinions and interpretations proffered in this book.

My particular thanks – again! – to Joe Fisher and his staff in the Glasgow Room of the Mitchell Library; Andrew Jackson and his staff in the Strathclyde Regional Archives; and Elspeth King and Michael Donnelly in the People's Palace Museum. It would be impossible to find a more courteous, knowledgeable and helpful set of librarians, archivists and curators anywhere in the country.

I would also like to acknowledge endless assistance from my editor at Lawrence and Wishart, Stephen Hayward. He has been a model of comradely chivvying, perceptive editing, useful suggestions and general encouragement. Similarly, Tony Lane, general editor of this series, has been most helpful with intelligent and pithy editorial comments. It has been a pleasure to work with them both. A special thanks is also due to my daughter Mairi, who took the pure brilliant cover photograph. I am also grateful to Professor Thomson and Margaret Thomson Davis for permission to quote from their books and to Mike Shand for the maps.

Finally, a great big huge thanks to Kathleen Clark and Mae Donaghey who cheerfully word-processed endless drafts of this book. Their Glasgow good humour and sensible suggestions have been magic, by the way.

Seán Damer,
Glasgow,
January 1990

Introduction

In the summer of 1968 I graduated in sociology from the University of Edinburgh and immediately moved to Glasgow to start work as an Assistant Planning Officer in the Corporation's Planning Department. I knew little or nothing about Glasgow. To me, it was a vast, dirty, unfathomable tenemental city whose denizens were unpredictably violent. The only two places I can remember being in in Glasgow before 1968 are Hampden Park and the State bar. This was a momentous time to come to Glasgow. The Corporation was busy knocking the tenement city down and the vision of the future was already to be seen in the Gorbals high-rise flats. It was a vision which I and other young graduates in the Planning Department found distinctly alarming.

I had brought one sociological preoccupation with me from Edinburgh to Glasgow: this was a fascination with studies of working-class communities and culture which I had derived from the one course at Edinburgh which had really excited me – urban sociology. This was taught with enthusiasm and panache by a Londoner, Brian Elliott, whose anthropological training had left him with an abiding interest in working-class culture. Brian himself had taught at the University of Glasgow before going to Edinburgh, and had also remarked the absence of a literature on the city's working class. In retrospect, I can see that my interests also reflected a rejection of the sanitised culture of the bungaloid suburbia of Edinburgh in which I grew up. As a child, I was always much happier visiting my grandparents in working-class inner-city Tollcross.

As disquiet about high-rise, high-density building

grew, and protest from those about to be 'comprehensively redeveloped' increased, it is hardly surprising that I became more and more interested in those working-class communities which were being wiped off the map of Glasgow: the Gorbals, the Calton, Townhead, Cowcaddens, Govan, Springburn – an endless list. I began to look for the anthropological or sociological literature which would tell me something about these communities; I am still looking. It is a fact that sociology students at the University of Glasgow can find a more extensive literature on the slum-dwellers of San Juan or Harlem than they can of their own city. An ethnography of Glasgow working-class life is conspicuous by its absence, a damning indictment of the practice of anthropology and sociology in the city's two universities.

In any event, I raved on about my preoccupations to my friend, Glasgow butcher Emmet Price, whom I had got to know while a student at Edinburgh. (The fact that Emmet is now a lecturer at the Bell Technical College in Hamilton tells you something about butchers from Anderston.) 'Urban sociology,' said Emmet, 'I'll give you urban sociology!' So, one Friday evening shortly after my arrival in Glasgow we met and Emmet took me right down Argyle Street from where he lived up near the Kelvingrove Museum. We dodged up and down pends, into back-courts, through alleys, with Emmet providing a running commentary. The most striking of the many memories I have of that trip is of four men playing cards on top of an orange box in a back-court; it was a serious game, with whole wage-packets involved. I also remember the squalor of the backs, and the racket coming from the tenements: singing, fighting, children screaming, televisions and wirelesses blaring, a persistent cacophany. And all the while Emmet was talking of his childhood in Anderston, the vicious sectarianism, the struggle to keep one's head above water, the rotten housing.

Eventually we arrived at the Shandon Bells pub. (To anyone of Irish extraction this name is of immediate significance: 'The Bells of Shandon' is a famous ballad from Cork.) In we went. As we stood at the bar, a wee man sitting on a bar-stool greeted Emmet. He was the ultimate Glasgow bauchle, an elderly man of indeterminate age, with a face like Flanders and a bonnet perched at an unlikely angle on his head. He was all of five foot four inches. 'Haw big man,' he said, 'Who's the boay?'

'This is my friend Seán from Edinburgh,' said Emmet, and continued with an elegant introduction I remember to this day. 'A Seán tae a Wullie, a Wullie tae a Seán.' Wullie shook my hand.

'Another fucking Fenian, eh, Emmet?' said the Wullie. I was struck dumb.

'Very good,' said Emmet, 'as a matter of fact Seán was in the army.'

'Ahm no feart,' says Wullie, looking me up and down with contempt, 'no even o the Wild Linoleum Boy!'

As I fell about the place laughing, Emmet explained my interests to Wullie, and from then until closing time I listened to the two of them swop stories about Anderston in the bad old days. I was absolutely spell-bound; I had never heard such vivid, witty, and pungent language in my life. I was hooked. In the morning I applied for my naturalisation papers. I've never looked back since.

1 Images and Realities

I have been collecting media representations of Glasgow since 1968, and it was not long before I realised that something systematic was going on. From the *New Statesman* to the *Guardian* and the *Sunday Times* to the BBC, not to mention the tabloids, a coherent imagery of this city was presented, an imagery whose parameters were so fixed that they constituted a stereotype. The stereotype was of a filthy, slum-ridden, poverty-stricken, gang-infested city whose population consisted of under-sized, incomprehensible, drunken, foul-mouthed, sectarian lumpenproletarians who were prone to hit each other with broken bottles and razors without warning. To make matters worse, Glaswegians were infected with the Red Peril; Glasgow was a robustly socialist city. Its people actually believed in all that stuff about the Red Clyde. This imagery was also produced and reproduced by some Glasgow writers and academics in a series of books of which *No Mean City* is the classic.[1]

First published in 1935, and reissued no less than 27 times with more than half a million copies in print, *No Mean City* was the result of collaboration between an unemployed baker from the Gorbals, Alexander McArthur, and an English journalist, H. Kingsley Long. The former had written his memoirs which the latter then tried to put into shape. It is hardly surprising that this 'ghosting' resulted in a badly plotted and ill-written book. It tells the story of the rise and fall of Johnnie Stark, a young man from the Gorbals who becomes a gang-leader and 'razor king' – what would now be called a street fighter. The novel is notorious for its graphic descriptions of squalor and violence in the Glasgow of the

5

1920s. It not only inspired a series of poor imitations, but also sells well to this day. In spite of the fact that there are over 300 novels dealing with Glasgow, it – or its title, as is astutely observed by Moira Burgess, the bibliographer of the Glasgow novel – is *the* Glasgow novel inevitably quoted by outsiders.[2] It is small wonder that Glasgow became Britain's ghetto, and that people from Ealing to Edinburgh believed that it was populated by dangerous animals.

This imagery was reinforced by major television 'documentaries' in recent times, like the notorious 1977 BBC television film about the Lilybank housing scheme in the city's East End. In this programme academics Kay Carmichael and David Donnison succeeded in the supreme achievement of reducing a Glasgow working man to tears in front of the nation through their arrogant and patronising behaviour. More recently, in 1983, there was the BBC2 series, 'Glasgow: Portrait of a City'. Whatever the intentions of the makers of this series, there can be no doubt that yet another series of totally negative images of the city was presented to viewers. Glasgow had such a bad image nationally that it repelled potential industrial and commercial investment, as the Toothill Report had observed as early as 1961, pin-pointing poor local housing as a key factor: 'There remain the bleak areas of roughcast boxes in many housing estates...'[3] Many local authority and Scottish Office reports have made the same point since.

This imagery was to change dramatically. On 7 August 1988 Glasgow made the front cover of the *Sunday Times* colour supplement. The legend was: 'Can This Be Glasgow?' Instructively, the twelve photographs on the cover were of places or buildings, not people. Alan Massie's article extolled the 'Glasgow's Miles Better' image. What had happened in the five years since the BBC2 series to reverse the old stereotype? The short answer is that the image-builders had been at work. The long answer is what this book is all about. In the meantime, a striking iconography of this change in image is easily accessible. These are the photographs of the 'old' Glasgow taken by Oscar Marzaroli in the 1950s and 1960s, and the 'new' Glasgow taken by Colin Baxter in the 1980s, and both widely available as postcards. Marzaroli's pictures are in black-and-white. The city is grey, rainy, smoky, gritty. There are many ordinary Glasgow people doing ordinary Glasgow things: women in the steamie, a couple of winos with their vino collapso, kids playing in the street, football fans at the match, CND demonstrations. There is a sense of vitality to Marzaroli's photographs, and a strong sense of commitment to his subjects. Colin Baxter's pictures are in colour. They are soft, dreamlike, sunny, pretty, and contain very few people. Even his picture 'Partick – Rain', which has some people in it, is very pretty. There is an air of detachment about them all, and a slight air of unreality. They mirror precisely the miles-better Glasgow, while Marzaroli's pictures are the ones which to me immediately signify this city. His photographs are in good faith, Baxter's in bad faith.

In what did the change of image consist, precisely? Before answering this question, it is essential to remember the reality underlying the images. What the image-builders were trying to do was to sell the city's investment potential. This was and is the underlying rationale. This is what the Glasgow Garden Festival was all about. The images were the bait, as is made perfectly plain in a quotation from the glossy promotional prospectus, 'Glasgow Action: The First Steps', of June 1987:

> Environmental enhancement without self-sustaining development in the city's economy would not retain and develop human talent. But progress in the areas of economic opportunity was unlikely without enchancement of the city's environment and image. These would be essential if companies were to be persuaded to locate in Glasgow, if visitors were to be attracted, and if skilled individuals were to choose to live and work in the city.[4]

What the image-builders subsequently did was very clever. The first major step was the coining of the slogan 'Glasgow's Miles Better' by an advertising agency in

1984, and the hard-sell campaign by the city's Lord Provost Michael Kelly.[5] Then they went on to sell two vital attributes of Glasgow: its beauty and location, and its people. Beauty? Yes, beauty. Glasgow is a city of fine Victorian architecture, and great charm and elegance. It has its Charles Rennie Mackintosh to compare with the Gaudi of Barcelona or the Loos of Vienna. In this sense, it is a truly European city. Glaswegians themselves have always known this; they could see through the dirt and the grime. They knew that while all slums might have been tenements, not all tenements are slums. But the English (and the planners) did not know this, as the visual master-status of Glasgow was one of slums and desolation. When the tenements and older office and business-blocks began to be stone-cleaned in the 1970s, the elegance of their lines became visible to outsiders, and scales fell from their eyes. Ten years later they fell at an even faster rate when they discovered that a spacious West End or South Side tenement flat was available at a fraction of the cost of its equivalent in London. And that there were good restaurants, pubs, parks, galleries and theatres in the city. And that in half-an-hour you could be at Loch Lomondside or sailing on the Clyde, or in one hour you could be heading up Ben More, or that in two hours you could be lost in Glencoe. This recognition of the beauty of Glasgow and its surrounds was given a boost by the fine film which BBC television made of the 1983 Marathon in the city. It showed vistas of elegant parks, fine tenements, the Clyde and Kelvin rivers and the surrounding countryside. All of which had been known to Glaswegians for a century at least.

And then there were the people. Besides being congenitally friendly, Glaswegians are among the best talkers in the world, the most articulate debaters, the wittiest story-tellers, the best one-liners, the best purveyors of what they themselves call the 'lightning repartee'. But like Liverpudlians, with whom they have much in common, Glaswegians are fiercely independent, no respecters of status, no takers of prisoners. Life in the heavy manufacturing industries and working-class neighbourhoods of Glasgow has been too tough to permit of a phoney sentimentality. Thus the culture of its workers, male and female, is one which contains a contradictory mix of unbelievable warmth and friendliness and incredible combativeness. You will be approached democratically, but you are expected to hold your own.

Possibly the first glimpse of the attributes of Glaswegians seen at a national level was Stanley Baxter's immortal television series 'Parliamo Glasgow'. But ironically, this series perhaps helped to reproduce the esoteric aspects of the city's image, a place where the natives routinely said 'Erraperraweeherrizgaundoonraroad' – glottal stops and all. It was a younger generation of entertainers and actors and writers and musicians and poets who convinced outsiders of the reality of the warmth and wit of Glaswegians. I am thinking of entertainers like Billy Connolly, actors like Bill Paterson, Terry Neason and Robbie Coltrane, writers and poets like Liz Lochhead, William McIlvanney, James Kelman, Alasdair Gray, John Byrne and Tom Leonard, pop musicians like Jim Kerr of Simple Minds, Eddi Reader of Fairground Attraction, Jimmy Somerville of the Communards, bands like Deacon Blue, Love and Money, Hipsway and Texas and painters like Ken Currie, Steven Campbell and Adrian Wiszniewski, to name but a few. There have been folk bands like the Whistlebinkies and the Battlefield Band. And there has also been the new wave of Scottish movies like those by Bill Forsyth and Peter McDougall, many set in Glasgow. Television drama from Glasgow has scored notable successes, the most memorable of which, of course, is 'Tutti-Frutti'. STV's 'Taggart' is nationally networked, it must be remembered, and presents – intentionally? – powerful images of the 'new', trendy Glasgow to viewers south of the border, while presenting Taggart himself as the ultimate macho Glaswegian: rough, tough, sharp and dour, but witty.

Now these people were not in business to sell an image of the 'new' Glasgow. They were and are artists doing their job. But their very talents unintentionally helped the image-makers to package the 'new' Glasgow, to convince outsiders that the city was 'Miles Better', to emphasise the friendliness of Glaswegians, to discuss Mayfest and a thriving theatrical culture, to stress its wonderful Garden Festival, to point to the Merchant City, to boast of its being European City of Culture in 1990. Much of this package took off on the back of GEAR, the Glasgow Eastern Area Renewal Project. This was a large-scale project which had the ambitious task of 'revitalising' a huge area of the city's East End, and which has been extoled by everyone from academics to Prince Charles and Margaret Thatcher. It is held out as an example of what can be done with a devastated inner-city area, where the old industries have collapsed, where the housing was obsolete, where unemployment was through the roof and where the people were thoroughly demoralised. What else was there to sell in this 'new' Glasgow?

A first point is the cleaned-up and modernised tenemental neighbourhoods. It is wonderful to see Woodlands, Govanhill and Partick as restored residential and shopping areas. Then there are attractive shopping centres like Princes Square, the Parkhead Forge, the St Enoch Centre and the Buchanan Street Pedestrian Precinct – if you like that sort of thing. There are numerous art galleries, theatres and museums, with the Burrell Collection being Scotland's single biggest tourist attraction. This new gallery commands international respect. There is the Clydeside Walkway and the Kelvinway, leading on to the West Highland Way. There is the Cycleway from Glasgow to Balloch on the shores of Loch Lomond, built by young people on the YTS scheme. There are beautiful parks. There is the Scottish Exhibition and Conference Centre. There is the huge new £19 million Forum Hotel complex towering over the Clyde beside this Centre, with planning permission granted for a Hilton in an inner-city riverside site. (In fact, there are now five large and relatively new hotels in Glasgow's city-centre.) There is a plethora of new boutiques, delicatessens, clubs and pubs. There are numerous Barrett-style housing developments, many on attractive sites. There are handsome old buildings and bridges which have been cleaned, painted and spotlit. There are excellent national and international communications systems, permitting anyone who so wishes to shuttle up-and-down to London daily.

Above all, there is a new climate, a climate of optimism, of excitement, even. It is a city where the incoming young professional could find a stimulating – and relatively cheap – life-style, with all the cachet of being in the legendary rough, tough Glasgow. These are images of the 'new' Glasgow, summed up in the excruciating Saatchi & Saatchi slogan, 'There's a Lot of Glasgowing On in 1990', which cost the city's ratepayers a great deal of money. As we have seen, the whole objective was to attract these young professionals, and to keep the few indigenous ones who remained.

There is, of course, a tension between the old and the new imageries. The *No Mean City* image dies hard, for Glasgow *is* a tough city, if not in the way that the authors of that awful book portray. This tension is expressed very clearly in William McIlvanney's Glasgow thrillers. Although he has been writing successfully for more than twenty years, he has only recently won fame with his two novels featuring the complex, reflective policeman Laidlaw – *Laidlaw* (1977) and *The Papers of Tony Veitch* (1983). Indeed, it could be said that the hero of these books is Glasgow rather than Laidlaw. McIlvanney's pithy comments about the city are evocative:

> It [Glasgow] had always been so sure of itself, so full of people who didn't open doors tentatively, who had a cocky walk. It was a hard city.

> It was Glasgow on a Friday night, the city of the stare.

...in Glasgow openness is the only safe-conduct pass. Try to
steal a match and they'll ambush you from every close. They
hate to be had. Come on honestly and their tolerance can be
great.

That's what I love about Glasgow. It's not a city, it's a
twenty-four-hour cabaret.

McIlvanney's imagery is relentlessly masculine, if not
uncritically so. His cops and robbers spend an inordinate
amount of time philosophising about the morality of
violence. Indeed, they are on the same continuum of
entrapped masculinity. They know the rules, they may
not like them, but they cannot escape them, and so, being
men of honour, they continue on the path of self-
destruction, the ultimate wages of the sin of machismo.
For all that McIlvanney is infinitely more subtle and
complex – and gifted – than the writers of *No Mean City*,
it seems to me that he does not transcend the 'barbarian'
image of Glasgow. If the model of the Glaswegian in *No
Mean City* is the savage, McIlvanney's is the *noble*
savage. Nobody denies that Glasgow is a tough city and
that its people – women as well as men – are tough, but
that toughness was a necessary and unwanted outcome
of historically harsh working conditions and harsher
living conditions. Although he is well aware of this
historical process, McIlvanney never really does it justice
in his fiction, because of his *idée fixe* about the 'hard men'
and his constant representation of them as the 'norm' of
working-class life. His vision of Glasgow is not only
male-dominated, it is fundamentally romantic, for all the
gritty realism and wit of his prose.

Before turning to a critique of the imagery, one simple
point needs to be made. Many of the recent innovations
in Glasgow are to be welcomed. Glaswegians are entitled
to garden festivals, riverside walkways, more and better
galleries, good restaurants, decent, comfortable pubs,
civilised drinking hours, good entertainment, a wide
range of shops, food and goods, and, in general, a clean,
attractive and safe city. Nobody denies them that; it is

their right as citizens. But the question has to be asked: Glasgow's Miles Better for Whom?

The short answer is: not for the bulk of Glaswegians. Much of the prestigious commercial development is in the Central Business District, or immediately adjoining it. The 'Merchant City' is typical. It is a complete invention of environmental consultants. Nobody in Glasgow had heard this term ten years ago. At the moment it is still a very small area to the east of the city centre in which hardly any working-class people live. Neither industrial nor service workers could afford the prices of the new or converted houses in the area bounded roughly by Bell Street, the Candleriggs, the High Street and the Trongate. Nor could most of them get mortgages even if they wanted one. The 1989 price for a one-bedroomed flat in Mackintosh Court in the 'Merchant City' was £40,000 – plus £2,000 for a parking space. The Garden Festival was a fun experience, but the wild talk of dozens of permanent jobs being generated by it has proved pure mythology. And the site, which never left private ownership, will be devoted principally to luxury housing. If one analyses the academic reports on the much-vaunted GEAR, whatever its achievements, making inroads into local unemployment is not one of them. Precisely fourteen long-term unemployed East Enders got jobs as 'small entrepreneurs' out of GEAR, generating another sixteen jobs.[6] Such employment as has been created in Glasgow is practically all in service industries, and it hardly needs repeating in the 1990s that these are the worst paid, least unionised, most seasonal jobs, with the longest hours and the poorest conditions in terms of health and safety, and which predominantly employ women on a part-time basis. It is patently a dubious proposition to state that such jobs are better than no jobs, even though unemployed Glaswegians may want them desperately.

Glasgow's statistics for poverty and unemployment are quite staggering.[7] While there is no official government definition of poverty, the Income Support level is often

taken as a reasonable measure. In 1987 there were about
140,000 people claiming supplementary benefit. That is,
about 20 per cent of the population. If we include
dependents and those eligible for benefit, but not
claiming, the proportion rises to about 40 per cent of the
population. This represents an increase in claimants of
some 20 per cent since 1981, a period during which the
city's population declined by 7.6 per cent. And it should
be noted that benefit rates have decreased slightly in real
terms since 1981, while the average earnings index has
increased substantially more than the increase in state
benefits, thus exacerbating the gulf between the 'haves'
and the 'have-nots'. About 30 per cent of the households
with children in the city are single-parent, a good
indicator of poverty as about two-thirds of them are
living at or below the supplementary benefit/income
support level. About a quarter of the city's employed male
workers and two-thirds of its female workers are on low
pay – reflecting the point made above about service
industries. In 1988 no less than 66 per cent of public
sector tenants and 51 per cent of private sector tenants
were receiving Housing Benefit. The official (1989)
unemployment rate is 17.1 per cent – 23.1 per cent for
men and 9.1 per cent for women. If we take into account
the numerous recent government changes in how
unemployment rates are calculated – all designed to
bring down the figures of the unemployed – then the true
unemployment rate is on the 26 per cent level.
Homelessness increases by leaps and bounds.

In the four large peripheral estates, Easterhouse,
Drumchapel, Pollok, and Castlemilk, still housing some
125,000 people between them, 'Glasgow's Miles Better' is
a sick joke. In neighbourhoods out there, and in the
smaller and now forgotten slum-clearance housing
schemes like Barrowfield, Teucharhill, Blackhill,
Moorepark, Ruchill and Possilpark, unemployment is
well over 60 per cent. If we talk of 'multiple deprivation',
then 45 per cent of the population of Glasgow now lives in
Areas of Priority Treatment (APTs). In these areas,

heroin is a readily available commodity, as is the violence, money-lending and prostitution associated with the drug trade. In such schemes, despair is normal. Their tenants are truly peripheralised in Thatcher's 'booming' Britain. They are unable to visit the bonnie, bonnie banks of Loch Lomond or climb Ben More, for their poverty effectively imprisons them in their housing schemes. On the very day that I am writing this (1 July 1989), a study of unemployed families has been published showing that the adults spent only 15 per cent of their time outside the house, and that both adults and children spent more than half of their week sleeping or watching television.[8]

The 1988 changes in the social security system have had a devastating effect on vulnerable groups, especially the introduction of the social fund in place of the old system of one-off grants for essential items. And, of course, there is also the introducton of the poll tax, although that is being strongly resisted in Glasgow where an estimated 30 per cent of the population has refused to pay. Whatever indicators of poverty and deprivation one takes, or however one shakes the cocktail, the fact of the matter is that Glasgow is still far and away the most deprived city in the United Kingdom. Behind the stone-cleaned façades of the old working-class neighbourhoods lurks a grim reality of persistent poverty and racism. A recent report has painted a shocking picture of racial harassment in Glasgow, shattering the complacent illusion that it doesn't happen in Scotland.[9] This is the side of Glasgow life which the image-builders do not want to discuss. Nor do they wish to discuss the even grimmer reality a mere twenty miles down the Clyde: the Faslane submarine base, a nuclear arsenal currently housing the Polaris vessels, soon to be replaced by the Trident system, which constitute a vital part of Britain's 'nuclear deterrent'. It would hardly help the image of Glasgow if it were to be admitted that it is going to be miles better to die there in the event of a nuclear war.

What needs to be discussed now is the large-scale

industrial restructuring of Glasgow in the post-war years, for the new images could not be peddled without some kind of reality lying under the surface of the glitz. In the post-war years, the international economic system revolutionised itself yet again, principally by means of opening up the 'Third World' countries. In metropolitan Europe this means the rapid contraction of traditional, labour-intensive, manufacturing industries. Nowhere was this more true than on Clydeside, where shipbuilding and heavy engineering went into deep crisis, faced with a world glut of shipping, a result of the war, on the one hand, and the rapid expansion of cheap shipbuilding in places like Japan, Taiwan and Korea, on the other. Quite simply, large numbers of Glasgow workers became redundant to the needs of rapidly restructuring capital. So did their communities – the old tenemental neighbourhoods of the Gorbals, Govan and Springburn. These places were perceived as obsolete. A new broom was needed to open up the city for new forms of industry and new kinds of workers. As we have seen, the mechanism for this large-scale restructuring was the Comprehensive Development Areas programme of the 1960s. 29 CDAs were declared in Glasgow, and these were in full swing when I arrived in 1968. But, in spite of large-scale demolition and construction, massive problems of poverty and deprivation remained. In 1971 a well known Department of the Environment Study characterised Glasgow as the most deprived city in Britain. It had 578 'multiply-deprived' Enumeration Districts compared with 170 in Birmingham, 101 in Edinburgh, 93 in Manchester and 60 in Liverpool.[10] (This was one of the first of a whole series of similar studies producing more or less elaborate versions of the same findings.) To make matters worse, the drift of population out of the city was rapidly accelerating. It was during this period that there was a spate of media reportage on Glasgow, all tending to reproduce the 'shock city' imagery, a combination of bevvy-and-violence, and runaway industrial decline and dereliction. The television series which made films about Glasgow included 'This

Week', 'Panorama', 'Arena', 'World in Action', 'Man Alive', and 'Nationwide'. Television luminaries who had a go at Glasgow included Bernard Falk, Jonathan Dimbleby, Gus MacDonald and Joan Bakewell. From the late 1960s onwards, Glasgow became a jungle into which the media fearlessly ventured to portray the wild animals.

It was under these circumstances that state intervention became inevitable. The key mechanism was the establishment by the Scottish Office in 1971 of the West Central Scotland Steering Committee, whose task was the establishment of the strategy for restructuring the region, in economic, physical, and social terms. These were subsequently followed by important innovations by Strathclyde Region, including the Regional Report, the Structure Plan and various joint social and economic area initiatives. A major outcome for the purposes of this discussion was the establishment of GEAR in 1976. GEAR's approach to the problems of vast tracts of the East End was an holistic one; it took an overview of industrial, housing, planning, environmental and social problems. It was to try and enhance local employment prospects by, *inter alia*, making the area a more attractive one in which to invest. GEAR was packaged very cleverly. It was billed as the first effort at 'comprehensive regeneration' of a whole inner-city area utilising a 'multi-agency' approach. In this sense, it was a prototype of the subsequent inner-city partnerships in England.

Glasgow District Council and Strathclyde Regional Council adopted 'corporate management', and produced reams of 'strategy' documents. In 1973 the District Council's Housing Management Department introduced housing co-operatives and announced a 'homesteading' experiment in Easterhouse whereby tenants could opt to buy their houses at rock-bottom prices and do them up themselves whilst fighting off the local Comanches. In 1976, the Regional Council's Chief Executive's department designated whole areas of the city as 'Areas for

Priority Treatment' (APTs), whose deprived residents would benefit from corporately managed and rationalised welfare services delivered in the neighbourhoods of most 'need'. Community Councils and Area Committees were established to keep locals in touch with the corporate strategies. It was a period of innovation and experimentation, and the Labour Party, which dominated both Glasgow City Council and Strathclyde Regional Council, was in the vanguard. Socialism went with the old and 'negative' image of Glasgow, and was quietly abandoned. And in the background, the emigration continued, manufacturing jobs declined by leaps and bounds, and the figures for unemployment, poverty and deprivation continued to increase dramatically.

The result was that by the beginning of the 1980s Glasgow had a captive unemployed and somewhat demoralised labour force, willing to take on practically any employment for something better than the parsimonious level of Supplementary Benefit. Glasgow is indeed a pleasant place in which to live and work. As long as you don't have to live in the peripheral estates, that is. It is entirely comprehensible that entertainment and the arts should flourish. The yuppies have to have something on which to spend their inflated salaries. (And a cynic might mutter something about bread and circuses.) What has happened in Glasgow is that the managers of the service sector, the restaurateurs and disco proprietors, the yuppies in finance, the civil servants fleeing from the South-East of England, the residents in and patrons of the 'Merchant City', are able to enjoy their enhanced life-style *at the expense of* the thousands of unemployed and low-paid workers living in the aptly-named peripheral estates. The latter are an embarrassment in Thatcher's Britain.

Does this mean the end of the legacy of the Red Clyde? Does it mean the death of the witty and pugnacious Glasgow punter? Is The Patter on the way out? Are Glaswegians giving up on these attempts to hijack their city? No way. To return to William McIlvanney at his best – Detective Inspector Laidlaw is speaking:

Even when this place was the second city of the British Empire affluence had never softened it because the wealth of the few had become the poverty of the many. The many had survived, however harshly, and made the spirit of the place theirs. Having survived affluence, they could survive anything. Now that the money was tight, they hardly noticed the difference. If you had it, all you did was spend it. The money had always been tight. Tell us something we don't know. That was Glasgow. It was a place so kind it would batter cruelty into the ground. And what circumstances kept giving it was cruelty. No wonder he loved it. It danced in its debris. When Glasgow gave up, the world could call it a day.[11]

Glaswegians do not know the meaning of the term 'give up', because they are a unique people among the urban dwellers of Britain, with a unique history. To understand why they see through the 'Miles Better' stuff, and why they are unsurprised about being the 'European City of Culture', it is necessary to know a little of the People's History of Glasgow.

References

1. A. McArthur and H. Kingsley Long, *No Mean City*, Corgi, 1978 (first published 1935).
2. Moira Burgess, *The Glasgow Novel: A Survey and Bibliography*, 2nd edition, Scottish Library Association and Glasgow District Libraries, 1986, p.44.
3. Scottish Council (Development and Industry), *Inquiry into the Scottish Economy 1960-61*, Paisley: James Paton, 1961, p.148.
4. Glasgow Action, *The First Steps*, June 1987.
5. Dr Kelly went on to become Chairperson of the Drumkinnon Development Company, currently involved in a £40 million development plan for the derelict Drumkinnon Bay on Loch Lomondside, near Balloch. See *Lennox Herald*, 20 October 1989.
6. D. Donnison and A. Middleton (eds.), *Regenerating the Inner City: Glasgow's Experience*, Routledge and Kegan Paul, 1987, p.80.
7. The subsequent figures are derived from (i) Strathclyde Regional Council, *Poverty in Strathclyde: A Statistical Analysis*, June 1988, and (ii) up-to-date figures made available to me in June 1989 by the Chief Executive's Department; I am most grateful for the assistance of Chris Harvie of that department.
8. 'Survey Reveals Dole Prisoners', *Guardian*, 1 July 1989. The study is CPAG, *Living on the Edge*, 1989.

9. Bruce Armstrong (ed.), *A People without Prejudice? The Experience of Racism in Scotland*, Runnymede Trust, 1989.
10. cf. Sally Holtermann, 'Areas of Urban Deprivation in Britain: An Analysis of 1971 Census Data', *Social Trends*, No.6, 1975.
11. William McIlvanney, *The Papers of Tony Veitch*, Coronet, 1984, p.224.

2   People and Work

I live at the top of a steep street in the Partick area of Glasgow which has featured in at least half-a-dozen films. The views to the south-east and south-west are stunning. On a still night I can clearly hear the clang of hammers, the rattle of drills and shouted messages from the Kvaerner Shipyard in Govan, about a mile away across the River Clyde. Kvaerner's used to be Govan Shipbuilders, which used to be Upper Clyde Shipbuilders of work-in fame, which used to be Fairfield's of even greater fame. The noise and the nocturnal flash of welders' torches is reassuring – romantic, even; it reminds me of Glasgow's history and shows that, as an industrial city, it is not yet dead.

It is a cliché to associate Glasgow with shipbuilding; everybody knows that. The phrase 'Clydebuilt' is internationally known. The pubs of Partick and Govan are full of shipbuilders, and even more ex-shipbuilders who claim to have told Billy Connolly all his jokes. The cranes still punctuate the skyline. People still turn out to see a launch. But the reality is much more complicated than shipbuilding alone. To understand Glasgow it is necessary to understand the labour process in the city in the period of modern history, by which I mean from 1800 onwards. Glasgow was a city embracing a particular form of industrial development, quite different from, say, that of Liverpool in the same period. It was this highly localised form of industrial development which produced a distinctive working class and a distinctive type of working-class culture. These gave Glasgow its unique stamp, and while in 1990 the forms of industrial production may have changed, the legacy of the previous forms is alive and kicking – some might say only too literally!

I include three elements in the notion of 'labour process': the dominant forms of industrial production, the labour force which staffed them and the group which controlled production. In Glasgow the combination of these three elements was unique in these islands. The form of production which came to dominate Glasgow in the Victorian years was heavy engineering. Although Glasgow's industrial *image* is as a shipbuilding city, this was but one of many heavy engineering activities. Thus the key element in the labour force was the engineering trades, and their syndicalist politics, which sought workers' control of industry and government solely through shop-floor organisation, dominated the local labour movement until at least the end of the First World War. But the cultural origins of the Glasgow working class in West Central Scotland, the Scottish Highlands and Ireland resulted in a unique and explosive mixture in the broader working-class movement which was not readily controllable by the labour aristocrats of the engineering trades. Finally, Glasgow was characterised by a middle class of industrial entrepreneurs of extraordinary vision, energy and ambition, who by 1900 had turned Glasgow into the workshop of the world and justified the title 'Second City of the British Empire'. Their impressive achievements have been well documented;[1] similarly, there is any amount of biographies of these industrial barons.[2]

It is to be noted here that, for most of the nineteenth century, practically all of the shipbuilding and much of the heavy engineering production was located *outside* the official boundaries of the city of Glasgow. They were located in immediately adjacent burghs such as Kinning Park, Partick and Govan. These burghs had finally all been incorporated into the city by 1912. Here, 'Glasgow' refers to the built-up area of city and adjacent burghs.

Glasgow Heavy Industry

At the beginning of the eighteenth century, it would be safe to say, Glasgow, although the second city of Scotland, with a population of approximately 15,000, was a parochial place with horizons stretching little further than the West Highlands and the Islands, and relatively isolated from the rest of the United Kingdom.[3] Its merchants had already established regular if small-scale links with the West Indies and the east coast of North America, and sugar and tobacco were being steadily imported. This created pressure for deepening the Clyde, which was barely navigable up to Glasgow. The city's merchants' response was to start the development of a harbour at Port Glasgow ten miles down-river, and this was fully functioning by 1700 while, simultaneously, a modest quay system was initiated at the Broomielaw nearer the city centre.[4] A small but thriving textile industry also existed, centred on wool and linen, and handloom weaving was widespread, both within the city and the surrounding counties. The fundamentally Presbyterian nature of Glasgow can be gauged by the fear and loathing with which it treated Prince Charles Edward Stuart's army on its way back from Derby in 1745. Glaswegians were heavily fined for their lack of support for the Jacobite cause, and hostages were taken by the Highlanders on their doomed retreat north. The archetypal Glasgow merchant of the period is Bailie Nicol Jarvie of Sir Walter Scott's novel *Rob Roy*, described here by a young Englishman visiting the city for the first time:

> ...a man whose good opinion of himself amounted to self-conceit, and who, disliking the English as much as my father did the Scotch, would hold no communication but on a footing of absolute equality; jealous, moreover; captious occasionally...tenacious of his own opinions in point of form...and totally indifferent, though the authority of all Lombard Street had stood against his own private opinion.[5]

Throughout the eighteenth century Glasgow's maritime trade with Ireland, the rest of Europe, North America and the West Indies expanded steadily. The transatlantic trade followed a triangular pattern, Glasgow-mainland Europe-North America/West Indies, or vice versa. While there is no evidence to suggest that Glasgow merchants were directly involved in the slave trade, Scottish planters in the West Indies certainly were slave owners, and kept black women as concubines. James M'Lehose, the husband of Robert Burns's 'Clarinda', was a case in point. Further, slaves were certainly known in the city. As early as 1650 the 'Scripture Rules' in the Merchants' House of Glasgow, which had to be observed in local buying and selling, contained the following rule:

> Thirdly, do not buy men for slaves, this the lord reproves in Amos 2, 6, 'They sold the righteous for silver and the poor for a pair of shoes;' and so in Deut. 27, 'Thou shalt not steal thy brother and make merchandise of him.'[6]

The implication is clearly that Glasgow merchants were involved in the slave trade. In 1776 a black slave sued his master in the Court of Session for his freedom,[7] and the Glasgow newspapers of the second half of the eighteenth century contained many advertisements for slaves for sale or for runaway slaves.[8]

Tobacco became increasingly important in overseas trade, and by the last third of the century it absolutely dominated imports to the Clyde. Glasgow was Britain's major tobacco processing centre. This in turn led to more pressure to make the Clyde navigable right up into the city, as by now Port Glasgow, the city's port, and Greenock, at the estuary of the river, were engaged in a trade war. Thus, by 1771, systematic and eventually successful attempts were being made both to deepen and widen the Clyde. Glasgow's Tobacco Lords became the most important section of the middle class as they were also the city's bankers.[9] Through highly developed entrepreneurial skills they expanded their influence by using their profits to set up banks, which rapidly extended credit, which in turn stimulated further trade and banking. They bought their way into the landed gentry by a classic series of dynastic inter-marriages, thus consolidating their status. When the tobacco trade collapsed in 1776, as a consequence of the American War of Independence, these merchants rapidly moved back into the West Indian trade, this time, significantly, concentrating on cotton. They left their mark in a series of handsome Georgian streets and mansions developed to the west of the old city centre at Glasgow Cross; traces of their elegence remain. Suffice it to say that the trade was so lucrative that tobacco merchant Stephen Mitchell was able to leave a bequest of £66,989 in 1874 to found the city's famous and superbly stocked Mitchell Library. The issue here is not the detailed history of the Tobacco Lords, but the accumulation of wealth and the formation of a class of entrepreneurs which would underwrite the impending agricultural and industrial explosion in Glasgow and the surrounding area.

The key phase of industrial expansion in Glasgow paralleled that taking place elsewhere in Britain: it was based on cotton. The city's estimated 4,000 handloom weavers at the turn of the nineteenth century made a painless transition from linen to cotton and in the hinterland of West Central Scotland there were about 20,000 handloom weavers.[10] Textile manufacturing came to dominate Clydeside industrial production from the late eighteenth century until the middle of the nineteenth century. The cotton industry expanded very rapidly in Glasgow and its hinterland. In 1818 there were eighteen steam-weaving factories in Glasgow containing 2,800 looms. The take-off of these steam-powered 'manufactories' heralded the slow and pitiful death agony of the hand-loom weaving industry, although there were still as many as 30,000 looms working in 1831, employing considerably more people through the family-based domestic system. Families with their wealth in land, both old and new, invested in the textile industry, and it began to produce its own capitalists who in turn would be ready for the next phase of industrial expansion. It is sometimes overlooked when discussing these chains of capital accumulation that the textile industry also produced a skilled labour force: the millwrights and mechanics who maintained the machinery and who were endlessly trying to develop more efficient steam engines. A spin-off from the textile industry was the development of the chemical industry, vital to bleaching and dyeing. Charles Tennant's famous chemical factory at St Rollox in Springburn was established in 1798 and, within three decades, was the biggest in the world. Its huge chimney – 'Tennant's Stalk' – at 435 feet 6 inches the highest in the world, spewed out pollution all over northern Glasgow, and was an early symbol of the close inter-relatedness of the Clydeside economy.

The fuel for the steam-powered mills was coal, and iron the raw material for the steam-engines. West Central Scotland was fortunate in having ample supplies of coal and iron ore, and open-cast mining for both was widespread in Glasgow and hinterland in the eighteenth century. Open-cast coal mining was so common within what are now the city boundaries of Glasgow that it is still not at all unusual for a tenement to begin to subside gently into an old pit-working! As late as 1871 there were still fourteen working pits in Glasgow, and another thirty in the adjoining areas of Bridgeton, Shettleston and Baillieston.[11] As the various histories of Scottish mining recount, working conditions in these pits throughout the nineteenth century – and well into the twentieth century – were horrific, with the most brutal exploitation of women and children being normal until the middle of the nineteenth century.[12] But mining technology was archaic at the time of the rapid expansion of the textile industry, so, faced with an escalating demand for coal, the coal- and iron-masters, who were typically one and the same man, were driven to innovate rapidly in terms of drainage, ventilation and extraction. As early as 1825 there were eighteen iron foundries in Glasgow.[13] John

Dixon and his son William, the biggest iron- and coal-masters in the region, gave their names to 'Dixons' Blazes', five non-stop blast furnaces in their massive Govan Colliery and Ironworks in Hutchesontown on the south side of the Clyde, built in 1839. It was a potent symbol of the new manufacturing, lighting up the night sky and adding its quota to the din and effluent which were by now beginning to pollute the old city. The nocturnal glare also had other uses. An 1849 comment was that:

> ...The bright glare cheers the long winter night, and at the same time does the work of a score of policemen, by scaring away the rogues and vagabonds who so plentifully infest other and darker parts of the city.[14]

William Dixon also owned the pit at Blantyre, outside Glasgow, where the terrible disaster happened on 22 October 1877. Of 233 men and boys working in the pit on that day, 207 were killed in an explosion. The event is remembered in a well known folk-song, 'The Blantyre Explosion', whose first three verses go (in a version sung in Ireland):

> On Clyde's bonny banks where I lately did wander,
> Near the village of Blantyre I happened to stray,
> I espied a young woman, she was dressed in deep mourning
> So sadly lamenting the fate of her love.
>
> I boldy stepped up to her; said I My young woman,
> Come tell me the cause of your trouble and woe.
> I do hear you lamenting the fate of some young man,
> His name and what happened him I'd like for to know.
>
> With sighing and sobbing she at length then made answer,
> John Murphy, kind sir, was my true lover's name,
> Twenty-one years of age and a mild good behaviour,
> To work in the mines of High Blantyre he came.

Note the name of the miner; in fact, the majority of the slain men were Irish. Dixon's pit was notorious for poor ventilation and bad management. The local miners'

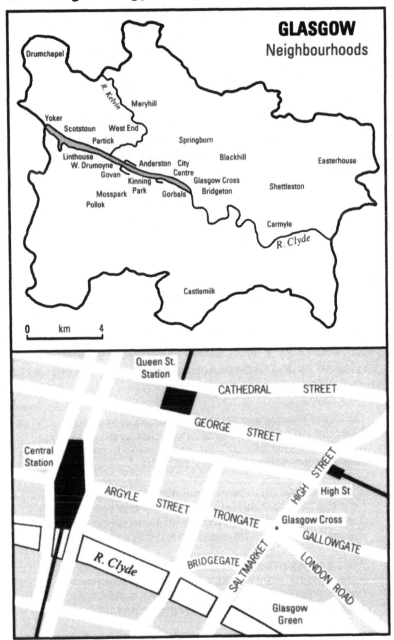

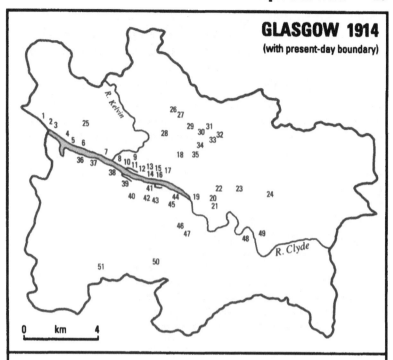

GLASGOW 1914
(with present-day boundary)

R. Kelvin

R. Clyde

0   km   4

Location of Main Engineering Works & Shipyards

1. Barclay Curle's West Yard
2. Yarrow & Co.
3. Blythwood Yard
4. Connel's Scotstoun Yard
5. N. British Diesel Engine Works
6. Barclay Curle's Clydesholm Yard
7. Meadowside Shipbuilding Yard
8. Pointhouse Shipbuilding Yard
9. J & G Thompson's Boiler Works
10. Kelvinhaugh Slip Dock
11. Queen's Dock
12. Stobcross Slip Dock
13. J & G Thompson's Engine Works
14. Lancefield Foundry
15. Anderston Foundry
16. Anderston Cotton Works
17. Tod & McGregor's Engine Works

18. Bergius Engine Works
19. Templeton's Carpet Works
20. Barrowfield Iron Works
21. Dalmarnock Iron Works
22. Camlachie Foundary
23. Parkhead Forge
24. Shettleston Iron Works
25. Barr & Stroud, Anniesland
26. Saracen Foundary
27. Clydesdale Iron Works
28. Canal Foundary
29. Cowlairs Railway Works
30. Hydepark Locomotive Works
31. Atlas Locomotive Works
32. Frederick Braby & Co.
33. Arrol Brothers
34. St. Rollox Railway Works

35. St. Rollox Chemical Works
36. Linthouse Shipbuilding Yard
37. Fairfield's Shipbuilding Yard
38. Harland & Wolff
39. Princes Dock
40. Clutha Iron Works
41. Kingston Dock
42. James Howden & Co.
43. Scotland St. Iron Works
44. Randolph, Elder & Co.
45. Kinning Park Foundry
46. Glasgow Locomotive Works
47. Sentinel Works
48. Clydebridge Steel Works
49. Clyde Iron Works
50. Argus Foundry
51. Holm Foundry

leader, Alexander McDonald, was hard put to it to restrain the pitmen from taking summary vengeance on Dixon and his managers.[15] And Dixon, ironically, was regarded as a model employer in many respects.

The greed of the local iron- and coal-masters, who were notorious (Dixon excepted) for operating the 'truck' system of company stores with hiked prices where the workers could get goods on credit, is celebrated in another contemporary folk-song, aimed at Eadie and Miller, the owners of the New Monkland Colliery at Airdrie, and the Langloan Iron Works:

> You truck masters all, pay attention to me,
> Especially Gartsherrie and Summerlee;
> And as I am sitting and thinking great long,
> If you will listen to me I'll sing you a song.
> As for some of our masters they are great men,
> And one of them a ruler of our native land,
> I wonder what's the reason he does not stop,
> The infamous system of a truck shop.
>
> The reason is obvious and plain to be seen
> The profits are great altho' they are mean –
> They rob the poor man in every stage,
> And they very soon make him a small enough wage,
> There is one in Drumpeller that place o' great fame,
> But to sing about it, could I think shame,
> For a collier there told me that works under ground,
> That they subtract from him five shillings a pound.[16]

The production of iron ore and coal soared. Pig-iron production doubled between 1847 and 1870, as did coal output between 1854 and 1870.[17]

The increasing production of coal and iron stimulated the rapid development of a transportation network, initially by river, then by the Monklands Canal, built in 1793 to connect the heartland of the extractive industries to the west of Glasgow with the Clyde. A railway network was also quickly constructed, resulting in yet more demand on the iron industry, which began to innovate until Neilson's hot-blast system, developed between 1828 and 1832, permitted the more efficient and rapid production of good quality iron from the abundant local deposits of blackband ironstone. This in turn led to a further series of innovations which revolutionalised the production of pig iron.

The next factor in the equation was the explosion of shipbuilding, itself directly related to this ready availability of iron. By the 1840s the Clyde was dredged sufficiently well to allow ships right up to the Broomielaw, Glasgow's quay, and by 1870 ships of 3,000 tons could come up. The *Comet* was launched on the Clyde in 1812, and sailed to Oban via the Crinan Canal that same year, to be followed by another 42 steam vessels in the next eight years.[18] By the 1830s there were more than 70 steamers per day going up and down the Clyde, and between 1850 and 1859, 42 fast steamers were built in the competition with the railways for passengers from lower down the Clyde.[19] The shipbuilding industry was stimulated by the export trade in coal and iron, and by the very large coasting trade, the biggest in Europe. The Clyde specialised in iron-built ships, and by 1870 was far and away the biggest producer in the world. The development of the Bessemer process for mass producing steel between 1856 and 1858 further drove forward naval architecture by enabling the building of lighter, more flexible, yet stronger steel ships.

Thus there was a series of interlinkages between iron, coal, steel, engineering and shipbuilding which led to Glasgow becoming the undisputed workshop of the world and the 'Second City of the Empire' in the last quarter of the nineteenth century. The shipbuilding boom took off on constant innovations in construction and propulsion. The sheer scale of this enterprise is admirably summarised by Anthony Slaven in the following two quotations:

For twenty years from 1851 to 1870 the Clyde shipbuilders poured out the prodigious figure of over 70 per cent of all the iron tonnage launched in Britain.[20]

The record of the Clyde in shipbuilding between 1870 and 1913 is quite astonishing. Between these dates her slipways consistently poured out a third of the total British tonnage. Launchings averaged 250,000 tons each year between 1871 and 1874, and this was more than doubled to 565,000 tons between 1909 and 1913. In the peak year of 1913 the Clyde built and launched almost three-quarters of a million tons of shipping, some 756,973 tons, a feat never to be equalled. This represented not only one-third of British tonnage, but almost 18 per cent of world output, and was more than the production of the entire shipbuilding industry of either Germany or America.[21]

The achievement is all the more astonishing when it is realised that as late as 1851 the textile industry was still by far the biggest employer in Glasgow. But in the succeeding half-century the engineering and metal trades soared ahead, as the following table demonstrates:

Table 1: Structure of Employment (per cent) in Glasgow, 1851 and 1901

	1851	1901
Textiles	46.98	27.56
Metal Manufacture	3.46	10.28
Mechanical Engineering	3.00	34.79
Instrument Engineering	0.38	3.02
Shipbuilding, Marine Engineering	0.47	3.04
Other Metals	1.08	5.07
	55.37	83.76

Source: adapted from W. Forsyth, 'Urban Economic Morphology in Nineteenth Century Glasgow' in A. Slaven and D. Aldcroft (eds.), *Banking, Business, and Urban History*, John Donald, 1982, p. 171.

It can readily be seen that the trades associated with heavy engineering expanded very rapidly during this period, while the textile sector declined steadily. Further, for all Glasgow's *image* as a shipbuilding city, these trades only accounted for a small proportion of the total workforce.

So by the end of the nineteenth century Glasgow, and the Clyde, was dominated by heavy engineering, including shipbuilding and ship-repairing, and exported its products all over the world. A boat-trip down the Upper Clyde at the outbreak of the First World War would have revealed the following shipyards: on the north bank at Pointhouse, A. & J. Inglis; on the south side at Govan, Harland & Wolff (three separate yards); at Meadowside, on the north bank, D. & W. Henderson; on the south bank at Govan, the Fairfield; on the north bank at Partick, Barclay Curle's; on the south side at Linthouse, Stephen's; on the north bank at Whiteinch, J. Reid and Ritchie, Graham, & Milne; and further along the north bank at Scotstoun, Connell's. And these yards were all within the city boundary of Glasgow. To take but one example, between 1853 and 1950 Stephen's yard built 634 ships, including barques, brigantines, dredgers, barges, steamships, schooners, yachts, tugs, tankers, passenger motor-vessels, coasters, destroyers, cruisers, banana-boats, refrigerated motor-vessels, minesweepers, aircraft carriers and passenger-cargo boats.[22] Although Glasgow was never a seafarers' city to the extent of Liverpool, a list of the city's steamship lines in the inter-war years would include Anchor, Carron, Clan, Clyde Shipping, Donaldson, Ellerman City, Furness Withy, LM&S Railway, LNE Railway, MacBrayne and Williamson Buchanan.[23]

At the turn of this century, besides shipbuilding, Glasgow's heavy engineering industry included building girders for bridges and cranes, engine-building and boiler-making, locomotive manufacture, rivet-, tube- and boiler-making, iron and brass-founding, lead-pipe and sheet making, coppersmithing, crane building, rail making and chain making. There were also ancillary trades like cabinet-making, saw-milling, nautical instrument manufacture, boat-building and tarpaulin-making.[24] The products of all these trades were exported, as were pre-fabricated cast-iron buildings like tea-houses and bungalows, sewing-machines, clothes woven in Bridgeton (including saris), Turkey Red dye patterns, brands and stamps, and carpets. (The carpets in the British, Australian, New Zealand and South African

Houses of Parliament were all woven in Glasgow.)[25]
Glasgow's industrial development, in short, was ultimately related to Britain's position as the world's
dominant military and economic power.

The Glasgow Industrialists

Many of the men who were behind Glasgow's industrial
take-off were locals – Napier and Tennant, for example –
while a few were incomers: the Dixons were from
Northumberland, the Elders from north-east Scotland.
But through a series of careful marriages, and the
inter-locking of firms, they formed an industrial
bourgeoisie which was initially highly competitive.
Napier's foundry at Camlachie and shipyard at Lancefield Quay were responsible for training several
generations of engineers, including David Elder, who
was known as the 'Father of Clyde Shipbuilding'. Elder
served his time as a pattern-maker, and later
draughtsman, as did his son after him.[26] He designed
machine-tools as well as engine components. Thus they
took practical skills into management with them. These
engineers and shipbuilders were church-goers to a man.
Alexander Stephen, of Stephen's of Linthouse, was a
Free Church member, for example, while the Elders were
Episcopalians.[27] Whatever their doctrinal differences,
they all shared several characteristics. They all
subscribed to a Protestant work ethic, and were
prepared to muck in with their men. They were
engineering innovators and inventors, and hard-headed
in their business calculations. And they were all highly
paternalist managers of their workforce.

There was no challenge they would not take on.
Alexander Stephen built an iron schooner of 70 tons, the
Aurora del Titicaca, in his Linthouse Yard in Govan in
1869. It was built in parts, none longer than 18 feet, or
heavier than 150 lbs – for they had to be carried on the
backs of mules up to Lake Titicaca at 12,545 feet in the
Andes, and assembled there![28] The Elders built floating

docks for Java, Saigon and Callao. The Transport Museum in Glasgow contains many models of the most exotic Clydebuilt ships, including circular dreadnoughts.

But these shipyard developers did not set up their businesses on the Clyde for nothing. They developed where they did because they were on what we would now call 'greenfield sites', close to rich deposits of coal and iron-ore, to which they could attract a labour force from the Scottish Lowlands and the thousands of Highland and Irish peasants fleeing devastation in their rural areas. And they could control this labour force by using skilled workers as the 'NCOs of labour', by setting piecework, by setting Protestant against Catholic and, quite simply, by lock-outs. Violently anti-trade union, they worked hand-in-glove with a stratum of highly skilled engineers, whom they regularly consulted about work in progress, with whom they were often members of the same Masonic – and, sometimes, Orange – Lodges and to whom they offered the 'social wage' of good pay rates, steady employment even during hard times, company houses, pensions and all the paraphernalia of the 'labour aristocracy'. There was little love lost between these engineers and the 'black squad' of riveters and caulkers, and none at all between them and the mass of unskilled labourers.

The public face of the shipbuilders' philanthropy was impressive. If we take the Govan shipbuilders alone, Alexander Stephen built 120 houses for his regular workers at Linthouse, set up the Stephen's Boys Club, complete with summer camps, outings, etc., and established bursaries for local schoolboys.[29] He opened a co-operative store which was *not* a company store run on the truck system.[30] He ran his shipyard almost as a family – with himself as paterfamilias, of course. The Elders, father and son, were of the same stamp. They encouraged their apprentices to go to evening classes to 'improve' themselves, paid the fees of those who couldn't afford them – and noted the ones who didn't attend. They established an accident fund for their workers, by voluntary contribution.[31] They also established 'domestic economy' classes for their workers' womenfolk, where they could learn economic cooking from a professional cook, darning and mending, starching and ironing, and where they could be given lectures on cleanliness, ventilation and childcare. (And, I daresay, the perils of socialism.) A pamphlet containing all these handy tips was printed, and the whole experiment attracted the keen attention of the US Consul. He wrote a report on it which appeared in *Scientific American*, and also the *British Medical Journal*, one of the few occasions in recent times that women's domestic labour has been seen as worthy of 'scientific' attention by men.[32]

Stephen was also a confirmed teetotaller. It was at his insistence that there were no pubs in the Linthouse area, adjacent to his yard – thus demonstrating his power over his workers. Hence the nearest pub, just over the Govan border in Elderpark Street, was called The Number One![33]

Men like Elder and Stephen were well known and well respected in both the local communities of Govan and Linthouse, and in Glasgow at large. Alexander Stephen, for example, was created Lord Dean of Guild, and thus an automatic Town Councillor, in 1881.[34] When Elder died in 1869 these shipbuilding communities stopped work and turned out on the day of his funeral, as an eye witness recounts:

> The funeral was one of the most impressive sights I ever witnessed. The busy works south of the Clyde were shut, forge and hammer at rest and silent as the grave. The forest of masts along the river were draped in flags, lowered half-mast, in sign of mourning. A very army of workmen dressed like gentlemen, followed his body column after column. Respectful crowds lined the streets as if gazing on the burial of a prince, and every one of us, as we took the last look at his coffin and left his grave, felt that we had left a friend behind.[35]

After the death of her husband John, Mrs Elder gave the Elder Park to the people of Govan as a memorial, in 1885.

The memorial volume celebrating this event is a master-piece of sycophancy and hagiography.[36] But the description of the razzamatazz surrounding it gives us an insight into how the employers tried to inculcate into their workers – or at least their skilled workers – a world-view of the shipyard-as-community. The speeches by such luminaries as Lord Rosebery are a skilful blend of consensus politics and the most vulgar jingoism. But it is plain that building ships could be a profitable business, for the volume recounts that apart from the £50,000 which was the cost of the park, in 1883 Mrs Elder also gave £5,000 to help endow a Chair of Civil Engineering at the University of Glasgow; £12,500 for a new Chair of Naval Architecture; £15,000 for the Queen Margaret College for Ladies, designed to emulate Girton College, Cambridge; £27,000 for the Elder Library, opened in 1903 by Andrew Carnegie; £5,000 to the Building Fund of the Technical College (later the University of Strathclyde), and £5,000 to establish a lectureship in Astronomy there; and £50,000 to establish the Elder Cottage Hospital, and the Training Home for Cottage Nurses. Her public benefactions were estimated to be in excess of £200,000, equivalent to £8 million in 1990.

The legend on the statue of John Elder in the Elder Park in Govan says it all. On the eastern side the inscription reads:

BY HIS MANY INVENTIONS, PARTICULARLY IN
CONNECTION WITH THE COMPOUND ENGINE, HE
EFFECTED A REVOLUTION IN ENGINEERING
SECOND ONLY TO THAT ACCOMPLISHED BY JAMES
WATT, AND IN GREAT MEASURE ORIGINATED THE
DEVELOPMENTS IN STEAM PROPULSION WHICH
HAVE CREATED MODERN COMMERCE.

On the southern side:

HIS UNWEARIED EFFORTS TO PROMOTE THE WEL-
FARE OF THE WORKING-CLASSES, HIS INTEGRITY
OF CHARACTER, FIRMNESS OF PURPOSE AND KIND-
NESS OF HEART
CLAIM

EQUALLY WITH HIS GENIUS, ENDURING
REMEMBERANCE.

After running Robert Napier's yard from 1864 to 1870, Englishman William Pearce joined Elder's and took over as sole partner in 1878; he proved a spectacularly successful manager. The shipyard, known as the Fairfield Shipbuilding and Engineering Works since 1890, specialised in both naval vessels and fast transatlantic liners. No less than 55 warships were built between 1870 and 1909, and another twelve were engined in the Fairfield.[37] Pearce carried on the paternalist practices of his predecessors, although he was a much more flamboyant character. He was successful enough to acquire a personal fortune in excess of £1 million, be created a knight and later baronet, and to be offered a safe Tory seat. He was a noted bon viveur and, hints one biographical sketch, a philanderer. Upon his death in 1888, at the early age of 53, his family followed Mrs Elder's precedent, and donated the Pearce Institute to Govan. Opened in 1906 by Lady Pearce, the Institute served as a unique type of community centre, with its Men's and Women's Clubs, gymnasium, restaurant, Fairfield Hall and Clyde Room. It is still there, and is still well used. The plaque on Pearce's statue across the road from the Institute, near Govan Cross, handsomely outdoes Elder's in fulsome language – one wonders whether this is deliberate:

Sir William Pearce, Bart., M.P.,
died 1888 aged 55 years.

AS A SHIPBUILDER AND ENGINEER, HIS ORIGIN-
ALITY OF THOUGHT AND MARVELLOUS SKILL IN
EXECUTION CONTRIBUTED LARGELY TO THE
DEVELOPMENT OF THE NAVY AND THE MER-
CANTILE MARINE. IN TOKEN OF HIS EMINENCE IN
HIS PROFESSION, HE WAS CREATED A BARONET IN
1887.

HIS EXTENSIVE AND ACCURATE KNOWLEDGE LED
TO HIS APPOINTMENT TO SERVE ON THE ROYAL

COMMISSIONS ON TONNAGE, LOSS OF LIFE AT SEA
AND DEPRESSION OF TRADE. HIS CAREER FUR-
NISHED A STRIKING EXAMPLE OF WHAT GENIUS
COMBINED WITH ENERGY, INDUSTRY, AND INDOMI-
TABLE COURAGE MAY ACCOMPLISH, EVEN IN A
SHORT LIFETIME.

The south panel on the statue notes that Pearce was also
a Commissioner of Police in the Burgh of Govan,
Honorary Colonel of the 2nd Volunteer Battalion,
Highland Light Infantry, a Commissioner of Supply, a
Justice of the Peace, Deputy Lieutenant of the County of
Lanark, an MP and, of course, Provincial Grand Master
of the Glasgow Freemasons. When he died in 1888 he left
£1,069,669. As the late Calum Campbell, the historian of
the Govan working class, remarked, 'This represented
roughly sixteen thousand times the full annual income of
a shipyard worker.'[38]

It was the very rigidity of their paternalism, their
inability to delegate, the calcified organisational structure of their firms, their resistance to new technologies,
which brought these family-based dynasties to the wall
in the inter-war years. But that is to anticipate matters.
In the decades just before the First World War, when
these engineers and shipbuilders were at the peak of
their power, Glasgow was some city to behold. It was
dominated by huge units of industrial production – the
workforce in Beardmore's Parkhead Forge was over
4,000 in 1913, in 56 separate shops, while Fairfield's
Shipbuilding and Engineering Works in Govan reached
8,473 in December 1913. These, and other gigantic
enterprises like Weir's of Cathcart, the four locomotive
works in Springburn, the Barclay, Curle Yard at
Whiteinch, the Meadowside and Pointhouse yards at
Partick, the Tharsis chemical plant at Garngad, Barr
and Stroud at Anniesland, the Linthouse yard in Govan,
the Saracen Foundry, the Clutha Ironworks at Plantation, the Templeton Carpet Factory, were surrounded
and supplied by myriad small shops. The banging,
clanging, sawing, welding and drilling went on day and

night. No less than 80 per cent of the world's sugar-crushing and refining machinery was made in Glasgow in the years immediately before the war, while the Clyde, including the Glasgow yards, produced 18 per cent of world shipping.[39] Similarly, the city produced 71 per cent of the world's locomotives, and these were shipped to Russia, India, China, the Sudan, Argentina, South Africa, the Rhodesias, Paraguay and Australia, *inter alia*. Some of these engines are still in service. The journey of these locomotives from the various railway works in Springburn, initially on horse-drawn, later on traction-engine-drawn, low-loaders, to the Finnieston Crane was a frequent sight in Springburn, and one which helped give the area its very definite profile as a railway community. Glasgow novelist Margaret Thomson Davis, a writer noted for her painstakingly accurate research, paints an evocative picture of such a journey:

> The big gates of Hyde Park swung open at last and there were appreciative gasps from the crowd as the gigantic work of art fashioned in shining steel, a thing of power and beauty, moved forward...A spontaneous cheer went up from people lining the pavements and leaning from open windows as the locomotive made its slow, dignified progress over the cobbles of Vulcan Street, vibrating as it did so every dish on every shelf in the surrounding houses. The traction engines billowing yellow smoke from their copper-capped stacks continued to ease the engine forward and the cavalcade of officials came after it at a brisk walking pace or in vehicles. Round the elbow bend of Springburn Road it went and down the hill past St Rollox and slowly, slowly it trundled under Inchbelly Bridge while everyone held their breath. There seemed no more than one inch at most between the chimney cap and the bottom of the girders.[40]

Contemporary prints and photographs portray a jam-packed, filthy-dirty metropolis bristling with chimneys belching smoke out into an already over-polluted atmosphere, the streets black with people. The photographs of the pre-war engineering shops show vast structures large enough to contain whole locomotives, boilers, ships' engines, turbines, gun-turrets and barrels.

Pictures of the River Clyde show it similarly packed with shipping, the masts and spars of sailing ships intermingled with the funnels of steam-packets, paddle-driven ferry boats, the 'puffers' of the Highland coastal trade, and transatlantic passenger vessels dwarfing the smaller tenders, tugs and 'cluthas' which ferried workers up and down the Clyde. The many photographs of male workers of the period show men universally wearing large 'bunnets', or cloth caps, and crossed 'mufflers', or scarves. I have not seen a single photograph in which one of these workers is wearing a coat. The photographs of female workers – much fewer in number – tend to show cheerfully smiling women, with their hair in buns, wielding the universal mop and pail, and wearing protective aprons. They also show – a point ignored in the academic literature – women working routinely in three shipbuilding trades, as tracers, french-polishers and riggers.[41] In the latter trade, women were responsible for making hatch-covers, spray-sheets and awnings. What of these workers? Where did they come from, over one million of them?

The Glasgow Working Class

For all their resourcefulness, Glasgow's industrial barons would have been unable to benefit from the readily available natural resources, or from the west-facing River Clyde, had vast reserves of labour not been available. More than that, these reserves had to be landless and propertyless, and their connections with their rural roots severed, so that they could be inducted into the discipline of industrial production. These reserves of labour were ready and waiting at the start of Glasgow's industrialisation. They came from three areas: Lowland Scotland (particularly the South-West), the Scottish Highlands and Ireland. They flocked into Glasgow in such numbers that the city had the fastest population growth in the whole of Europe in the nineteenth century. Between 1811 and 1901, the population of the city increased seven-fold, from 100,700 to 761,709, while between 1800 and 1900 that of the built-up area increased twelve-fold, from 85,000 to 1,071,000.[42]

Lowland Scots

The bulk of the migrants to Glasgow in the last quarter of the eighteenth century were Scottish-born Lowlanders from the surrounding counties of Dunbartonshire, Renfrewshire, Lanarkshire, Ayrshire, Dumfriesshire and Wigtownshire. These were people dispossessed from the land, rural labourers, former colliers and handloom weavers. But they were not without a history of struggle behind them, and in fact carried a radical political tradition with them which went back at least as far as the struggles against rural enclosures in the late seventeenth and early eighteenth centuries.[43] (In spite of being serfs, in a legal sense, until 1799, living in wretched tied cottages and working in appalling conditions, the Lanarkshire miners were noted for their militancy.[44] This combative tradition they brought to the Glasgow Trades Council on which they were represented until the First World War.) All these groups were heavily involved in the radical politics of the time from the Friends of the People in 1792-93 to the United Scotsmen of 1797–1802, and later the Chartists.[45] They had read Tom Paine's *Rights of Man* and planted their liberty trees. It was this Jacobin and republican tradition to which Robert Burns was appealing in his poem, 'The Tree of Liberty', which was published in Glasgow:

> For Freedom, standing by the tree,
>   Her sons did loudly ca', man;
> She sang a song o' liberty,
>   Which pleased them ane and a', man.
> By her inspired, the new-born race
>   Soon drew the avenging steel, man;
> The hirelings ran – her foes gied chase,
>   And banged the despot weel, man.

One suspects that the professional Scotsmen who attend the annual Burns saturnalia in such droves wouldn't know what a Tree of Liberty was if it fell on top of their heads.

The common people of the South-West of Scotland, then, possessed what Scots historian James D. Young has called '...a passionate levelling egalitarianism' which seems to have carried a much deeper implantation of the ideas of the French Revolution than had taken root in England.[46] Indeed, one would have expected this as a result of the 'Auld Alliance' between Scotland and France. Young has documented the strength and pervasiveness of this movement in Scotland.[47] It certainly reached into Glasgow as we know from the strike of the Calton weavers in 1787, when after a two-month long strike against starvation wages, the military were called out and, following a violent confrontation, six weavers were shot dead.[48] The Lord Provost and Magistrates of Glasgow fell over themselves to congratulate the military and gave the officers a dinner in the Tontine Hotel.

But the weavers did not abandon the struggle, and fought in their illegal trade unions and in the courts for decent wages. These struggles were linked to wider political demands for the abolition of private property and for national independence.[49] It was estimated by the authorities that in Glasgow and the surrounding region there were over 100,000 workers in illegal 'combinations' in 1812.[50] Earl Grey, discussing the radical reform agitation in the House of Lords said, on 16 June 1817:

> Glasgow was one of the places where treasonable practices were said, in the Report of the Secret Committee of both Houses, to prevail to the greatest degree; but there could no longer be any doubt that the alleged treasonable oaths were administered by hired spies and informers.[51]

This culminated in the first General Strike in Scotland in 1820, in what was known as the 'Radical Rising', so there was a direct link between the local republican tradition and the battle for trade union recognition. This radical spirit was so well recognised in Glasgow that it led to a somewhat bitter joke:

> Those whose purses could not afford tea or coffee used a substitute for the latter sold in the city under the name of 'Radical Coffee', so called because it was favoured by some of the disaffected; it consisted of horse beans, rye or wheat, partially carbonised and ground down.[52]

While the 1820 revolt failed, it still did not put an end to militant unrest. It is plain that this republican spirit carried over into the militant Chartist struggles of the 1840s in Glasgow and surrounding areas, as is evident from the masthead quotation from the French revolutionary La Fayette in the local weekly newsaper, *Chartist Circular* (1839-42): 'For a Nation to Love Liberty, it is Sufficient That She Knows it; and to be Free, it is Sufficient That She Wills it.'[53] In fact, it is probable that the very radicalism of these Lowland areas was due in part to the presence in them of numbers of Highlanders and Irish well before the major traumas of the Clearances and the Famine.

The Highlanders

The connection between Glasgow and the Scottish Highlands is centuries old. In our period, and right up until well after the last war, it had potent symbols. Before the railway over Argyle Street was built in 1879 Highlanders used to congregate every Sunday evening at the north-west corner of the Broomielaw Bridge. The area was known as the 'Gaelic Cross', and missonary speakers would hold services in Gaelic.[54] The sheltered arcade in Argyle Street under the Central Station railway bridge has, for decades, been known as the 'Hielanman's Umbrella', as that was their next meeting-place. The local regiment was the Highland Light Infantry (Glasgow Highlanders). Then there was the Highlanders' Institute, with its popular dances and ceilidhs, shut only in 1979. There were many clan and county associations in the city. And there was the legendary, ubiquitous 'teuchter' polis, or policeman. (The word 'teuchter' is a mildly derogatory Lowlanders' word for a Highlander. Its etymology is totally obscure and I have never heard a satisfactory explanation.) What are the origins of these connections?

The central historical connection is trade, by both land and sea. The old drove roads for cattle came down Loch Lomondside to Glasgow via Drymen, although communication with the north-west Highlands and the Islands was easier by sea. To say that Glaswegians' original attitude towards the Highlanders was hostile would be to put it mildly. Generally, they were seen as uncouth savages, and basically feared. There was, of course, some historical justification for this, for not only did the Highland clansmen raid travellers passing through their territories, they had been used in the repression of the Covenanters in Glasgow in 1677 during the religious wars.[55] And as we have seen, they were thoroughly unwelcome guests during the 1745 Rising. They were referred to quite simply as the 'Irish', as was their language, until well into the eighteenth century. This reference to their historical origins was meant to be abusive, to classify the Highlanders and their language as 'foreign', that is, non-Scots. But Glasgow's geographical location inevitably meant that it became the trading centre for the Highlands. Sir Walter Scott provides an evocative picture of the meeting of the two cultures:

The dusky mountains of the Western Highlands often sent forth wilder tribes to frequent the marts of St Mungo's favourite city. Hordes of wild, shaggy, dwarfish cattle and ponies, conducted by Highlanders as wild, as shaggy and sometimes as dwarfish as the animals they had in charge, often traversed the streets of Glasgow. Strangers gazed with surprise on the antique and fantastic dress and listened to the unknown and dissonant sounds of their language, while the mountaineers, armed even while engaged in this peaceful occupation with musket and pistol, sword, dagger and target, stared with astonishment on the articles of luxury of which they knew not the use, and with an avidity which seemed somewhat alarming on the articles which they knew and valued.[56]

By the eighteenth century Highlanders appear in Glasgow civic affairs in ever-increasing numbers, as tradesmen, merchants and academics. In 1760, the Black Bull Inn in Argyle Street was built specifically for the city's Highlanders by the Glasgow Highland Society. It was soon the informal hub of the Highlanders' labour market.[57] They maintained a distinct sub-culture within the city by virtue of their different language, the Gaelic; for many, their fundamentalist Presbyterianism; and their culture and history. They were not a rural proletariat like the people of South-West Scotland. They were clanspeople from a patriarchal, warrior, semi-feudal system which had been systematically destroyed after Culloden. They carried with them memories of a simple but arcadian past which came to be increasingly romanticised in the urban environment. In 1835, according to a church census in Glasgow, there were 22,234 Highlanders with many more who could not or would not be counted.[58] According to the 1851 census, the number of Glasgow residents born in the 'classic' Highland counties were as follows: Argyll: 11,858; Invernessshire: 2,434; Ross and Cromarty: 815; Sutherland: 447; Perthshire: 6,683, making a total of 21,737, or 6.6 per cent of the city's population of 329,097. This figure does not include the many thousands more born in Glasgow or elsewhere of Highland parentage, which would easily push the proportion above 10 per cent. Throughout the eighteenth century many Highland Societies were founded in Glasgow, and these were partly benevolent, partly social, clubs. The first Gaelic Church was established in Ingram Street in 1770, the second in Duke Street in 1798 and the third in the Gorbals in 1813.[59] In that year Glasgow also had two Gaelic schools.[60]

According to the censuses, the number of Scots Gaelic

speakers in Glasgow was as follows. (1891 was the first census in which systematic questions about Scots Gaelic-speaking was included):

1891	1901	1911	1921	1931	1951	1961	1971	1981
17,978	18,517	16,544	16,744	16,276	12,566	12,165	12,865	9,472

Source: Censuses of Glasgow.

The numbers of Gaelic speakers remained fairly constant until after the Second World War. This was reflected in Gaelic publishing, which jumped from 38 items in the second half of the eighteenth century to 252 in the nineteenth century.[61] Of course, it is to be remembered that not all Gaelic speakers were literate in their own language, any more than 'Highlander' was a homogeneous category. There was a tendency, for example, for Catholic Islanders from South Uist and Barra to live in the Kinning Park area on the South Side, while the main Protestant contingent lived – and still lives – in the Partick area. These religious and clan and territorial groups all had their different clubs and pubs, and indeed there are still a few pubs in Glasgow, like the Ben Nevis Bar and the Park Bar in Argyle Street, where you can hear Gaelic spoken routinely every night of the week.

The Glasgow City Police was founded in 1800, when there were 83 officers, or about one for every thousand inhabitants, growing to 523 officers in five divisions in 1848.[62] From the earliest days Highlanders have been prominent in the force. In selecting randomly from the Register of Police Officers from 1881 until 1890, I found the following proportions of Highland-born officers to all recruits: 1881-84 (the years covered by the particular register), 163 out of 582; 1884-89, 203 out of 570; and 1889-90, 127 out of 265; or 28, 35.6 and 47.9 per cent respectively.[63] While there were not a few recruits from both the north and south of Ireland and, of course, from elsewhere in Scotland, it is plain that Highlanders formed the single biggest grouping in the force, at least for the period in question. Names like Neil Cameron,

Hector Campbell, Roderick Chisholm, Murdoch MacLeod and Donald MacDonald abound. Places of birth like Tain, North and South Uist, Assynt and Lochbroom recur frequently. 'Former occupations' of recruits include gamekeeper, labourer, forester, shepherd, fisherman, seaman, blacksmith and many ex-soldiers. (Interestingly enough, a very large number of these police officers were disciplined at least once for being the 'worse of liquor'!) It is not difficult to see why so many Highland men became policemen. From the founding of the Black Watch regiment in 1739, there has been a military tradition in the Highlands; between 1756 and 1815, 23 regiments of foot and 26 of 'fencibles' (reserves) – some 50,000 men in all – were raised in the Scottish Highlands.[64] Many men naturally joined a uniformed, disciplined force on leaving the colours. Then there was forced rural depopulation throughout the Highlands in the late eighteenth and nineteenth centuries, and many men joined up because there was no other work. And the Glasgow police have actively recruited in the Highlands and Islands for a long time. Until relatively recently, the height qualification for the force was 5 feet 10 inches, and substantial numbers of men of this stature were to be found mainly amongst the healthy and sturdy stock of the north and west of Scotland. In 1900 the Glasgow police force was reckoned to be the strongest body of men in the world; they were world champions at tug-of-war. PC Kennedy, 6 foot 2 inches tall and 28 stones in weight, was the biggest policeman in the world and held over 200 prizes for throwing the hammer, putting the shot and tossing the caber.[65] In any event, the 'teuchter polis' rapidly passed into the folklore of the Glasgow working class as a somewhat slow but utterly fearless giant who would go into the backcourt with a malefactor, take his tunic off and have a 'square-go'. By the start of the First World War he was an established figure in the Glasgow streetscape.

The majority of Highlanders, however, became ordinary workers who, with their Irish cousins, formed the human raw material of Glasgow's industrialisation. They were sucked into the mills, factories, docks and shipyards. In an interesting study of the Govan area, Calum Campbell shows that in 1891 Highlanders were twice as likely to be labourers than one would expect from their numbers in the population.[66] They were concentrated in semi-skilled and unskilled occupations, with many Highland women working in the textile mills and in bleaching and dyeing. Even more Highland women worked in service, as domestics and maids for Glasgow's bourgeoisie. To this day, many West End flats have bed-recesses in the (large) kitchens, with numbered bells, where the 'Highland girl' used to sleep. Like the Irish, the Highlanders were overcrowded in the worst slum housing. But they managed to maintain their cultural identity, often unfortunately as a result of being set in sectarian strife against their Irish neighbours by the industrialists we have discussed earlier. Interestingly enough, it has been put to me that this sectarianism was an *urban* phenomenon; this sectarian hatred did not exist in the Highlands themselves. For example, the Chief of the Clan Fraser has been a Catholic for centuries, while ordinary clanspeople are predominantly Protestant. This did not appear to present a problem to anyone.[67] By the same token, the Catholic and Protestant communities in South Uist live together harmoniously; their differences are theological, not social.

The key cultural attribute which the Highlanders brought with them to the city, and one vital in the formation of the Glasgow working class, was their bitter hatred of the landlords and lairds who had driven them violently off the land during the Clearances. The history of the Highland Clearances, and the controversies surrounding them, has been written elsewhere.[68] But it would not be too fanciful to suggest that the British state attempted systematic cultural genocide against the Gaels, and nearly succeeded. It was the *deliberate and calculated nature* of the Clearances coupled with their ruthlessness which distinguished them from rural depopulation elsewhere. It is very difficult for the modern city dweller not of a Highland background to understand the agony of being summarily wrenched from land which had belonged to one's ancestors and clan for generations. It is best to let the Gaelic poets express the deep feelings of the dispossessed:

Gur gbochd leam an cunntas	I find sad the account
Tha nochd as mo dhuthaich,	tonight from my country,
Mo chairdean 'g an sgiursadh	my friends are being scourged
Aig umaidhean Ghall;	by Lowland poltroons;
Le bataichean ruisgte	with sticks at the ready
'G an slachdadh mar bhruidean,	being beaten like cattle,
Mar thraillean gun diu dhiugbh,	like slaves quite uncared for
'G an dunadh am fang	being shut in a fank.
An sluagh bha cho cairdeil,	The folk who were friendly,
Cho suairce 's cho baigheil,	and kindly, warm-hearted,
Rinn uachdarain straiceil	have now been pressed sore
Am fasgadh cho teann;	by landlords' conceit;
Tha saors' air am fagail,	their freedom has left them,
Tha 'nraointean 'n am fasaic,	their fields are deserted,
'S na caoraich an aite	sheep have taken the place
Nan armunn 's a' ghleann.[69]	of free men in the glen.

Or:

Gu'n chuir iad fo na naosgaichean,	They handed over to the snipe
An tir a b' aoidheil sluagh,	the land of happy folk,
Gu'n bhuin iad cho neo-dhaonn	
tachail,	they dealt without humanity
Ri daoine 'bha cho suairc'.	with people who were kind.
A chionn nach faoidte 'm bathadh,	Because they might not drown them
Chaidh an sganradh thar a' chuain;	they dispersed them overseas:
Bu mhiosa na bruid Bhabilion,	a thralldom worse than Babylon's
An caradh sin a fhuair.	was the plight that they were in.
Cu'n mheas iad mar gu'm shnathainn iad	They reckoned as but brittle threads
Na cordan graidh 'bha teann,	the tight and loving cords
A' ceangal cridh' nam beann.	that bound these freemen's noble heart
Ri duthaich ard nam beann.	to the high land of the hills.
Gu'n d' thug am bron am bas orra.	The grief they suffered brought them d
'N deidh crabhaidh nach bu ghann;	although they suffered long,
'S an saoghal fuar 'g an sarachadh.[70]	tormented by the cold world.

But although the Glasgow 'teuchters' were notorious for a certain Celtic melancholy, not all their poems and songs are sad. The following is an extract from Iain MacPhadein's 'An T-Eileanach', a sharply observed series of poems and readings about Glasgow at the turn of the century. The poet is taking the micky, to coin a racist phrase, out of the Irish; the poem is called 'Sing of the Saltmarket', sung to the tune of 'Johnny Stays Long at then Fair':

Na O'Rork's na M'Gorks 's iad a' mort nan O'Branigans;
Bh' aig Kelly *shillelah* 's e 'g éirigh air Flannigan,
Michael Mulhoul gu 'n dhall e O'Rafferty,
    'S leag iad M'Cafferty fhein.

Nuair thòisich an tuasaid bu chruaidh a bha 'n sadadh;
Bha slaodadh air cluasan is struaiceadh air claiginn;
Gach fear air a bhualadh is spuaic air a mhalaidh,
    'S e glaodhaich air caraid gu streup.

O'Brian's O'Ryan's, O'Reilly's O'Ligerim;
O'Brearie's O'Learie, O'Shearie 's O'Sigerim;
O'Hara, M'Ara, O'Larra 's O'Liderim;
    Barney M'Fiddie 's M'Dade.

Nuair shéid iad na fideagan chiteaoh 'nam cabhaig iad,
A' couban 'gan deoin 's gach froig am falach;
Gu 'n tug iad an anin 's ha tuill fo thallamh,
    Mar radian is abhag 'nan déidh.

*   *   *

The O'Rorks and M'Gorks set to kill the O'Branigans,
Kelly with shillelagh making for Flannigan,
Michael Mulhoul blinded O'Rafferty,
    and McCafferty down on the ground.

When the fighting began there were hard blows a-plenty,
there was tugging of ears and tearing of skulls,
not a man but was hit, a lump on his forehead,
    and calling a friend to the fray.

O'Brian, O'Ryan, O'Reilly, O'Ligerim,
O'Brearie, O'Learie, O'Shearie, O'Shigerim,
O'Hara, M'Ara, O'Larra, O'Liderim,
    Barney M'Fiddle, M'Dade.

When the whistles were blown they took to their heels,
crouching in corners in order to hide,
down with their heads in holes underground,
like rats with a terrier in chase.[71]

By the last quarter of the nineteenth century the Highlanders were active in any political movement for Highland land reform and crofters' rights. They therefore backed successively the Crofters' Party, the Scottish Labour Party, the Liberal Party and the Scottish Land Restoration League.[72] They were prominent in the agitation for the Crofters' Commission which was established in 1883. By the beginning of the twentieth century they were being drawn into socialist politics via the Independent Labour Party (ILP) and became active in the rents struggle in Glasgow, and their main neighbourhood, Partick, played a prominent role in the famous 1915 Rent Strike.[73] While retaining a distinct sub-cultural identity, the Highlanders were by now an integral part of the Glasgow working class.

The Irish in Glasgow

Put at its simplest, without the Irish there would have been no industrialisation in Glasgow, or elsewhere in Scotland for that matter. They laid the roads and railways, they dug the canals and the dams, they constructed the tenements, factories and mills, they mined the coal and iron ore, they laboured in shipyard and dock, they wove, spun, and bleached and dyed the textiles. (Indeed, the latter industry was almost entirely staffed by women from Ireland and the Highlands.) They worked in town and country, in summer and winter. They, men, women and children, are the unsung heroes of the Industrial Revolution in Scotland; their reward has been relentless sectarian vilification and violence.

Anti-Irish racism in Britain has a long history which has been inadequately studied.[74] The English have never forgiven the Irish for refusing to accept the benefits of colonial rule, and for daring to fight doggedly against it for centuries. This led to the Elizabethan and Cromwellian massacres in Ireland, and to the long attempt by the English to portray the Irish as moronic savages. This antipathy has a particularly hard edge in Scotland, especially in the West Central region, including Glasgow. There are essentially two reasons for this. The first is the consequence of the Plantation of the counties of Antrim and Down in Ulster with Lowland Scots Protestants in the seventeenth century. It was the Irish rising against these Planters which led to the Cromwellian massacres. The Irish were portrayed systematically as 'rebels' against the 'legitimate' rule of the outsiders. The second reason is the legacy of the vicious religious wars in Scotland, which started in the sixteenth century with the Reformation and continued with the massacres and counter-massacres of the Covenanting years in the second half of the seventeenth century. For complex historical reasons, including the geographical proximity of Ulster and economic links, these events are burned deep into the psyche of Scottish people, both Catholic and Protestant, above all in the Glasgow area.

Although the 'Scots' were originally Irish, the first Christian missionaries in Scotland were also Irish, and there has been population exchange and trade between the two countries for at least a couple of millenia, there were few Irish in Glasgow itself before 1800. As far as the city's history is concerned, the critical event was the Irish Famine of the 1840s. As James Handley, the historian of the Irish in Scotland, says of the migratory Irish peasant:

> Self-improvement was the impulse that transported him to Scotland in pre-famine days. Self-preservation was the urge that drove him onwards in the black night of pestilence.[75]

Dr Handley's evidence makes it plain that the provisions of the English government's Irish Poor Law Bill of 1838 were deliberately aimed at quickening the pace of Irish depopulation. The failure of the potato crop, wholly or partially, every year between 1846 and 1850 finished the business. Even then, it is vital to repeat that Ireland was a net exporter of food during these years. The ensuing tragedy was a result of English governmental policy. The population of Ireland was calculated to be 8,175,124 in

1841. By 1850 some 900,000 Irish had emigrated, and some 1,250,000 had died of the 'great hunger' or associated fever.[76]

The Irish fled to Britain, to Merseyside and Clydeside in particular, but also to London and other regions. The 'better-off' used Liverpool and Glasgow as jumping-off points for the onward journey to Canada and the United States. The poorer stayed. The floods of desperate, starving, penniless, sick and ill-clad refugees provided a most important stimulus to the early Glasgow steamship-building industry. A trade war between the cross-channel shipping companies raged with the consequence that fares became ridiculously low. At their lowest during the 1840s, the Belfast-Glasgow steerage fare was 3d, the Derry-Glasgow fare one shilling. The passengers were jammed on these paddle-steamers like cattle. In one twelve-day period in 1847 no less than 12,940 poor Irish people were landed directly in Glasgow, or via the Ardrossan rail-link, by four steamers making thirteen trips.[77] These boats were very small. One boat, the *Londonderry*, of 277 tons, carried 1,778 passengers on one of these trips. An idea of the degree of overcrowding can be gained from a comparison with the *Waverly*, the paddle-steamer with which every Glaswegian is acquainted from trips 'doon the watter'. Although built in the classic pattern of Clyde paddle-steamers, the *Waverley* is only forty years old, with all modern navigational and life-saving equipment. She displaces 372 tons, and has a passenger certificate for an average of 842 passengers. Her absolute maximum is 1,120 passengers. It is small wonder that the conditions on these early ferries were disgusting, that the passengers reeled off them, and that not a few died *en route*.

According to the 1841 census, there were 44,000 Irish-born people in the city of Glasgow, that is 16 per cent of the total population. In 1851 the figure was 18.2 per cent.[78] But as Handley points out, these figures, and the figures for the Irish in Scotland as a whole, do not

include the many people born in Scotland of Irish parentage. Given the long-standing connection between Ireland
and the West of Scotland, he estimates that there was
probably the same number again of Irish extraction. That
would mean 36.4 per cent of the city's population in 1851.
In other words, we could say that by mid-century about
one-third of Glasgow's population was of immediate or
fairly recent Irish extraction. The proportion for the surrounding region would be very similar. But a sizeable
proportion of the Irish immigrants were Ulster Protestants and, according to one estimate, by the 1860s they
constituted one-quarter of the Irish population of Glasgow.[79] This of itself would have served to keep the flames
of sectarianism burning brightly.

The working and living conditions of the Irish in Glasgow and its region were appalling, and Handley documents these at length.[80] In Glasgow, they concentrated
initially in the narrow wynds of the High Street, the Saltmarket and the Bridgegate. As they sought work in the unskilled sectors of the construction, engineering, mining,
shipbuilding and textile industries, they were used by
employers against existing workers to bring wages down,
in the classic strategem described by Marx as the 'reserve
army of labour'. In these circumstances, it was hardly surprising that the Irish were accused of being strike-
breakers, and that sectarian conflict was exacerbated.
And make no mistake about it, the Irish and their Catholic
religion were bitterly resented by the native Scots. In the
popular eye, the words 'Irish' and 'Catholic' were synonymous in Glasgow and its hinterland, until at least the
First World War. But the massive and ever-increasing
pool of cheap labour constituted by the Highlanders and
the Irish was precisely what enabled the industrialisation
of Glasgow to proceed at such a breakneck pace. The sectarian conflict both kept labour costs down, and militated
against effective trade unionism. The Irish, however,
rapidly came to gain a grudging respect on two counts:
firstly, they were grafters, and secondly, their community
was marked by high standards of moral behaviour. They

might get drunk and fight each other as well as the Protestants but, by-and-large, they were law-abiding people.

Like the Highlanders, the Irish brought their culture with them. In the first instance, they brought a dreadful poverty. Their very need for clothes led to the establishment of 'Paddy's Market' in the Bridgegate area as early as the 1820s.[81] This colourful second-hand clothes and household-goods street market is still going to this day. Then they brought a bitter hatred of the English – the 1798 Rising and the fearful repression afterwards were within living memory. Their greatest desire was Home Rule for Ireland. They carried a further hatred of the landlords who had driven them off the land. This was to be deepened in the second half of the century by the Land Wars in Ireland, in which the peasantry, under the leadership of Michael Davitt, clashed head-on with the landlords. And they brought their music and song, perhaps even more so than the Highlanders, whose musical self-expression was somewhat constrained by a Calvinist disapproval of any form of pleasure. In general, the Irish were a more exuberant people than the Highlanders. The reason is simple; they had never been beaten. But they were equally capable of expressing their love for their land, and their anguish in their exile. The following verse from the beautiful song 'Slieve Gallion Braes' is the version sung by the late and much-loved Irish traditional singer, Mary Wall:

> It was not the want of employment at home,
>> That caused all the sons of Old Ireland to roam;
> But those tyrannising landlords,
>> They would not let us stay,
> So farewell unto ye bonny, bonny Slieve Gallion Braes.
>> But the rents were getting higher,
> And we could no longer stay –
>> So farewell unto ye bonny, bonny Slieve Gallion Braes.

The Irish emigration peaked between 1850 and 1875; in 1874 there were still daily sailings between Glasgow and Dublin, and regular services between Glasgow and Belfast, Derry, Sligo, Westport, Ballina, Portrush,

Limerick, Cork and Waterford.[82] Thereafter, it steadily declined, although it was still not insubstantial, standing at 30,687 Irish-born Glasgow residents according to the 1891 census, 33,997 in 1901 and 26,562 in 1911.[83] But by 1891 the vast majority of Catholics in Glasgow and West Central Scotland were native-born, a fact overlooked by Protestant bigots who right up until the Second World War were prone to talk of the 'native stock' being 'swamped' by Irish 'aliens'. It is probably true to say that like the Highlanders, the Irish maintained a distinct cultural identity up until the First World War, with their own pubs and clubs and, of course, many church organisations not to mention the Celtic Football Club. Their potential for political mobilisation is indicated by claims made for IRA membership in Glasgow in 1920.[84]

A key factor in the relative social isolation of the Irish was their location in the labour market. Out of sheer prejudice the skilled trades routinely excluded the Irish up until the First World War, and in many cases, until 1939. The phrases 'Irish need not apply' and 'No Irish' were well-known on the Clyde. From the Famine until 1914 the Irish were concentrated in unskilled manual jobs – although it is accepted that a lot of jobs termed 'unskilled' did in fact contain a skilled element, if not to the level of tradesman. Within Glasgow, Irishmen were to be found in abundance as dock, wharf and shipyard labourers; as builders', masons' and bricklayers' labourers; and as road and general labourers. But these were precisely the occupations most subject to both seasonality of employment and casualisation.[85] They were, not surprisingly, the lowest paid. Foundry labourers in Glasgow were getting between 17 and 19 shillings per week, when they were working. Railway labourers got between 18 and 20 shillings. And dock labourers got 7d per hour, from 1890-1907, while shipbuilding and boilermaking labourers got fourpence-halfpenny per hour.[86] That is to say, if a shipbuilding labourer worked an eight-hour day, six days a week, he would get 18 shillings per week. But a shipyard labourer never worked six days a week in the first decade of this century; there were 10,000 of them, far too many for the available jobs.[87] Their labour was totally casualised. Irishwomen worked in steam laundries, as chars and in the textile industry, both in spinning factories and in sweated labour in the home. The stark reality for these families was unrelenting poverty.

It is also the case that while their Catholic religion undoubtedly helped the Irish in their daily struggle for survival, it also impeded them on two counts. Firstly, an unknown but certainly considerable amount of the cash surplus of the Irish community went into building churches and schools, and supporting their priests. A glance at the Catholic churches of Glasgow of this period reveals substantial and not inexpensive buildings. While richer Catholics like publicans and small businessmen undoubtedly contributed handsomely in the years before the First World War, the bulk of the money must have come from the poor. Secondly, the very triumphalist, introverted, authoritarian and anti-intellectual nature of Irish Catholicism played its part in preventing Irish workers from making common cause with their Protestant brothers and sisters in the labour and trade union movement. The Catholic Church was paranoid about socialism. This was not helped, of course, by the fact that the Irish were actively *excluded* by the elite trade unionists like the engineers and boiler-makers. In spite of this, by the end of the century the Glasgow Irish are beginning to appear amongst the leaders of the 'new unionism', like the dock labourers, and become more and more visible politically as the twentieth century advances.

Working Conditions

So if we could say that by 1913 the Glasgow working class was fully formed, and that its key characteristic was that it was an *industrial* working class, a major caveat would have to be its complex internal structure.

The class was fissured – more deeply than any other in Britain – by skill, gender, religion, and regularity of employment. (The *politics* of this will be discussed in Chapter 4.) Let us take shipbuilding as an example. At the top was a stratum of highly-skilled engineers, pattern-makers, boiler-makers and the like – sober, respectable, Presbyterian, valued and consulted (sometimes) by their employers. They were the labour aristocrats of Glasgow, and they knew it; they had a good conceit of themselves. Red Clydesider Harry McShane, an engineer himself, describes them thus:

> Every member of the ASE [Amalgamated Society of Engineers] was a time-served man, and in the union there was a stand-offish attitude: a sort of craft pride, and a pride of union. The members really believed themselves to be the aristocrats of labour, and they dressed differently and better than other workers. Like all craftsmen they wore blue shirts and bowler hats on weekends but during the week they wore a deep-sea cap, like the ones they wore at sea. They all thought they were marine engineers![88]

The classic example of someone from this stratum is David Kirkwood, later Lord Kirkwood of Bearsden.[89] Below this was another layer of highly skilled workers, tradesmen of a slightly lower status; iron- and brass-moulders, shipwrights, joiners, blacksmiths, hammermen, plumbers, riggers. They were mainly local Protestants. Some of these workers, the joiners, for example, were better paid than the engineers, but the latter had a higher status because of the greater security of their work.[90] Then there were the skilled workers of the 'black squad' – riveters, holders-on, platers, anglesmiths and caulkers. These were substantially Protestant, but the Irish and the Highlanders were appearing in this group by the end of the century because of these trades' need for brute strength, if for no other reason. Then there were hordes of so-called unskilled labourers, a category actually containing a wide range of skills, as for example, stevedoring or red-leading. By the beginning of the twentieth century, the bulk of the Irish and some of the Highlanders were still concentrated in the seasonal and casualised labouring jobs requiring little but strength and stamina.

In much industrial work in our period, a great deal of strength and stamina *was* needed. At the beginning of the period of industrialisation the working day was as long as the employers could make men and women work. But as the nineteenth century wore on, and workers began to organise, a twelve-hour day became the norm, with a six-day working week. The better organised trade unions, like the engineers, fought for a reduction of the working week; in 1868 they worked a 58-hour week. At that time, the wages for a skilled man were about 27 shillings per week.[91] By the beginning of the twentieth century, most skilled trades worked a 54-hour, five-and-a-half day week, while an engineer's weekly pay in 1913 was between 32 and 36 shillings. Harry McShane describes the situation in his memoirs:

> Up to 1914 our week was 54 hours. All working people, including boys and girls, started at 6 a.m. and finished at 5.30 p.m., and worked until noon on Saturdays. During the war it had been extended to a 12-hour day and Saturday and Sunday working. The six o'clock start was miserable: you had to get up at five, and you couldn't go out or do anything at night because you would tire yourself for the morning. When I worked at Dalmuir during the war I had to get out of the house before five to get the ferry to Anderston Cross and the train to Dalmuir; there were no lights on the train, nobody spoke, and the only sign of life was the spark from somebody's pipe. To get the hours reduced would be a victory for us all as well as helping unemployment.[92]

This makes the constant evening political work of socialist leaders like McShane even more extraordinary.

But the 54-hour week was a privilege gained only by powerful unions of the skilled trades like the ASE. It is to be remembered that many workers, lacking such organisation, worked much longer hours. The masons' labourers, a socially despised but radical group, the majority of whom were Irish, worked a theoretical

51-hour week for 5d per hour, or 21s 3d per week.[93] But the 51-hour week was the masons' and bricklayers' week: the labourers worked much longer getting the job ready for the tradesmen the next morning.

A reporter attended a labourers' union meeting in 1889:

> In rather a flowery speech one of the orators contrasted the scenes amidst which they had passed the years of their childhood with the squalid misery to which they were now condemned. He pointed out that whilst they had been formerly accustomed to view the green fields and smiling valleys in their boyhood, to hear the singing of the birds, and listen to the gentle murmurs of the wind among the trees, that they had been forced by the greed of the capitalists to leave these beloved scenes, and betake themselves to the cities, to compete in the labour market that was already overstocked. They were compelled, he said, to live in hovels where their employers would not keep their dogs. Their children were forced to breathe the poisoned air of the back-slums of Glasgow, and to have their ears polluted and their minds corrupted by the most immoral people. The Being who had called them into existence had endowed them with reasoning facilities, and it was for them to think out the matter for themselves, and to see that they received a just reward for their labour. It was plain from the applause with which this speech was greeted that the large audience sympathised with his sentiments, and looked back with longing eyes to the happy times which he had so glowingly described.[94]

The nature of industrial work in Glasgow's factories and shipyards in the years before the war has received relatively little attention from academics compared with, say, the conditions of the coalminers. While the etchings of Muirhead Bone give a good general impression of shipyard work, and a size of its scale, it is the paintings of Stanley Spencer which do justice to the detail. His huge canvases, in the collection of the Imperial War Museum, were executed on the Clyde during the Second World War, but much of the work remained unchanged. We see boys red-leading ventilators, labourers hauling metal frames, rivet-boys heating rivets, with the holder-on inside a mast and the riveter hammering away, arc-welders – a new trade – at work, platers bending a keel plate, male and female riggers splicing ropes and cables and making tarpaulin hatch-covers, plumbers bending a pipe, blacksmiths hauling a white-hot beam from a furnace, burners cutting plates, pattern-makers carrying a template, and in this particular painting, 'The Template', a nice touch – a woman with her baby.

In the period before the First World War, a great deal of industrial work was highly dangerous. There was no such thing as Health and Safety at Work regulations; the life of a worker was literally cheap. Some of the works must have appeared like Dante's *Inferno*. Here is a description of Tennant's St Rollox Chemical Works in 1858, by a visiting businessman:

> The most extraordinary part of the works is that in which the sulphuric acid is made. In going into this place we pass between two mountains of sulphur, each of which contains 5,000 tons. We then enter a devil's den, with an immense row of glowing furnaces on each side of us and huge lead pipes above our heads and around us. And after we have been half roasted and our lungs struggling with the atmosphere, loaded with sulphuric gas, our good mentor takes us up a flight of narrow wooden steps until we ascend some hundred feet above the surrounding buildings. It would be utterly impossible to describe the surprising scene that meets the view. Immediately beneath us there are fifty-eight lead chambers for receiving the sulphurous gas, and converting it into vitriol; each of these immense aereal reservoirs hold 21,000 cubic feet of gas. These chambers are approached by many miles of wooden stages, from which, down to the south and west, the huge city forms a most glorious picture with the cathedral in the foreground, with the impress of 700 years.[95]

The terrible costs of working in this particular inferno were revealed some thirty years later, in 1889, in a newspaper interview with one of the chemical workers:

> You speak of the work being unhealthy. How does it affect the men?

If a man goes to the works young he will be past working before he reaches forty years of age...For instance, you will easily know a chrome-worker from the fact that, as a rule, the bridge of his nose is completely eaten away. In some cases, where they have not been so long employed amongst the chrome, you will notice that the nose is often partly decayed and in holes, and it is very seldom that you will find a chrome worker who is not more or less affected in this part.[96]

The majority of the chemical workers were Irish; they were paid an average of 15s 6d per week, a pitiful wage. Tennant himself lived to the ripe old age of 83; the gross value of his estate was £3,151,974 18s 1d. And that did not include his factories, nor his houses in Glasgow and London, nor the 5,200 acres of his country estate at 'The Glen' in Peebleshire.[97]

The dreadful conditions in these chemical plants were the subject of Keir Hardie's famous attacks on Lord Overtoun in 1899. Overtoun was the proprietor of a large chemical works on the Glasgow-Rutherglen border, and also a noted philanthropist and man of religion. Keir Hardie, in a series of articles in the socialist newspaper *Labour Leader* – subsequently reprinted as pamphlets – exposed the fearful working conditions in Overtoun's chemical works.[98] He confirmed that the workers rapidly lost the cartilage in their nose working with these noxious chemicals, but also suffered from 'chrome holes' being burnt in their body, and respiratory diseases. Moreover, they worked a twelve-hour day, seven-day week – with no time off for meals, and in foul conditions. Keir Hardie's stinging, and successful, exposé of Overtoun's hypocrisy was the talk of Glasgow at the end of the nineteenth century. His pamphlets were printed in runs of 80,000 at a time.

Death and fearful injury were also daily occurrences in the shipyards. In 1883 the 500-ton *Daphne* capsized at her launch from Stephen of Linthouse's yard, with nearly 200 fitters, joiners, riveters and labourers aboard, of whom 124 were drowned.[99] The *Govan Press*, a weekly

newspaper covering the major shipbuilding neighbourhood, reported a fatal accident in practically every issue
in the years up to the First World War; crushing, or
falling from staging, was common. The following report
of 25 May 1900, was typical:

> On Tuesday morning at about 8 o'clock when John
> Sanderson (44), carpenter of 104 Smith Street, Whiteinch,
> was engaged in working on a staging on vessel 414 in course
> of construction at Fairfield Yard, and while removing from a
> side staging onto the strings of the vessel which was 3 feet
> broad and about 5 feet below the staging, he overbalanced
> himself on reaching the strings, and fell backwards, a
> distance of about 18 feet, to the ground, whereby he was
> severely injured internally, and from which injuries he died
> shortly after he was admitted to the Western Infirmary.[100]

Old shipyard workers have told me stories of rivet-boys
slinging red-hot rivets high up the staging to be caught
by the holder-on in a small bucket; this was a routine
occurrence, not a circus trick. But if he missed the rivet,
and it fell on a worker below, it could burn a hole clean
through him. I have been told similar stories of men
working on a fitting on the outside of a ship's hull, on the
staging high above the ground, when a burner on the
inside started cutting a hole through the plate without
warning. Occupational deafness among platers and
riveters was commonplace, as was respiratory disease
from the muck flying about inside the hull. The 'black
squad' wasn't given its name because of its ethnic origins
but because of the filthy nature of its work. And, in terms
of the weather, none of the Glasgow shipyards was
enclosed before 1913. Quite simply, shipbuilding, heavy
engineering and the other forms of Glasgow's industrial
labour were hard, dirty, and dangerous – and low-paid,
relative to the rest of Britain – up till 1913. It was seen as
men's work and not for the faint of heart. The following is
a list of accidents in the various Springburn railway
works as reported for a short period in 1899 by a local
newspaper:

March 9th – Caledonian Railway Works. Man crushed by waggon. Dies in Royal Infirmary.

March 9th – Springburn Goods Station. Engine driver falls onto rails and fractures leg.

March 16th – Cowlairs Works. Man's trousers caught by revolving wheel. Severe lacerations above right knee.

March 16th – Clydesdale Iron Works. Man struck on chest by hammer. Dies fortnight later.

May 11th – Hyde Park railway works. Man drilling steel plate which overturned and fell on top of him. Severe internal injuries.[101]

It is plain from the evidence that many of these accidents were a result of fatigue induced by the long hours of work. The oral history of Springburn says:

In December 1891, 275, or 83.34 per cent of the Caledonian Railway's 334 passenger drivers and firemen worked more than twelve hours a day on 1331 occasions. In other words, most drivers worked more than twelve hours nearly five times that month, without a rest of eight hours before their next shift.[102]

Whatever the legitimate pride of these workers in their skill, their employers routinely put profits before people.

Glasgow's population and industrial growth throughout the nineteenth century had been not so much rapid as cataclysmic. But it was not until the last quarter of the nineteenth century that it had assumed its characteristic form as an engineering and shipbuilding city, dominated by huge units of production, substantially geared to the export trade. It was a vast city of distinct industrial neighbourhoods, urban villages and occupational communities, some of which like Govan, Springburn or Parkhead were practically company towns. Its working class was rumbustious, tough and unpredictable, fired by the hatred of the property-owning classes brought to it by

its Highland and Irish migrants. But it was also a class
with a good deal of confidence in itself and a great deal of
craft pride as Glasgow entered the twentieth century.
Glaswegians knew that it was they who had made the
place the 'Second City of Empire', and they didn't give a
damn for anyone else, and certainly not the English. It
was a thoroughly *Scottish* city. It was an introverted,
rough-and-ready place and one had to be tough to survive,
but Glaswegians had learned that the hard way. Their
culture was formed, their communities were formed, their
politics were formed. These were – and remain – imper-
meable to the casual interloper.

References

1. A. Slaven, *The Development of the West of Scotland: 1750-1960*,
Routledge & Kegan Paul, 1975; M. Moss and J. Hume, *Workshop of
the British Empire: Engineering and Shipbuilding in the West of
Scotland*, Heinemann, 1977.
2. e.g. J. Hume and M. Moss, *Beardmore: The History of a Scottish
Industrial Giant*, Heinemann, 1979; J.M. Reid, *James Lithgow –
Master of Work*, Hutchinson, 1964; P.L. Payne (ed.), *Studies in
Scottish Business History*, Cass, 1967; W.J. MacQuorn Rankine, *A
Memoir of John Elder, Engineer and Shipbuilder*, Blackwood, 1871.
See also the 'Profiles of Clyde Shipbuilders' in the *Glasgow Chamber
of Commerce Journal* in 1970-71 and the biographical sketches in
Clydeside Cameos, Sketches of Prominent Clydeside Men, 1885. I am
grateful to Joe Fisher of the Glasgow Collection in the Mitchell
Library for bringing the latter references to my attention.
3. T. C. Smout, 'The Glasgow Merchant Community in the 17th
Century', *Scottish Historical Review*, No. 47, 1968, quoted in A. Gibb,
Glasgow: The Making of a City, Croom Helm, 1983, p.53.
4. Slaven, op. cit., pp.28-30.
5. Sir Walter Scott, *Rob Roy*, Nelson, n.d., p.253.
6. See these rules displayed in the reconstructed Merchants' House in
the 'Early Glasgow' exhibition in the People's Palace Museum. I am
grateful to Elspeth King, Curator of the Museum, for drawing this
and the following two references to my attention.
7. 'Negro Slavery in the City of Glasgow' in Senex (Robert Reid),
Glasgow, Past and Present, 1856, pp.402ff.
8. See, *inter alia*, the adverts in the *Glasgow Journal* of 1 April 1773
and 30 December 1745, and in the *Glasgow Courant* of 10 May and 6
September 1756, and 28 August 1758.
9. The story of these tobacco merchants is told in T.M. Devine, *The
Tobacco Lords*, Edinburgh, John Donald, 1975. There is only one

mention in this book of a Glasgow merchant being 'involved...in the slave trade to the Carolinas'. (p.62). There must have been more.

10. Slaven, op. cit., p.97.
11. A. Campbell, *The Lanarkshire Miners: A Social History of their Trade Unions, 1775-1974*, Edinburgh, John Donald, 1979, p.112.
12. Ibid., and R. Page Arnot, *A History of the Scottish Miners*, Allen & Unwin, 1955.
13. Moss and Hume, op. cit., p.12.
14. Senex, op. cit., pp.139-40.
15. A.L. Lloyd, *Come All Ye Bold Miners: Ballads and Songs of the Coalfields*, Lawrence & Wishart, 1978, p.352. Two versions of the song are given on pp.179-81, while another song is given on p.182.
16. Ibid., pp.264 and 359.
17. Slaven, op. cit., pp.121 and 123.
18. W. Power, *Pavement and Highway: Specimen Days in Strathclyde*, Glasgow, Archibald Sinclair, 1911.
19. Ibid., pp.187-8.
20. Slaven, op. cit., p.132.
21. Ibid., p.178.
22. John Lee Carvel, *Stephen of Linthouse: A Record of Two Hundred Years of Shipbuilding*, Glasgow, Alexander Stephen, n.d. (c.1950), pp. 183ff.
23. *Glasgow. Burns Country. Dunoon. Rothesay. Arran*, Ward, Lock & Coy, Illustrated Guide Book, n.d. (c.1940).
24. A. Craig, *The Elder Park, Govan: An Account of the Life of the Elder Park and of the Erection and Unveiling of the Statue of the John Elder*, Glasgow, James Maclehose, 1891, pp.8-9.
25. See the exhibits and captions in the People's Palace Museum, Glasgow (as at autumn 1989).
26. Rankine, op. cit.
27. Carvel, op. cit., p.87.
28. Ibid; p.47.
29. Ibid.
30. Ibid.
31. Rankine, op. cit.
32. Ibid., p.198.
33. I am grateful to my friend Brian Martin, a Govan boy, and time-served engineer in Barclay Curle's, for this information.
34. Carvel, op. cit., p.89.
35. Craig, op. cit., pp.36-7.
36. See footnote 23. The figures for the bequests are from this source, and from Mrs Elder's own memorial volume: Sir A. Craig, *The Statue of Mrs Elder, Govan, etc.*, Glasgow, John Cossar, 1912.
37. *The Fairfield Shipbuilding and Engineering Works*, London, 'Engineering', 1909, p.19. ('Engineering' was the journal of the profession.)
38. Calum Campbell, *The Making of a Clydeside Working Class: Shipbuilding and Working Class Organisation in Govan*, Our History Pamphlet No.78, 1986, p.14.
39. Moss and Hume, op. cit.
40. Margaret Thomson Davis, *Rag Woman, Rich Woman*, Corgi, 1988, pp. 172-3.

41. See photograph opposite p.92 in 'Engineering', note 37 above, op. cit., for an example.

42. Computed from Gibb, op. cit., p.124 and Slaven and Aldcroft (eds.), op. cit., p.124.

43. Thomas Johnston, *The History of the Working Classes in Scotland*, 3rd edition, Glasgow, Forward Publishing Company, n.d., Ch. VII.

44. Ibid., Chs. XIII-XVI; see also Campbell, and Page Arnot, op. cit.

45. Johnston, ibid.

46. James D. Young, *The Rousing of the Scottish Working Class*, Croom Helm, 1979, p.44.

47. Ibid., Chs. 2 and 3.

48. Ibid., and Elspeth King, *The Strike of the Calton Weavers, 1787*, Glasgow Museums and Art Galleries, 1987.

49. Young, op. cit.

50. *Second Report from the Select Committee on Artisans and Machinery*, PP, Vol.V, 1824, p.70, quoted in Young, p.99.

51. Quoted in Peter Mackenzie, *Reminiscences of Glasgow and the West of Scotland*, 3 vols., Glasgow, John Tweed, 1867, p.125.

52. T. Ferguson ital., *Public Health and Urban Growth*, Glasgow, Centre for Urban Studies Report No. 4, 1964, p.4.

53. Ibid., see also Johnston, op. cit. A copy of the front page of the *Circular* was reproduced in the exhibition 'The French Revolution and the Scottish People', Mitchell Library, Glasgow, summer 1989.

54. 'The Streets of Glasgow' in *Glasgow Sketches*, 1889, book of newsaper cuttings in the Glasgow Room, Mitchell Library, ref. no. G330.193.01444 MIL. The pages in this cuttings book are not numbered. Again, thanks to Joe Fisher for this reference.

55. Robert Bain, 'The Gael in Glasgow', *Celtic Monthly*, Vol. XIX, 1911, p.66. I am grateful to my colleague Kenneth MacDonald of the Department of Celtic in the University of Glasgow for drawing this, and the following references, to my attention. The original 'Covenanters' were those Presbyterians who signed the National Covenant in Edinburgh in 1638 against Charles I's attempts to enforce Anglicanism, including a new 'Popish' prayer-book, on Scotland. The name also applied to those who fought against the king and for religious freedom in the subsequent religious wars.

56. Scott, op. cit., p.221.

57. Ibid.

58. C.W.J. Withers, *Gaelic in Scotland, 1698-1981: The Geographical History of a Language*, Edinburgh, John Donald, pp.184ff. This is the key reference for those wishing to plot the movements of the Celtic diaspora.

59. Bain, op. cit., p.106.

60. Ibid.

61. See footnote 55.

62. John Ord, 'The Origins and History of the Glasgow Police Force', Paper No. 6 to the Old Glasgow Club, 1906, in *Old Glasgow Club: Transactions, Vol. 1, 1900-1908*, Glasgow, Aird & Coghill, 1908.

63. These and subsequent data were derived from the *Register of Police Officers* in the Strathclyde Regional Archives. The appropriate reference is: (1881-1890): SS 22/55/11-13.

64. Allan Macinnes, 'Scottish Gaeldom: The First Phase of Clearance' in T.H. Devine and R. Mitchison (eds.), *People and Society in Scotland, Vol. 1, 1760-1830*, Edinburgh, John Donald, 1988, p.83.

65. Douglas Grant, *The Thin Blue Line: The Story of the Glasgow Police*, John Long, 1973, p.51.

66. Campbell, op. cit., p.8.

67. Personal communication, Mr Iain Fraser.

68. John Prebble, *The Highland Clearances*, Penguin, 1963; James Hunter, *The Making of the Crofting Community*, Edinburgh, John Donald, 1976; Eric Richards, *A History of the Highland Clearances*, 2 vols, Croom Helm, 1982, 1985; J. M. Bumsted, *The People's Clearances: Highland Emigration to British North America*, Edinburgh University Press, 1982.

69. The Gaelic stanzas in the first poem are from 'Na Goitearan sgitheanach', in Neil Macleod, *Clarsach an Doire*, 5th edn., Glasgow, A. MacLabhrunin, 1924.

70. Those in the second stanza are from Iain MacA'Ghobhainn's 'Spiorad a' Charthannais' in Iain N. MacLeoid, *Bardachd Leodhais*, Glasgow, 1916, rep. 1953. Translations of both poems by Derick Thomson, *An Introduction to Gaelic Poetry*, Gollancz, 1977, pp.228 and 243.

71. Iain MacPhaidean, *An t-Eileanach*, Glasgho, Alasdair MacLachrainn agus a Mhic, 1921, p.94. My thanks again to Kenneth MacDonald for providing the translation from the Gaelic.

72. J. G. Kellas, 'Highland Migration to Glasgow and the Origin of the Scottish Labour Movement', *Bulletin of the Society for the Study of Labour History*, No. 12, Spring 1966.

73. S. Damer, 'State, Class, and Housing: Glasgow, 1885-1919' in J. Melling (ed.), *Housing, Social Policy and the State*, Croom Helm, 1980.

74. But see *Nothing But the Same Old Story: The Roots of Anti-Irish Racism*, Information on Ireland, 1984, and G. Finn,' Multicultural Anti-Racism and Scottish Education, *Scottish Educational Review*, 19, 1987, for a good beginning.

75. James Handley, *The Irish in Scotland*, Glasgow, John Burns & Sons, n.d., p.157.

76. Ibid., p.175. T.A. Jackson, *Ireland Her Own: An Outline History of the Irish Struggle*, Lawrence & Wishart, 1976, pp. 243-4, provides an account of the foodstuffs produced in Ireland during the Famine, exported to England and re-exported to Ireland. I am grateful to Charlie Johnston for this reference.

77. Handley, op. cit., p.15.

78. Ibid., Ch. 3; and Slaven, op. cit., pp.144-5.

79. Tom Gallagher, *Glasgow – The Uneasy Peace: Religious Tension in Modern Scotland, 1919-1914*, Manchester University Press, 1987, p.27. My own feeling is that this figure is a substantial over-estimate.

80. Handley, op. cit., Ch. VI.

81. The story of this market is told in Moira MacAskill, *Paddy's Market*, University of Glasgow Centre for Urban and Regional Research Discussion Paper No.29, 1987. There is a market of the same name in Liverpool.

82. See the advertisements in the *Glasgow Herald* during March 1874.

83. Gallagher, op. cit.

84. Kevin O'Connor, *The Irish in Britain*, Torc Books, 1972, p.41, claims that there were 4,000 volunteers on the IRA register in Glasgow in 1920. This claim is clearly a highly exaggerated one, but there can be little doubt that there was considerable sympathy for militant republicanism in Glasgow's Irish community. Again, my thanks to Charlie Johnstone for this reference.

85. J. Treble, 'The Seasonal Demand for Adult Labour in Glasgow, 1890-1914', *Social History*, Vol.3, No.1, 1978.

86. Ibid., 'The Market for Unskilled Male Labour in Glasgow, 1891-1914' in Ian McDougall (ed.), *Essays in Scottish Labour History*, Edinburgh, John Donald, 1986.

87. *Glasgow Sketches*, op. cit.

88. Harry McShane and Jean Smith, *No Mean Fighter*, Pluto Press, 1978, p.42.

89. David Kirkwood, *My Life of Revolt*, Harrap, 1935. Many Glaswegians believe that this self-congratulatory autobiography would be more aptly entitled *My Revolting Life*!

90. McShane and Smith, op. cit., p.42.

91. G. Hutchison and Mark O'Neill, *The Springburn Experience: An Oral History of Work in a Railway Community from 1840 to the Present Day*, Edinburgh, Polygon, 1989, p.6.

92. McShane and Smith, op. cit., p.101.

93. *Glasgow Sketches*, op. cit.

94. Ibid.

95. Quoted in S. Berry and H. Whyte (eds.), *Glasgow Observed*, Edinburgh, John Donald, 1987, p.110.

96. *Glasgow Sketches*, op. cit.

97. S.G. Checkland, 'Sir Charles Tennant' in A. Slaven and S. Checkland (eds.), *Dictionary of Scottish Business Biography*, Vol. 1, Aberdeen University Press, 1986, pp. 285-89.

98. See the *Labour Leader* of 1899 and the series of pamphlets of that year by Keir Hardie printed by the *Labour Leader* under the general heading of 'White Slavery'.

99. Carvel, op. cit., p.76. See also extensive coverage in contemporary newspapers.

100. Quoted in A. Gray and R. Currie (eds.), *Clyde Shipbuilding c.1900*, Strathclyde Department of Education, Dunbarton Division, 1987, p.37.

101. Hutchison and O'Neill, op. cit., p.58.

102. Ibid., p.59.

3 Housing and Community

The population growth of Glasgow throughout the nineteenth and early twentieth centuries was, as we have seen, staggering. The city quadrupled in size between 1800 and 1850, and quadrupled again between 1850 and 1925, when it was home to 1,396,000 people. In the league-table of the world's largest cities in 1800, Glasgow was 80th in population terms. In 1850 it was twentieth, and in 1875 it was fourteenth, with Liverpool in thirteenth place. By 1900 it had slipped to being the sixteenth largest city in the world, Liverpool having dropped back, and Manchester and Birmingham having overtaken Glasgow. So we can see that Glasgow had strong contenders for the title of the 'Second City of the British Empire': Liverpool, Manchester, Birmingham and Dublin all claimed that distinction at one time or another, although, in a characteristically Eurocentric oversight, Calcutta, with its population of over one million by 1890, is excluded from the equation.[1]

In physical terms, Glasgow was still small in 1800, the City proper comprising only a couple of square miles centred on the Saltmarket, Bridgegate, High Street, Trongate, Stockwell Street and the Gallowgate. The Gorbals, Calton, and Anderston were still separate municipalities, while places like Bridgeton, Camlachie, Parkhead, Govan and Partick were suburban villages.[2] Thereafter, it expanded rapidly, with the main middle-class residential development taking place to the west, north of the River Clyde, in what was to become a classic European urban phenomenon: the West End/East End divide. Many of the street names in this development

71

celebrated admirals, generals and battles of the Napoleonic Wars: Nelson Street, St Vincent Street, Waterloo Street, Wellington Street, Brunswick Street, Hope Street, Cadogan Street – and Pitt Street, of course. The detailed nature of Glasgow's geographical development has been summarised by Andrew Gibb.[3] What is important to remember is that Glasgow was always a small city for the population it had to house.

What is more important to understand is that it was into this small area, the City Parish, that the waves of migrants flooded. There were two kinds of working-class housing in this area. The first was the classic Scottish tenement, solidly built of stone, of three or four storeys, entered by the 'close', which gave access both to the common stair and to the back-court. Off the stair were the numerous apartments and underneath them were the cellars, in which the working class lived.[4] The high densities of people-to-site thus obtained ensured that tenements were money-making machines for their landlords, as there was practically no limit to the number of people who could be crammed into them – and the landlords *did* cram them in. These houses ('flats' in England) were universally of one room, the 'single-end', or two rooms, the 'room-and-kitchen'. Their dimensions were very small, frequently 8 feet by 12 feet, sometimes only 8 feet by 10 feet. Few of these tenements had internal sanitation or water supplies, the sanitary facilities comprising a 'privy' in the back-court, the water coming from a hand-pump in the street. There were no sewers at all prior to 1790, and by 1832, they existed in only 45 streets. There were no foot pavements prior to 1777, although there were more than a hundred miles paved by 1836, mainly in the middle-class neighbourhoods.[5] These tenements constituted the bulk of housing for the common people, and were jammed on top of each other in a picaresque, impenetrable maze known as the 'Closes and Wynds'.

The second kind of working-class housing was known as 'made-down houses'. These were former middle-class houses, whose occupants had joined the westwards exodus. With the explosion of population, each room in this kind of dwelling had been turned into a separate house, frequently being sub-divided first by gimcrack partitions of a type well-known to this day. Sometimes access to this kind of house was provided by a circular, brick-built staircase tacked onto the back of the building; this was the case in Abbotsford Place in the Gorbals, for example, once that neighbourhood had lost its social cachet.[6] Several of the merchants' houses in the Bridgegate became made-down houses, the departure of their occupants having been accelerated by the frequent floods from the nearby River Clyde.

With the influx of migrants from Ireland and the Highlands increasing with each decade, the demand on housing became enormous. But during this period the supply never remotely met the demand. During the decade 1831-1841, for example, the population of Glasgow increased by 37 per cent – but the supply of housing increased by only 18.5 per cent.[7] Existing tenements became more and more over-crowded, subterranean earth-floored cellars were pressed into service as dwellings, old houses were rapidly 'made-down' and gerry-built tenements run up wherever there was space – even in the back-courts of existing tenements. These became the notorious 'backlands' of Glasgow – damp, filthy, disease-ridden warrens where the sun never shone, and where there was no water or sanitation.[8] The living conditions in these houses were unspeakable, and were notorious enough for Frederick Engels to reproduce a quotation about them in his famous *Condition of the Working Class in England* of 1844:

I have seen human degradation in some of its worst phases, both in England and abroad, but I can advisedly say, that I did not believe, until I visited the wynds of Glasgow, that so large an amount of filth, crime, misery, and disease existed in one spot in any civilised country. The wynds consist of long lanes, so narrow that a cart could with difficulty pass along them; out of these open the 'closes,' which are courts about fifteen or twenty feet square, round which the houses, mostly of three storeys high, are built; the centre of the court is the dunghill, which probably is the most lucrative part of the estate to the laird in most instances, and which it would consequently be esteemed an invasion of the rights of property to remove....In the lower lodging houses, ten, twelve, or sometimes twenty persons, of both sexes and all ages, sleep promiscuously on the floor in different degrees of nakedness. These places are generally, as regards dirt, damp, and decay, such as no person of common humanity would stable his horse in.[9]

In 1843 one of Glasgow's District Surgeons wrote of the area immediately to the east of the Saltmarket:

The tenements in which I have visited are occupied from the cellars to the attics, and almost altogether kept for lodging-houses, many of them being more fit for pig-stys than dwellings for human beings; and in not a few the donkey and the pigs rest at night in the same apartment with the family. The entrance to these abodes is generally through a close, not unfrequently some inches deep with water or mud, or the fluid part of every kind of filth, carelessly thrown down from unwillingness to go with it to one of the common receptacles; and in every close there is at least one of these places, situated immediately under the windows of the dwelling-houses, or together with byres, stables, etc., forming the ground floor, while the stench arising therefrom in summer pollutes the neighbourhood and more especially renders the habitations above almost intolerable. The beds are variously constructed, some being merely a portion of the floor divided by a piece of wood kept in its place with stones or brick...in other cases the beds are formed in tiers over each other, as in the steerage of an emigrant ship...Need I add to this, that the inhabitants with whom I have to deal are of the very lowest ranks in society; a few of them are labourers, but the greater majority are hawkers and beggars, thieves and prostitutes. At night whole families sleep in one bed; and as there are several beds in each apartment, several families are made to occupy it...In short, of the moral degradation, grossness and misery of these people, no adequate description can be given; and few, very few indeed, besides the District Surgeons know the actual condition of the pauper population of Glasgow.[10]

The surgeon was making an important point: the phenomenon of the urban slum was a new one. Its population was an unknown, unseen and unheeded by the middle classes. As Engels pointed out for contemporary Manchester, the very geography of the developing industrial city followed a class pattern, ensuring that the middle class was ignorant of the conditions of existence of the working class.[11] Only very few outsiders – the odd public health official, the police, ministers of religion and men preying on women – ventured into the slums in the first half of the nineteenth century. However, even in these early days, an astute Chief of Police related crime in Glasgow to the tenemental layout of the old city:

> The facilities for the committing of crime appear to be much greater than in London, Dublin, or Liverpool. In the latter cities nearly the whole of the houses and warehouses are self-contained; there are no common entries, no common stairs, and few, if any, sunk areas; while in Glasgow, the houses, with few exceptions, are divided into floors or smaller compartments, occupied by different tenants; there is to almost every tenement a common close or entrance, and a common stair to many of the tenements; there are sunk areas; and to nearly all there are back unprotected premises tenanted, or with right of access, by different individuals.[12]

In other words, it was impossible to tell when someone on the lam ran into a close from the street, whether s/he had run up the stairs to hide in one of the numerous houses, or jinked out into the back-court to escape through yet another close. Thus began what was literally a battle for the Glasgow police to penetrate and control the slum areas of the city. It was still going on in the 1930s when *No Mean City* was published.

Not surprisingly there was mass drunkenness in these areas of the city. In the 1840s, there was one pub to every 13.9 families in the City of Glasgow, with one to every 25.4 in the City plus suburbs.[13] And this does not take into account the numerous shebeens. Even less surprisingly, given the increasing pollution of the city's wells, there were frequent and terrible recurrences of epidemic disease. There were typhus epidemics in 1818, 1832, 1837, 1847 and 1851-52. There were cholera epidemics in 1832, 1848-49 and 1853-54, with a Relapsing Fever epidemic in 1843.[14] The death and infant mortality rate for these early years were extremely high:

Table 2: Glasgow: Death and Infant Mortality Rates, 1836-1840

	Death Rate	Infant Mortality Rate
1836	1 in 29	1 in 63
1837	1 in 24	1 in 65
1838	1 in 37	1 in 84
1839	1 in 36	1 in 72
1840	1 in 31	1 in 69

Source: *Reports of the Sanitary Condition of the Labouring Population of Scotland*, 1842, p. 168.

The cholera epidemics of 1848-49 and 1853-54 killed 3,772 and 3,885 people respectively. These epidemics, although they particularly ravaged the slums, were class-blind; they killed middle-class people as well as the poor. The City Fathers, therefore, had good reason to sponsor a series of Police Acts in the second half of the century, which attempted to control disease – and poverty – by increased sanitary controls. Thus, the common lodging houses became licensed and were subject to a battery of regulations concerning cleanliness, white-washing and the like. Two important measures of these Police Acts are worth noting.[15] The first was the Seventh Police and Municipal Extension Act of 1846, which not only brought the burghs of Anderston, Calton and Gorbals into the City of Glasgow, but also established the Town Council as the governing body of the city.[16] The second was the passing of the 1855 Corporation Water Works Act which was aimed at piping fresh water to the city from Loch Katrine.

In the meantime, by the 1840s and 50s, the skilled and better-paid workers of Glasgow were attaining a precarious measure of security. Of 20,076 individual accounts held in the National Security Savings Bank of Glasgow in 1842, 'mechanics, artificers, and their wives' held 6,734; 'factory operatives' held 1,574; and 'labourers and their wives' held 867.[17] In other words, almost half of the total were held by working people. But for the majority of the working class in the first half of the century, an unimaginable poverty, misery and squalor were the norm; in the spring of 1837 some 18,500 people in Glasgow were on Poor Relief.[18] Their situation was exacerbated by frequent downswings in the trade cycle, particularly in the textile industry. This could affect even the skilled workers, as a contemporary observer noted:

While, however, many of the working classes in Glasgow are able to live in comfort, and a number of them, by proper economy and prudence, to save money, it must be kept in view that they are subject to many causes by which even the most prudent and economical may be reduced to penury, such, for instance, as the want of employment; it may be from the inclemency of the weather, which almost every winter (and particularly during last winter) interrupts the masons, slaters, the outdoor labourers; the sudden convulsions and fluctuations of trade, by which the means of subsistence are frequently withdrawn from large masses; the high price of provisions; and above all, their liability to diseases, especially those of an epidemic nature.[19]

With the exception of epidemic disease, these factors were to remain true for Clydeside workers – as they were for Thames-side workers – until well into the twentieth century.[20] The reality of life for a low paid worker and her or his family was a constant and periodically unsuccessful struggle to avoid the abyss of penury. And this meant a lot of people, for in 1842 four-fifths of the population of Glasgow were working-class, while one-fifth was 'capitalists, bankers, professionals, and other educated men', a pattern which was to persist well into the twentieth century.[21]

For many Glaswegians, the prime cause of all the misery was perceived to be the Irish, and they were subjected to systematic racist abuse. But an intelligent observer noted in 1842:

It will be noticed that several of my informants specify 'the great influx of the lowest orders of Irish' into Glasgow as another cause of the destitution here. Doubtless the vast number of Irish immigrants must have affected the price of labour and rendered employment more scarce, and so have increased the amount of destitution in Glasgow, but not, I think, to so great an extent as is generally supposed; and it should be borne in mind that Glasgow otherwise has reaped immense advantage from the exercise of their lusty thews and sinews. When on this point, I may be allowed to remark that the poor Irish in Glasgow have completely verified the common adage, 'Give a dog a bad name, etc.'[22]

The Irish immigrants may have provided a handy scapegoat, but they were hardly to blame for the circumstances in which they found themselves. Given that the population had increased fourfold between 1800 and 1850, Glasgow's housing and living conditions in mid-century beggar description. A memorable picture of Glasgow in 1858 has been provided by 'Shadow', and the rotten housing, fearful drunkenness, prostitution and domestic violence he describes stands in vivid contrast to the glories of Glasgow's mid-Victorian industrial expansion.[23] He describes a 'house':

On the right is a sort of hole in the wall, which turns out to be the miniature home of a smart little woman in respectable attire. The formation of her head is good, and her eye beams with a genial intelligence. She is engaged in cooking. On one side of her is a neat little fire-place – the 'cheeks' beautifully whitened, and the little grate bars shine as Warren's blacking. At the other extremity of the apartment is a small bed in a recess. The rest of the 'make-up' of the household furniture consists of two stools, a table, and a few articles of crockery...Being granted liberty to measure the place, we here put the right heel against the toe of the left shoe, and find that six shoe-lengths determine the breadth. And between eight and nine the length, from the bed to the fire-place. The height of the room barely allows us to stand upright. In this hole the husband and wife have lived for one or two years, and until lately, two children; the youngest of the latter having been only some weeks dead of measles, after five months' illness. A shilling a week is paid for the apartment.[24]

Piecemeal attacks on problems of this scale were evidently not going to work, and the Corporation of Glasgow began a series of measures which were to establish its international reputation as a pioneer of municipal public health. An important step was the appointment of W.T. Gairdner as the City's first Medical Officer of Health in 1863. His view of his job was to become the orthodoxy for generations of public health officials in Glasgow:

> ...gross sanitary neglect inevitably leads to the production and multiplication of a class which is not only helpless and progressively in a state of degradation from generation to generation, but has in itself no power of redemption, so that as regards the community at large, it becomes a truly *parasitic* class, living on the classes above it, in such hovels as are provided for it, and absolutely precluded from every kind of spontaneous improvement, and therefore bound to become worse and worse with each generation.[25]

The problem for the city's middle class was what to do with this 'class', referred to in Glasgow as elsewhere in Britain as the 'dirty, criminal, and improvident class', the 'sunken tenth', the 'residuum' or the 'disreputable poor'. In the Glasgow Police Act of 1862 the 'ticketed houses' of Glasgow were established; the critical feature of this piece of legislation is that it gave the authorities the discretion to measure up the small houses of Glasgow, defined as being of not more than three apartments, and of not more that 3,000 cubic feet.[26] Then, at a rate of 300 cubic feet per adult, and 150 cubic feet per child under eight, the capacity of the house was calculated and the 'ticket', a round tinplate disc, displaying the legal maximum number of inhabitants was screwed to the door. The ticket might read four-and-a-half, as a child under eight was half a person! Thereafter, these ticketed houses were liable to be raided by the 'sanitary police', always in the middle of the night, to see if they were overcrowded. But in fact, as the authorities themselves admitted, these raids were as much to do with the moral policing of the poor as with public health; 'moral' health and 'public' health were to all intents and purposes one and the same thing.[27]

The 1860s saw two large-scale assaults on the district of the closes and wynds. The first was the result of the growth of the railway network, the second the actions of the City Improvement Trust. After ferocious competition, the Union company's new railway line ploughed straight through the Gallowgate and Saltmarket, sweeping away hundreds of small dwelling-houses, while a few years later the Caledonian did the same, on a lesser scale, on the south side.[28] The second, and more important development was that of the City Improvement Trust (CIT), established under the City of Glasgow Improvements Act of 1866. Under the terms of this statute the city was granted comprehensive powers to buy and demolish slum houses in an area of 88 acres, containing 51,294 people, in the old city centre. The average density within the area of the clearance scheme was 583 persons per acre, but there were neighbourhoods within it containing upwards of 1,000 per acre, – a truly staggering figure.[29] The city also had limited powers to lay out new streets and build new housing. The Act was hated by the landlords. Lord Provost Blackie, its architect, lost his seat at the next municipal election after a campaign by slum landlords, some of whom were town councillors In the event, the compensation which they received was generous. So the Trust went ahead, bought up, and demolished whole tracts of congested slums on a scale greater than any other British or European city:

> Between 1875 and 1888, slum clearances schemes in London displaced 34,693 people, around 0.9 per cent of the capital's 1881 population. In Glasgow, from 1866 to 1876, 28,965 people were displaced, representing 6.06 per cent of the city's 1871 population.[30]

The trust constructed a limited number of new tenemental streets containing houses of not less than two rooms, with running water and an inside toilet. It also constructed 'model' lodging houses for single men and women. The public health gains from this wholesale clearance were obvious; the death rates in the cleared areas plummeted. But the victory was a pyrrhic one for two reasons. Firstly, there was never any real intention to rehouse the thousands of the 'casual poor' and 'criminal classes' rendered homeless by the clearances, so they simply fled to the adjacent neighbourhoods in search of cheap accommodation and reproduced the overcrowding problem there. And secondly, the CIT itself became a major slum landlord! Not only was it frequently difficult to trace the owners of slum tenements, high interest rates made the cost of demolition prohibitive. Its 'improvements' may have looked good to Glasgow's middle class, but there were few tangible benefits for the poor. So, by the 1870s, had the situation improved for Glasgow's working class? There were some real gains. Firstly, the worst forms of epidemic disease – cholera and typhus – had finally been all but eradicated. Secondly, the shockingly high death rate was beginning to decline. And thirdly, there was an accelerating supply of decent small tenemental houses, with inside toilets – for those who could afford the rent.

Drink and Crime

The reality for the *mass* of the working people in Glasgow was a hell on earth – and that was also the way it was perceived by Glasgow's social and sanitary reformers, as we shall see in more detail in the next chapter. There are many accounts of life in the city in the second half of the nineteenth and the start of the twentieth centuries. Perhaps the most startling are the series of reports in 1870 and 1871, with the title 'The Dark Side of Glasgow', carried by the *North British Daily Mail*, one of the city's daily newspapers. These pieces were neither muck-raking nor sensational. They described what they saw and if they commented, it was usually out of pity for the victims.

We have already referred to the enormously high rate of drunkenness which characterised much of the old city. The reports note that quite apart from public-houses, there were 200 brothels and 150 shebeens in the central district of Glasgow alone; the differences between them were cosmetic:

> The effect of these shebeens has been to keep the streets in the neighbourhood in a continual turmoil; drouthy and disreputable characters and thieves turn night into day, prowl about till four or five in the morning, every now and then refreshing themselves at the shebeens until they become drunk and disorderly, and are carried off to the Police Office, making night hideous with their yells and imprecations. On these occasions the cross of Glasgow is a veritable pandemonium, and the rogues and vagabonds, when they have no innocents to fleece, wrangle and quarrel amongst themselves like a pack of hungry curs.[31]

The violence towards women which resulted from this drinking was shocking:

> The next shebeening episode of the night was the only too common one of assaulting a wife. The husband had made his escape ere the police were called in, and the wife was left to tell her own tale; but language was hardly necessary for this purpose. One side of her face was barely recognisable as human; it was literally reduced to pulp. The jaw was broken and caused the cheek to protrude in an ugly lump. The region of her eye was purple from a recent blow, but the organ itself was lost in a mass of swollen and discoloured flesh. The blow must have been a fearful one; from a great gash in her head the blood was streaming in torrents, and her hair was dripping with the gore, which had besmeared her face, arms, and dress.

The sexual exploitation of children was even more unspeakable:

> Another very painful feature in this dark picture is that parents systematically live by the prostitution of their children, at which they connive, and even assist; and, what we fear is too common, is that of mothers offering their daughters, as yet uncontaminated, for a consideration. We

could not have believed this had we not had one very painful opportunity of seeing it for ourselves; and, though we have never met with another instance of this description, we are informed that it is of frequent occurrence.

The paper's reports also reveal a highly-organised criminal culture in Glasgow, with 'Piggy's Close' in Princes Street being a central meeting place, along with Creilly's Crescent in the New Vennel, and MacLean's lodging-house being the favoured sleeping place. The crooks, just as in contemporary London, had their own 'cant' or language. Thus 'chumbs' were clumsy, inexpert thieves; a 'chiff' was a knife, (plainly the origin of the current Glasgow word 'chib') and 'lamps' were eyes, leading to the charming local expression 'I punched his lamps out'. Their range of activities was astonishing: 'moulders' forged coins which were passed by a 'swagsman'; a 'moll busser' was a ladies' pick-pocket, while a 'block busser' was a gents' pick-pocket and a 'ben-busser' pick-pocketed from gents' waistcoats – a top status job requiring both nerve and skill; 'thowan snatching' was stealing wet clothes off a line, to be sold in Paddy's Market, an activity for children organised in Dickensian gangs; a 'cracksman' was a burglar, while 'flumping' meant thumping someone in the solar plexus to wind him or her, then taking what she or he had. The paper describes an amazing range of confidence tricks, with the 'high mob', the true professional criminals, living in top hotels in the best of style after a successful job. It also makes it plain that many young boys and girls turned to crime after being driven from home by brutal beatings. These children slept rough under the wheelbarrows at the char kilns at Port Dundas on the canal, where they were persistently raided and batoned by the police. In fact, the newspaper makes it equally plain that in the war between the police and the crooks, there was no quarter given or expected. The police would routinely inform employers if one of their workers had been in prison, and harassment of the poor and prostitutes and 'known criminals' on the streets was normal. By the same token, any attempt by the police to arrest someone in the central district would attract a mob bent on releasing him or her by main force. The Glasgow City Police was formed in a tough school.

Of all the horrors exposed by the *Mail*, and other sources, perhaps the worst was baby-farming. This system depended on the fact there was a steady flow of illegitimate babies in Glasgow, born of the large numbers of single young women who had been seduced or raped by men. These women were frequently driven to distraction by their circumstances. The desperate measures to which they were forced to resort were highlighted as early as 1822, when a young woman called Helen Rennie was charged with murdering her child. She had been seduced by a waster, and had been obliged to put her child into the hands of respectable foster parents. It would seem that the father provided some help with the maintenance. Rennie visited the child every weekend for four or five years, showing every sign of maternal affection. Then suddenly the father fled Glasgow after some villainy and Rennie was so distraught at the prospect of maintaining her child on her own meagre earnings that she poisoned it with arsenic. The trial was sensational. Despite the fact that she had plainly killed her child, Rennie's youth and beauty, the fact that she was beside herself with grief and remorse and that her seducer was a wastrel, all told in her favour and, to public acclamation, she was found not guilty.[32]

The *Mail* found that in Glasgow (and Edinburgh, which the paper also investigated) the unwanted baby – or more correctly, the baby which it was impossible for most young working single mothers to rear – would be given to a woman who, for a small financial consideration or 'premium', would 'adopt' the baby for life. These baby farmers were frequently in league with back-street 'spae-wives' who would perform illegal abortions in equally illegal and secret 'lying-in' houses. The baby farmers would then occasionally murder the baby outright, or more often do it to death slowly by starvation and ill treatment, including beatings, and turning them into drug addicts with laudanum, a tincture of opium and alcohol. Some of these women were in a burial club and thus profited from killing the babies. One woman was cited who had adopted four infants, of whom three had subsequently died; all were insured. The *Mail* established that this practice was commonplace in Glasgow. It ran a dummy advert in the local press, offering a financial premium to anyone willing to adopt a healthy baby; it received 400 replies. On placing a similar advert without the premium, it received only two. The paper also watched one of these lying-in houses for three months, tailed the women who left it and found horrors like the following.

A neighbour of the woman who adopted four children, three of whom died, said of her:

> 'On one occasion when I happened to look in,' he says, 'Mrs X was at supper. The poor child looked up and eagerly stretched out its little hand for a morsel of bread. It appeared to be starving of hunger; but with a volley of coarse abuse the infant was ordered to lie down. My wife and I,' continued Mr..., 'were sorry for the little mite, and spoke to Mrs X about being so cruel to the child. He was a mere skeleton, with the bones like to come through the skin, and he had bed sores; but she made him lie on the bare boards of the bed with nothing under him. She said the doctor ordered him to be laid on the bare boards for his health. She made him lie in filth and never cleaned him. She beat him cruelly. The neighbours heard the children's cries and heard her beating them. She said she was only clapping her hands. It was a mercy when death put an end to the little sufferer's troubles.'

The combination of through-going sexism and noxious public health in mid-Victorian Glasgow thus resulted in the deliberate slaughter of children. The Parliamentary Select Committee appointed to enquire into baby-farming as a result of the *Mail*'s exposé heard that:

> The registration of deaths without a medical certificate is very common in Glasgow. In the Bridgetown district, for example, there were in the year 1868 1,614 deaths, of which

633 were not certified. In 1870 there were 1,662 deaths, of which 739 were not certified. Almost all of these were cases of the deaths of children. This system affords a terrible facility for child murder. The amount of benefit derivable from burial societies is generally much more than will suffice to bury a young child.[33]

How was it possible that such appalling crimes were not reported to the authorities? The *Mail*'s commissioners supplied an answer which is worth quoting, for it gets to the core of slum-living in a way which generations of subsequent sociological studies singularly failed to do:

... there are reasons which make non-interference the policy most usually followed. The poor in large cities like ours are of necessity packed together into the smallest available space, and if they cannot afford to enlarge their borders it is clearly a matter of self-interest to preserve a good understanding between themselves and the neighbours by whom they were hedged about. The comfort and happiness in a great measure of these little back colonies of our wynds and alleys depend upon the keeping of the peace, and the stirring up of strife is very naturally avoided in circumstances where safety and happiness depended upon good fellowship and friendly feeling. We have been told again and again that the dread of making disturbance amongst neighbours in close association causes such cruelties as those we are narrating to be winked at and passed over in silence.

The essence of tenement living was that a *common* way of adapting had to be found, or individuals and families would have gone under – as many did. If we see 'culture' as the collective adaptation to everyday working and living circumstances, then much of this horror becomes more comprehensible. This argument is worth pursuing in more detail, for much of the twentieth-century literature, both fiction and non-fiction, which attempts to grapple with tenement living in Glasgow falls either into a sickly sentimentality, or a *No Mean City*-like shock-horror-show.

The World of Women

The social conditions outlined above remained almost normal until the First World War, common until the Second, and were not unknown in the post-war years. I have several friends who were brought up in a single-end in the 1950s, including one who lived in a ticketed house. Right up until the Second World War, economic vulnerability was *normal* for the Glasgow working class; to be out of work was a common experience. As we have seen, much work was casualised so, for the vast majority of unskilled workers, poverty was *normal*. Even for skilled workers like engineers it was not uncommon to be laid off, or to work short-time, or to be out on strike or to be locked out, as happened to the engineers for thirty weeks in 1897.[34] Thus average wage rates camouflage the fact that actual wages were all too often much lower. Further, shipbuilding was also affected by trade cycles and bad weather, as we have seen. Many shipbuilding tradesmen were also employed only as piece-workers, that is, they were paid per piece of work finished, not by the hour or the day. Finally, many shipbuilding trades were paid fortnightly until 1906, a source of great frustration to the tradesmen, and even more to their women. It also meant riotous drunkeness in the shipbuilding areas on the Saturday night of pay-day. Until 1914, an accident at work, a lay-off or a spell of bad weather could spell ruin for many working-class families. Thus poverty, or the threat of poverty, was the common link between all members of the Glasgow working class. The city operated upon a low-wage economy. Harry McShane's élitist engineers quoted on p. 59 may have given themselves airs and graces, and they may have had some money in the Glasgow Savings Bank, but they would all have known someone, perhaps a family member, who had toppled into that ever-threatening abyss. As older local workers say: 'We were only a wage away from the gutter.' The culture which emerged among the less secure workers, the vast majority, was a culture of survival. What seems to have been entirely overlooked in the historical and sociological literature was that this was a culture sustained by women.

In working-class areas, the tenement stair was self-evidently a natural setting for the social organisation of the women left behind when their men were at work or in the pub, and their sisters were working in textile factories or in service. The women in a stair *had* to learn to co-operate. Many tenements, for example, had a common wash-house in the back-court, fired by a large boiler. There was a strict rota for its use – as there was for washing the common stair – and rows about the location of the key were the stuff of Glasgow music-hall jokes for decades. It was very important for a harassed housewife to be able to get in and get her washing done at the appropriate time. There were dense social networks of women in the working-class tenemental streets paralleling that so well described for contemporary London by Ellen Ross.[35] The women borrowed and lent from each other – the proverbial cups of sugar, or small sums of money for the rent or the messages (shopping). It was the women who spoke to the factor about that empty house two closes away for a married daughter or son. (The factor in Scotland was and still is the person who managed tenement property, which was owned by someone else. He collected the rent, and was, theoretically, responsible for organising the repair and mainte- nance which was actually so seldom done in the older properties. He would be an 'agent' in England. The factor was not a very popular person in Scotland, and in Glasgow, was the butt of endless music-hall and pantomime jokes.) It was the women who sold goods which fell off the back of a passing cart. It was the women who got the intelligence of a new consignment of fruit and veg at the local shops, and told their neighbours. It was the women who crowded warrant sales, bought up all the distrained goods for a song, threatening and warning off dealers and outsiders, and giving the goods back to the victims. It was the women who helped each

other at the 'steamie', the Corporation communal
wash-house, an important institution evocatively captured by the Wildcat Company's recent stage play of the
same name. It was the women who assisted each other at
childbirth or in procuring an abortion. It was the women
who washed and laid out the dead. It was the women who
defended their sisters against drunken, violent men, or
who patched them up after a battering. It was the women
who looked after each other's children. It was the women
who operated an elaborate shadow economy in these
neighbourhoods, involving, *inter alia*, money lending,
reselling pawn tickets and that Glasgow classic, the
'menage'. ('Menage' pronounced 'menodge' is a Scots word
deriving from the French *ménage*. It refers to a weekly
pay-in system organised by a network of local women for
the purpose of saving money. In Liverpool, it is called a
'tontine'.[36]) In short, it was the women who produced and
reproduced the culture of the tenements. Thus in talking
about working-class culture in Glasgow, an immediate
qualification has to be made; there were two working-
class cultures – that of men and that of women. Men and
women came together only in bed, and even then it was
only too often a violent collision.

But there was the obverse of this sisterly, supportive
series of densely impacted social networks – usually
glossed over as 'community spirit', a thoroughly
misleading term. And this was the fact that you could not
get away from your neighbours in a tenement close. If
you had for a neighbour a roaring drunk, a violent man,
an exuberant party-holder, a shebeen- or a brothel-
keeper, a bagpiper, a sectarian bigot or a filthy dirty
demented old person, you had had it: you couldn't escape.
And these were all burdens borne essentially by women.
Theoretically, of course, you could escape – but where to?
Most working-class families did not have the money for
the rent in the new, bigger, airier tenements. The older
tenements, with their small houses, clustered round the
big shipyards, docks, locomotive works and engineering
shops, were effectively prisons for their inhabitants. As

Jim McLean says in his bitter but accurate song about the
old Glasgow: '...tenement living was a bloody disgrace.'[37]
That is putting it mildly.

The problem with much of the writing about tenement
living in Glasgow is that it fails to understand that the
good and the bad, the progressive and the reactionary,
the humour and the tears, the struggle and the defeat,
the courage and the cowardice, the slum and the palace,
were part and parcel of the same phenomenon. Virtue
and evil co-existed in the tenements; they might face
each other across a landing. It was the sheer density of
living which necessitated this culture of survival. People
packed in on top of each other have to construct a 'moral
order', a way of co-existing, or there would be chaos. This
is what the *Mail*'s journalists were getting at in the
quotation on p. 86. They were right. There was not only
the real chance of physical violence from an offended
male neighbour, there was an even greater chance of a
'shirracking' from a female neighbour. This was a highly
public and very loud catalogue of vituperative complaints
against and character assassination of the guilty party,
which could assume ritual proportions. While it was all
part of the drama of the streets, anybody with any sense
wanted to avoid such a humiliation, wanted to avoid
hearing the self-satisfied 'Aye, ah read her her character
right enough!' The tenement dwellers called in the police
as a last resort, for they were the enemy; Glaswegians
sorted out their own disagreements. So it was for these
reasons that the women of the tenement streets put their
so-called 'community spirit' together; they had no other
options. Nobody in his or her right mind *wanted* to live in
a slum tenement. There were some people in Glasgow
who were not in their right minds, people like some of the
denizens of the wynds described above, people brutalised
beyond redemption by their poverty and despair. But
they were always a tiny minority. The vast majority of
slum dwellers wanted only one thing. Out.

The Legacy

Now it may be felt by the reader that all this history of the evils of life in the Glasgow working class over the last hundred years is irrelevant to the present. I do not think so, for the point is that the cultural patterns which were developed in those years have dominated working-class existence down to the present, although the industrial and housing conditions which gave birth to them have disappeared. Recognisable versions of these patterns thrive in Glasgow's remaining working-class tenement neighbourhoods, and even more vigorously in its interwar rehousing schemes, and in the big post-war peripheral schemes. Further, I have been struck over the years in reading documentary sources about Glasgow, and talking with old Glaswegians, that when they got the chance to speak out, working people knew perfectly well what was wrong with their existence. They made the same critical points over and over again. A key one was that it was impossible to feed a family properly on low and irregular wages. A Glasgow University physiological study in 1912 found that:

> ... those with a small income and those with an irregular income entirely fail to get a supply of food sufficient for the proper development and growth of the body or for the maintenance of a capacity for active work.[38]

Under these circumstances, it was, of course, the women who would go without to feed their men and children.

It was also thought iniquitous to have to bring up a family in a single-end. Imagine bathing six children of different sexes in a room measuring 10 feet by 14, where the only form of heating is the coal-fired grate. This was a normal part of week-to-week life for working-class parents, for those who bathed their children, that is. Then the appalling conditions of these small houses and the rapacity of the landlords and factors were frequently mentioned. And in spite of the efforts at slum-clearance made by the CIT, and in spite of the fact the numbers of new single-ends built after 1862 declined, the overall numbers of these houses remained large. A comparison of the 1861 and 1911 censuses of Glasgow shows that while the proportion of families living in single-ends and rooms-and-kitchens declined from 73.4 per cent to 66.3 per cent, the numbers living in such houses rose from 266,115 to 471,156.[39] And while it is to be remembered that all Glasgow slums, more or less, were tenements, it must be repeated that not all tenements were slums, a point to which we shall shortly return. Nonetheless, it is a shocking fact that in its heyday as 'Second City of Empire' and 'Workshop of the British Empire', nearly half a million Glaswegian workers and their families lived in such small houses. This was a unique situation in Britain and Ireland. To accuse these workers of being there because they didn't want anything better, or to label them as 'slum-makers', as so many middle-class contemporaries did, is intolerable cant.

Out of these conditions, then, came the classic Glaswegian 'wee bauchle' and 'wee wummin'. They *were* wee; their diet was totally inadequate, as we have seen. Not a few had rickets due to vitamin deficiencies and the lack of sunlight in the tenement streets. Nonetheless, Glaswegians knew how to enjoy themselves, and not only with drink, although that was always a central theme in the relaxation of working people. There were the numerous houses belonging to Highlanders and Irish people where there would be regular meetings to sing and play the music of the Hebrides or the Rosses. Then there were the 'free-and-easies', licensed back-court pubs with room for members of the audience to get up and do a turn – sing a song, tell a story, crack a joke.[40] They were patronised mainly, but not solely, by young male workers, and in 1872, there were nineteen of these foetid, smoke-filled mini music-halls within five minutes' walk of Glasgow Cross. These were, of course, the precursor of the singing pub, of which Glasgow happily still has many. The ribald nature of the jokes and songs offended the delicate sensibilities of the *Mail*'s reporters in 1872!

Then there was dancing; Glasgow has always been a dancing-mad city. Before the advent of the big dance-halls at the turn of the century, dances were organised in back-courts, on the pavement, in houses, in church-halls, in attics and cellars – anywhere where a musician or two could belt out a tune and people could dance. The most elementary form of dance was the 'clabber'. This was an informal pavement or back-court dance; these were common in tenemental Glasgow. There is a brief description of a 1921 clabber in *No Mean City*:

> In Rose Street, outside the corner public house, a little group had collected, and Bobbie Hurley's step quickened as he heard the sound of a mouth organ...Outside the...pub there were only two couples dancing, a young man and his girl and two other girls waltzing together. A ragged, bleary-eyed old fellow, lamentably undrunk [*sic*], was playing his mouth organ like an artist: many a vaudeville musician might have envied him his talent.[41]

A clabber could also be an impromptu concert in the back-court of the tenement; they were still common in Glasgow housing schemes right up to the 1950s. Here, a Blackhill woman describes them for that period:

> A 'clabber' was a get-together in the back-court. You'd put up a washing line and hing old blankets over it, sort of like a stage. We all brought our chairs out. Some would hing oot the windae, and everybody would give us a song or a dance, or something. Sometimes there would be a squeeze-box or a banjo or a penny-whistle, or a moothie. It was great.[42]

Kathleen Clark, who is word-processing this very text, can remember such clabbers in the back-court of her Springburn tenement in her childhood in the 1960s.

The *Mail*, somewhat condescendingly, describes a more organised form of dance in 1872:

> Glasgow literally swarms with cheap, low dancing places, where the youth of both sexes among the lower ranks of society meet regularly once or twice a week, to dance, drink, and enjoy themselves...A number of lads in a factory or mill,

less frequently in a warehouse, club together to hire a room, at from ninepence to one and sixpence a night, possibly in a public house, if not, in any building where a room can be had cheaply...The room was long, very low in the roof and narrow, with two wretched little sky-light windows, saw-dusted floor, and eight candles stuck in little tin brackets, two on each side of the room. At the further end, with the dark recesses of which it was some time before my eyes could pierce, stood a barrel, on which sat a youth fiddling, while beside him was a large white box...in which there were beer, whisky, and ginger-pop – the 'pop' being for the ladies...The floor was occupied by eight couples, engaged in a reel, and whooping and shouting like so many dervishes, while the sawdust flew about in a miniature whirlwind of dust, and the 'bussing' was frequent and hearty...[43]

As the nineteenth century wore to a close, commercial dance halls became much more common, and were well established by the interwar years. A similar pattern was followed by the legendary Glasgow music halls, the 'graveyard of English comedians'. It is no insult to Billy Connolly to say that he is in the best tradition of local music-hall humour.

It would hardly be possible to write of entertainment and the working class in Glasgow without mentioning football, the city's alternative religion. The two great clubs, Celtic and Rangers, were founded in 1887 and 1872 respectively. From the very beginning, they had religious/ethnic connotations, and it is impossible to discuss football in Glasgow without discussing sectarianism first.

Sectarianism in Glasgow can be defined as an insensate anti-Irish Catholic feeling, historically expressing itself as an active and pernicious discrimination in the housing and labour markets, not to mention physical violence. Its roots are old and deep and complicated, as was stressed earlier. The words 'Irish' and 'Catholic' were inter-changeable right up to the Second World War, although this was a misnomer because, as we have seen, the majority of Catholics in

Glasgow were native-born Scots before the end of the nineteenth century. Be that as it may, Protestants had the monopoly of skilled employment on the Clyde right up to the Second World War, and in some cases, beyond. There were very few Catholic engineers in Glasgow before 1914. Harry MacShane was an exception, as he himself allows. The Catholics were confined to the unskilled jobs. They were congregated in dock labouring, for example, but the foremen who hired the daily squads were typically Protestants.[44] Thus all the usual rackets associated with casualised dock labour – payment in pubs, buying the foremen drink, victimisation of trade unionists – were compounded by vicious sectarian discrimination.

Glasgow never had near-exclusive religious ghettoes to the extent of Liverpool, but there were plenty of neighbourhoods which were predominantly Catholic or Protestant. The Irish, being the poorest, were historically restricted to the worst housing, so they congregated in places like the Bridgegate and the Saltmarket, and subsequently in slum areas like the Garngad, immediately adjacent to the noxious Tharsis chemical plant, and the Gorbals. A major but not totally Protestant neighbourhood was Bridgeton. Fights round the boundaries of these territories were ten-a-penny; here is an 1884 account:

The Bridgegate may be called our local Donnybrook. A row can be got up here in almost no time, especially on Saturday night, and accordingly policemen are then stationed there as thick as blackberries. An Irishman who feels himself 'blue-moulded' for want of a beating has nothing to do but trail his coat along the street, and dare any man to tread on it, and he is soon thrashed to his heart's content. At times the district is so excitable that the appearance of an orange flower or ribbon is enough to produce something like an insurrection, which is productive of black eyes and bloody noses. A few years ago a powerful individual – still living, we believe – was distinguished by a mortal hatred of the Pope and the Papists, which, whenever he got a few glasses of whisky, he could not help showing, even at the expense of a beating. Accordingly, when he had drunk enough fairly to raise his 'dander', he deliberately stuck an orange ribbon in his button-hole, and marched down to the Bridgegate whistling 'Boyne Water', or 'Croppies Lie Down', varied with an occasional scream of 'To the Devil with the Pope'. Of course, he was set upon immediately; and although he might have the satisfaction of knocking down some half-a-dozen Papists in the struggle, numbers fairly floored him at last, and the matter ended by the enthusiastic Protestant being carried to the Police Office with his face so effectually battered that his mother would not have known him.[45]

While fights of this kind were common in Glasgow, persistent large-scale rioting of the kind common in Liverpool was virtually unknown in Glasgow by the beginning of the twentieth century. This had something to do with local politics, as will be discussed in the next chapter, and also something to do with the frequent and ritual expression of hostility between Celtic and Rangers, and their fans.

There is, of course, an extensive literature about Celtic and Rangers, but the point that needs making here is that Catholic-Protestant sectarianism in Glasgow has polarised round these two teams.[46] Their symbols were potent; Celtic flew the Irish tricolour, Rangers the Red Hand of Ulster. It is frequently said that Celtic is a Catholic team and Rangers is a Protestant team. It is certainly true that the Celtic Football Club has been the focus of the Irish Catholics in Glasgow since it was founded by an Irish Catholic priest, Brother Walfrid, in the East End. But to pretend that Rangers Football Club has a similar religious focus is a nonsense. As Glasgow writer and journalist Cliff Hanley said in the German film *The Big Teams*, Rangers isn't a Protestant team, it's an anti-Catholic team! Historically, that was certainly the case. There has always been a tie-up between membership of the Orange Lodge and supporting Rangers. But it is in fact wrong to say that Rangers have never signed a Catholic; over the years, they signed several. The problem was that they didn't play them. However, with the signing of former Celtic star Mo

Johnston in 1989, optimists feel that this pattern seems
to be at an end.

Respectability

I have stressed earlier that not all tenement neighbourhoods were slums. Glasgow also had areas of upper-
working-class and lower-middle-class tenements, as well
as those of the solid middle class. From 1900 until the
start of the First World War, for example, perhaps 6,000
room-and-kitchen houses with a bathroom were built by
private enterprises. Such a house – in a 'wally close' –
was the acme of working-class respectability. This latter
was a close with tiles on the walls up to a height of about
4 feet, as opposed to mere paint. (The term 'wally' refers
to the kind of china out of which the tiles were made.) In
his evocative book, *Dancing in the Streets*, Cliff Hanley
describes moving to this kind of house in the Gallowgate
of the 1920s:

> Instead of a long thin lobby, the new house had a square
> hall; and a bath, in a dim dark room off the hall shaped like
> a three-decker coffin. We had a big, opulent front parlour
> too, with a vast oval table supported in a tentative manner
> by a three-legged curly mahogany thing...Our new house
> was a posh affair, with a tiled close too – the ultimate seal of
> solidity in Glasgow society...[47]

The lower-middle-class version of this kind of house can
be seen perfectly preserved in the Tenement House
Museum in Buccleuch Street in the Garnethill area of the
city. It is essentially the way it was left when the tenant,
Miss Toward, a shorthand typist in a city shipping firm,
left to go to hospital in 1965. She remained in hospital
until her death in 1975, but kept her tenancy on. (Note
that in the nineteenth and early twentieth centuries
middle-class as well as working-class people ordinarily
rented their houses.) But the fact of the matter is that
such relatively good houses were beyond the reach of the
great majority of working-class families in Glasgow. At
the start of the First World War there were 11,000 empty

tenement houses in the city; working-class families simply could not afford the rents of the better houses. The Corporation of Glasgow, through the City Improvement Trust, had built a mere 2,199 council houses by 1914, housing perhaps 10,000 people, less than 1 per cent of the population of the city.[48]

So at the outbreak of the First World War, two-thirds of Glasgow's working-class families still lived in single-ends or rooms-and-kitchens which, if not outright slums, were grotesquely over-crowded. The world in which these families lived was by and large unknown to the contemporary middle class – except for the 'slumologists' who made periodic forays into 'Darkest Glasgow'. The Minutes of Glasgow University Settlement in Anderston at the beginning of this century provide a glimpse of the reality of the slums – and of the world-view of the Settlement workers:

> The children are paying more respect to our wishes, trying to please us, and the boys are even making an attempt at politeness, in raising their caps to us. This seems to me a step in advance, coming as it does spontaneously.

> The majority of the girls are not interested in anything – not even the tea they are having on Wednesday. They are constantly sighing for the good old days when they had dancing all evening.

> Last Monday, one of the girls was very drunk, and one or two others were not quite sober.[49]

Tea-rooms and Frills

I am well aware that so far I have not discussed the middle class and middle-class culture in Glasgow up till, say 1914. This is for three reasons. Firstly, they have been documented to death elsewhere. Their preoccupations are chronicled, *inter alia*, in the weekly magazine the *Bailie*, in the memoirs of J.J. Bell, in the massive literature on art in Glasgow, in a rake of novels and of course, in the *Glasgow Herald*, which was their

house journal.[50] Their point-of-view has also been put in
a camouflaged way in many of the previous books about
Glasgow, although the authors weren't honest enough to
say so.[51]

Secondly, the patterns of cultural expression of the
most important section of the middle class, the
industrialists, remain curiously elusive. For all their
powerful control over local engineering and shipbuilding,
their numbers were very small. Discussing Scottish
industrial capital at the beginning of the twentieth
century, Foster and Woolfson say:

> The controlling families, the Tennants, Colvilles, Lithgows,
> Stephens, Weirs and Yarrows were based on the Clyde and
> numbered no more than a dozen, were highly intermarried
> and combined holdings in coal, steel, shipbuilding and
> engineering. Their grip on the economy of Scotland was
> unchallengeable.[52]

It seems that apart from their interest in their work,
which certainly took them around Europe and elsewhere,
their outlook could be described as very parochial. Given
the Protestant work ethic to which they subscribed, they
possibly saw cultural activities as frivolous.

Thirdly, the cultural activities of the large, mercantile
middle class were not dissimilar to those elsewhere in
Britain. Guy McCrone captured their world perfectly in
his classic if turgid 'Wax Fruit' trilogy of novels about the
Glasgow middle class of the Victorian period:

> And frills were the things which counted with Bel. Frills.
> Any amount of them. A grand house expensively, solidly
> furnished. A financially solid husband, who went to a
> financially solid business – it was more genteel not to specify
> what kind of business – every morning in order to provide
> more frills. Clothes made by the best dressmaker. Well-fed
> children at the best local schools taking all the extras,
> getting all the frills. Good solid accounts in equally solid
> banks. Accounts that were never, never drawn to their limit.
> Seats in a well-built Victorian-Gothic church, where the
> minister delivered splendid sermons that told you where the
> unfortunates went who weren't as solid as yourself.[53]

For recreation, they did the usual sorts of things, albeit with a distinctly Scottish flavour. They seemed to play a lot of golf in exclusive clubs, indulge in massive banquets, go sailing on the Clyde, go to church a lot and inhabit the many posh tea-rooms with which late Victorian and Edwardian Glasgow was infested:

> Glasgow, in truth, is a very Tokio for tea rooms. Nowhere can one have so much for so little, and nowhere are such places more popular or frequented. Edinburgh, it is true, has some pleasant and charming rooms in haberdashers' shops, where most dainty lunches are to be had for a trifle. But the Glasgow man has a delicacy in entering places which ought, by rights, to be sacred to the other sex; and, if he does so, feels, perhaps, that he might be better dressed. In his own town he need have no such qualms. The tea rooms here are meant for him, and it is he who uses them mainly...It is believed (and averred) that in no other town can you see in a place of refreshment such ingenious and beautiful decorations in the style of the new art as in Miss Cranston's shop in Buchanan Street.[54]

Tea, however, did not appear to be so highly favoured by some West End ladies at the turn of this century:

> I do not know when afternoon tea was invented; in the days of which I am telling it may have been the usual thing in the drawing-rooms of Mayfair, but it certainly had not come into those of Hillhead, Glasgow. The ladies called on one another in the forenoon, being offered refreshment in the form of a glass of sherry, or Madeira, with a morsel of sultana or seedcake. Intense teetotallers draw depressing pictures of young matrons arriving home, after a round of calls, in a bemused condition, thereby acquiring a taste for liquor; while a cynic has suggested that the ladies did not pay calls in the afternoon, because they were then engaged in sleeping off those of the morning.[55]

And there was, of course, Sir William Burrell, the enormously rich shipping magnate, who eclectically pilfered art treasures from all round the world. On his death in 1946 he bequeathed these to the city. Prior to his death he had also left £450,000 for a gallery to house these artefacts. This is the famous Burrell Collection referred to in Chapter 1. Apart from this, the main legacy of the Glasgow bourgeoisie to the city has been rows of very elegant and very large dwelling-houses in places like Park Circus and Great Western Terrace, now all student halls of residence, architects' offices – or yuppie clubs, restaurants and discos. It seems a fitting testimony.

City Life

By the end of the nineteenth century, the communities of greater Glasgow – neighbourhoods like Plantation, Kinning Park, Govan, Saracen, Partick, Maryhill, Springburn, Bridgeton, the Gorbals – were fully formed. Each had its own reputation, each had its own icongraphy. Each was characterised by its 'Cross', the main road junction in the neighbourhood. The architects decorated the surrounding tenements with distinctive whigmaleeries: spires, clocks, phoney balconies, stone lozenges, fancy names. Sometimes the Cross, as at Bridgeton or Govan for example, would be marked by a handsome, painted cast-iron gazebo. The streets were jammed with trams, horse-drawn carts and cabs, and the first motor cars. At the turn of this century, the city centre was a permanent traffic jam. It was also black with people. Glasgow had a vibrant street life of shops, stalls, pubs, buskers, beggars, hawkers, tract-dispensers, hot-gospellers, soap-box orators, pick-pockets, prosti-tutes and mere spectators escaping the cramped single-ends for the free theatre of the pavements. William McIlvanney was absolutely right to say that Glasgow is a twenty-four hour cabaret. But the curious thing was that the inhabitants of this huge city frequently knew only their own neighbourhood. It was a city of urban villages, where a villager from Bridgeton had no business being in the Gorbals, except for work. Everything that was necessary for a full social life was usually available in your own territory – shops, pubs,

churches, pawnshops, public baths, small music-halls
and theatres, and workplace too, often enough. Thus for
the generations of Glaswegians who lived in the city
before the First World War, their urban world was
tightly circumscribed. The men who followed football
could escape regularly, but the women could not. They
were prisoners in their so-called 'communities'. For a
working-class family in those years, a trip to the
pantomime in the city centre was a major expedition. But
there was a ritual escape every year during the Glasgow
Fair, the local trades holiday in the last two weeks of
July. Hundreds of families would go 'doon the watter' on
a steamer to one of the many Clyde resorts – Dunoon,
Rothesay, Saltcoats or Brodick. These trips down to the
beautiful estuary of the River Clyde were much-loved
outings which still play a major role in Glasgow folklore.
The tendency to have a 'wee refreshment' was so
well-established that it led to one of the many colourful
Glasgow phrases for being drunk: 'steamboats'!

Thus the years before the First World War saw the
crystallisation of working-class culture in Glasgow in a
form which was to remain substantially unchanged for
another half-century, complete with its own private
language, 'the patter'. Its origins were in the slums of
Victorian Glasgow in the preceding half-century. The
dominant version of this culture was definitely *macho*,
brutally hard-drinking, aggressive with undertones of
real violence, massively exploitative of women and
children, unhealthy to a degree, disgustingly sectarian,
introverted – and yet at the same time astonishingly
democratic, friendly, witty, well-read, internationally
aware and politically conscious, as we shall shortly see.
Such are the contradictions of the historical process. The
less visible version of this culture was the world of
Glasgow women. Besides working hard in both waged
and domestic labour, they created the circumstances in
home and community, against what to outsiders
appeared impossible odds, and at terrible cost to
themselves, which permitted their men to indulge their

fantasies at the match and in the pub. They operated a sophisticated if subterranean economic and social system of which their men were totally ignorant – and in which they were totally uninterested. They are the unsung heroines of the making of the Glasgow working class; they deserve their own historian. Until she comes along, it can be noted that Glaswegians, both men and women, acted creatively on their grossly unfavourable working and living conditions to construct a culture which is uniquely tough, resilient, warm and witty. It thrived in a city whose wild beauty was again invisible to outsiders, but well-known to locals:

> Sometimes I ventured down to the docks at night when, with a metallic knock-knock trailing away, the shunting steam engines joggled their loaded coal trucks into position for the dockside cranes on rails to lift and cant into the ships' bunkers in the morning. Amid the clanking and puffing, punctuated by a cheery piercing whistle here and there, the glow of their fire-boxes jewelled the indigo velvet sky with sparkling shafts of gold, while the white superstructures of sleeping ships gleamed ghostly from their strategically placed electric lights at cabin level.[56]

References

1. Glasgow's position in the world is derived from the tables in T. Chandler and G. Fox, *3000 Years of Urban Growth*, Academic Press, 1974, pp.323 ff. For Calcutta, see Geoffrey Moorehouse, *Calcutta*, Penguin, 1988, p.272.
2. 'Introductory Chapter' by John Carrick to 'Senex' (R. Reid), *Glasgow, Past and Present*, Glasgow, David Robertson, 1884.
3. Andrew Gibb, *Glasgow: The Making of a City*, Croom Helm, 1983; see especially pp.95-104 and 118-24.
4. Further details about tenement construction and design are contained in Frank Worsdall, *The Tenement: A Way of Life*, Chambers, 1979.
5. James Cleland, *Statistical Facts Descriptive of the Former and Present State of Glasgow*, Glasgow, Bell & Bain, 1837, p.20.
6. The story of the decline and fall of this part of the Gorbals is told in J.R. Kellet, 'Property Speculators and the Building of Glasgow', *Scottish Journal of Political Economy*, Vol. VIII, 1961.
7. Edwin Chadwick, *Report on the Sanitary Condition of the Labouring Population of Great Britain, 1842*, edited by M. Flinn, Edinburgh University Press, 1965, p.5.

8. See S. Damer, *From Moorepark to 'Wine Alley': The Rise and Fall of a Glasgow Housing Scheme*, Edinburgh University Press, 1989, Ch. 3 for a detailed discussion of Glasgow's housing during this period.

9. Frederick Engels, *Condition of the Working Class in England*, Panther, 1969, pp.71-2. This quotation is slightly different from that in Engels, as he was quoting from a pamphlet written by Jelinger Cookson Symons, one of the Commissioners, *after* the investigation. The quotation reproduced here is from the original Report. In one or other of its forms, it has been cited in various academic studies of Glasgow but not, to my knowledge, in any more popular book.

10. Dr D. Smith, quoted in A.K. Chalmers (ed.), *Public Health Administration in Glasgow: A Memorial Volume of the Writings of James Burn Russell, BA, MD, LLD*, Glasgow, James Maclehose & Sons, 1905, pp. 10-11.

11. Engels, op. cit.

12. Captain Miller, quoted in Charles R. Baird, 'On the General and Sanitary Conditions of the Working Classes and the Poor in the City of Glasgow' in *Reports of the Sanitary Conditions of the Labouring Population of Scotland, 1842*, p.189.

13. Ibid., p.191.

14. Chalmers (ed.), op. cit., p.3.

15. On the Police Acts see, *inter alia*, Gibb, op. cit., Worsdall, op. cit., and H.F. Brotherstown, *Observations on the Early Public Health Movement in Scotland*, H.K. Lewis, 1952.

16. See discussion by Carrick in Senex, op. cit.

17. *Reports* (1842), op. cit., p.166.

18. Ibid., p.173.

19. Ibid., p.166.

20. Gareth Stedman Jones, *Outcast London*, Penguin, 1975.

21. *Reports* (1842), op. cit., p.162.

22. Ibid., p.185.

23. 'Shadow', *Midnight Scenes and Social Photographs Being Sketches of Life in the Street, Wynds and Dens of the City*, Glasgow, Thomas Murray, 1858; reprinted with an introduction by J.F. McCaffrey by the University of Glasgow Press, 1976. ('Shadow' was a pseudonym for Alexander Brown, a Glasgow letterpress printer.)

24. Ibid., pp.12-13.

25. W. T. Gairdner, 'Preface', in Chalmers (ed.), op. cit.; pp.vi-vii.

26. See Damer, op. cit. and also Chalmers (ed.), op. cit. and J. Butt, 'Working Class Housing in Glasgow, 1851-1914' in Chapman (ed.), *The History of Working Class Housing*, Newton Abbott, David and Charles, 1971.

27. See Damer, op. cit., pp.64-7.

28. John R. Kellet, *Railways and Victorian Cities*, Routledge & Kegan Paul, 1979. Ch. VIII deals with railway development in Glasgow.

29. Butt, op. cit., Senex, op. cit., p.xxvi.

30. Gibb, op. cit., p.143.

31. These reports are all contained in a book of cuttings entitled 'The Dark Side of Glasgow' in the Glasgow Room of the Mitchell Library, ref. no. G914.1435 GAR. All the following quotations are from this source. If no date is given, it is because it is not given in the book – although we

know it is 1870 or 71. Again, the pages of this cuttings book are not numbered. I am most grateful to Joe Fisher, the omniscient librarian of the Glasgow Room, for bringing this book to my attention. This and the following two quotations are dated 27.12.70.

32. Peter Mackenzie, *Reminiscences of Glasgow*, Glasgow, John Tweed, 1867, pp.356ff.

33. Cuttings book, 'The Dark Side of Glasgow', op. cit.

34. Gray and Currie, op. cit., p.3.

35. Ellen Ross, 'Survival Networks: Women's Neighbourhood Sharing in London Before World War 1', *History Workshop Journal*, 15, 1983. It is beyond my comprehension why similar research has not been done on women and tenemental life in Victorian and Edwardian Glasgow. This again is some kind of comment on the preoccupations of local academic sociologists. Maybe the fact that the majority of them are English and have no background or interest in working-class tenemental life has something to do with it...

36. It has also led to that classic Glasgow insult for an incompetent person: 'See him/her, s/he couldnae run a menage!'

37. Jim McLean, 'Farewell to Glasgow' in Farquhar McLay (ed.), *Workers City: The Real Glasgow Stands Up*, Glasgow, Clydeside Press, 1988, p. 21. This book contains Jim's song, and another by Adam MacNaughton, 'The Glasgow I Used to Know', which as the editor says, 'vividly illustrates the contrasting perspectives on life in Glasgow before the slum clearances at the close of World War II' (p.19). Adam's song constitutes the sentimental perspective, Jim's the savage.

38. D.E. Lindsay, *Report Upon a Study of the Diet of the Labouring Classes in the City of Glasgow, 1911-12*, University of Glasgow Physiology Department, 1913, p. 27. Emphasis in the original.

39. Computed from tables on p. 13 of *Glasgow Municipal Commission on the Housing of the Poor*, Minutes of Evidence, Vol. 1, Glasgow, William Hodge, 1904.

40. Described at length in the 'Dark Side of Glasgow', op. cit.

41. McArthur and Kingsley Long, op. cit., p.16.

42. Taped interview with Mrs G of Blackhill.

43. *Mail*, 11 March 1872.

44. The situation of the dock-labourers is described in *Glasgow Sketches*, op. cit.

45. Senex, op. cit., pp.108-9.

46. Bill Murray, *The Old Firm: Sectarianism, Sport, and Society in Scotland*, Edinburgh, John Donald, 1984. For a review see Bernard Aspinwall, *British Journal of Sports History*, 2, 1985. See also Gerry Finn, 'Irish Catholic Clubs and Scottish Football: A study of Scottish Racism, Religious and Social Prejudice, *International Journal of the History of Sport*, forthcoming.

47. Cliff Hanley, *Dancing in the Streets*, London, White Lion, 1979, p.32.

48. Butt, op. cit.

49. *Minutes* of the Executive Committee of Glasgow University Settlements, Glasgow University Archives, ref. DC170, March 29, 1901; January 12, 1904 and January 12, 1904 respectively.

50. See J.J. Bell, *I Remember*, Edinburgh, The Porpoise Press, 1932.

Novels would include Guy McCrone, *Wax Fruit*, Pan, 1984. There are many others; see M. Burgess, op. cit.
51. In this category I would include C.A. Oakley, *The Second City*, Blackie, 1946 and S.G. Checkland, *The Upas Tree*, University of Glasgow Press, 1976.
52. J. Foster and C. Woolfson, *The Politics of the UCS Work-In*, Lawrence and Wishart, 1985, p.83.
53. Guy McCrone, 'Wax Fruit' Trilogy, *Antimacassar City, The Philistines, The Puritans*, Pan, 1984, p.132.
54. J.H. Muir, *Glasgow in 1901*, Glasgow, William Hodge, 1901, pp.166-7.
55. Bell, op. cit., pp.83-4.
56. H. B. Morton, *Old Glasgow*, Glasgow, Richard Drew Publishing, 1987, p.103. The time is about 1920.

4   The Red Clyde

Of all British cities, Glasgow is that most associated with socialism. The 'Red Clyde' is still a redolent phrase and, although the phenomenon has inspired a massive literature, it is auguably the most misunderstood in twentieth-century British politics.[1] It is, of course, impossible to understand this period without a historical grasp of the wider politics in Glasgow in the three or four decades before the First World War.

Here I use the word 'politics' in the broadest sense of the term, as something more all-embracing than straightforward party politics. I therefore include the activities of temperance groups, friendly societies, Highland and Irish societies, church organisations, women's groups, the Corporation of Glasgow, employers' organisations, labour movement bodies, the Chamber of Commerce, Masonic and Orange Lodges and Ward Committees in the term. This alerts us right away to the fact that there wasn't just one form of politics in Glasgow, there were two: that of the middle class and that of the working class. Each of these will be taken in turn.

Liberalism and the Kirk

Put at its simplest, middle-class politics in Victorian and Edwardian Glasgow was dominated by the Liberal Party. Glasgow's was a particularly *Scottish* form of Liberalism, one heavily influenced by the democratic Presbyterian tradition and the most significant representative of this form of Protestantism was the famous Minister Thomas Chalmers, DD. While this is not the place to discuss the

'Disruption' in the Church of Scotland in 1843, it can be noted that Chalmers led the Secession from the Church of Scotland which, it must be remembered, was the established church in the country. Thus the establishment of the *Free* Church of Scotland meant driving a wedge into the old Tory connection between church and state as far as Scotland was concerned. The world-view of this new church corresponded substantially with the voluntarism of the Liberal Party. In Glasgow the vast majority of Free Presbyterian kirks were Liberal.

Briefly, Chalmers had an evangelical rather than doctrinal view of his religion in which securing sanitary and social reform for working people was an integral part of Christian philanthropy.[2] He wished to uplift the masses through the use of missionaries, and from the 1820s systematically sent divinity students into the slums with tracts. He was so active, especially in his own city-centre Tron parish, that in the 1820s Glasgow became known as 'Gospel City'.[3] A key dimension of this evangelical Protestantism was its anti-urbanism which made potent use of rural imagery and appealed to the simple yet pure life of the country people. Its heroes and heroines were the Covenanters, honest, God-fearing people ruthlessly harried and slaughtered by Royalists over the moss hags of Scotland. This imagery, reinforced as it was by the poetry of Robert Burns, struck a resonant note with at least some of the Highlanders and Lowlanders flooding into contemporary Glasgow. Yet at the same time Chalmers was an exceptionally hard-headed person, a true Calvinist who did not believe in the Poor Law. He believed that the poor must reform themselves through strength of character and was, therefore, opposed in principle to Poor Relief and philanthropy in general. This corresponded with the stress on self-help and individualism of Liberalism while running counter to the more humane beliefs of the radical Liberals.

Another critical dimension of this form of Protestantism was its strong temperance component. Chalmers

and his successors believed quite literally that the slums
represented hell on earth. But they also believed that
alcohol was responsible for the existence of these slums,
so if one could get rid of drink, one could get rid of the
slums. This attitude was to persist in Glasgow until at
least the Second World War, and indeed was an early
version of the notion of a 'culture of poverty'. This
emphasis on temperance was reinforced by organisations
like the Independent Order of Rechabites, which had
33,543 members in 63 'tents' in Glasgow in 1903.[4] This
important temperance and friendly society, catering
mainly for 'labour aristocrats', was essentially a
Protestant organisation whose officers were frequently
also involved in Masonic and Orange Lodges.[5]

Temperance was an important part of the socialist
tradition in Glasgow in the years before the First World
War, as it spanned a variety of organisations from the
Rechabites through the Co-operative movement to the
Independent Labour Party (ILP). Norma Denny argues
that:

> ...it was a short step from criticism of the public house
> landlord's exploitation of the worker to general anti-
> landlordism, and from attacks on 'the Trade' to demands for
> worker control of the means of production.[6]

While this is undoubtedly overstating the case, the
connection was definitely there. The endemic drunkenness of so much of the late nineteenth-century Glasgow
working class *was* a barrier to social reform and political
progress, and was perceived as such by working-class
leaders, many of whom came from a Calvinist, teetotal
background – John Maclean and David Kirkwood, for
example. But temperance was also an important aspect
of middle-class Liberal politics because it enabled its
practitioners to reach down into the working class and
find allies in the anti-drink movement.

A final aspect of democratic Protestantism which was
important in both middle-class and working-class politics
was its emphasis on universal education. The historic

connection between kirk and the successful Scottish educational system is well known, if perhaps over-emphasised.[7] Again, the importance attached to education squared exactly with Liberal notions of individualism, and the distinctively Glaswegian dimension of this was the long-standing connection between the University of Glasgow and the sons (not daughters) of Ulster Presbyterians, barred by their religion from studying at Trinity College, Dublin.

There was, of course, another side to these Presbyterian church-going Liberals – the authoritarianism common to those who believe that God has smiled personally upon their successful business careers. Glasgow's industrialists were a singularly ruthless bunch who kept a merciless grip on their workers. We have already seen how the prominent church-going Liberal, Lord Overtoun, treated his workers, but he was only one of a large number of similar employers, God-fearing to a man. Right up to the First World War, the shipbuilding and engineering employers kept control of their workers by the practice of issuing 'character notes'. Anyone without a 'character note' was deemed not to have a good character and would not be employed.[8] This practice was exactly paralleled in the tenement communities by the 'factor's line'. Without such a line, the inference was that someone was a bad tenant and so would not get the let of a new house.[9] It goes without saying that notes and lines were an excellent way of controlling socialists, trade unionists and other disruptive elements.

One cannot help gaining the impression that a strong strand in this Calvinist Liberalism was a barely camouflaged racism. If one reads the minutes of evidence of the numerous commissions of enquiry into the economic and housing conditions of the Glasgow working class, it is plain that the Irish get blamed for everything from the slums to low wages and bad weather. It is not so much a 'sub-text' as the actual text. While Joan Smith is without a doubt correct to say that sectarianism was much worse in Liverpool than in Glasgow, she underestimates the hold that anti-Catholicism had in Glasgow, where it was more subtle and commonplace than in Liverpool.[10] As we have seen, 'Irish' and 'Catholic' were interchangeable terms in Glasgow well into the twentieth century. A central tenet of Scottish fundamentalist Protestantism was and is a rabid anti-Papism which in the Orange Lodge or the utterances of Pastor Jack Glass of the Twentieth Century Reformation Movement in Glasgow, for example, becomes mindless paranoia wherein all notions of historical accuracy go out of the window.

Knights and Grocers

Perhaps we can make best sense of this Liberalism by looking at a couple of individuals, Sir Samuel Chisholm and Sir Thomas Lipton. Samuel Chisholm was born in Dalkeith in 1836 and died in 1923 in Glasgow.[11] A wholesale grocer by trade, he came to Glasgow in 1870 and was soon a prominent Liberal of the 'radical' persuasion and a prominent churchman. He first entered the Council in 1888 on a temperance ticket and, like many Glasgow industrialists, merchants and financiers, was proud to serve the city. He thereafter served more or less continuously as a Councillor, subsequently Bailie (magistrate), and was Lord Provost from 1899 to 1902. Chisholm was identified with a number of philanthropic causes, including the Foundry Boys' Religious Society. He was also heavily involved in a number of municipal issues in Glasgow, and chaired the important Municipal Commission on the Housing of the Poor in 1904. Chisholm's most enduring association, however, was with Glasgow's famous 'municipal socialism', as it was known both nationally and internationally.

Put simply, at the turn of the twentieth century Glasgow was the most municipalised city in the world, a fact of which the local middle class was inordinately proud.[12] The process had started with the municipalisation of the water supply in 1855, gas in 1867, the establishment of a municipal hospital in 1869, baths and wash-houses in 1878, a laundry in 1884 and the tramways in 1894. Christopher Smout has supplied an excellent discussion of these developments and the furore surrounding them.[13] The scale of the city's municipal enterprises was truly staggering. One witty quotation in Smout is well worth repeating:

> [In Glasgow a citizen] may live in a municipal house: he may walk along the municipal street, or ride on the municipal tramcar and watch the municipal dust-cart collecting the refuse which is to be used to fertilise the municipal farm. Then he may turn into the municipal market, buy a steak from an animal killed in the municipal slaughterhouse, and cook it by the municipal gas stove. For his recreation he can choose among municipal libraries, municipal art galleries and municipal music in municipal parks. Should he fall ill, he can ring up his doctor on the municipal telephone, or he may be taken to the municipal hospital in the municipal ambulance by a municipal policeman. Should he be so unfortunate as to get on fire, he will be put out by a municipal fireman, using municipal water; after which he will, perhaps, forego the enjoyment of a municipal bath, though he may find it necessary to get a new suit in the municipal old clothes market.[14]

The author of these remarks – made at the start of this century – might well have added that while this citizen was looking for a suit in the municipal old clothes market, his wife was washing his dirty one in a municipal wash-house and, finding that it was beyond repair, consigned it to the municipal incinerator while getting the fleas out of the 'new' one in a municipal fumigator, as their children were having municipal school dinners in the municipal school. And in the event that the citizen's wife dropped dead in the process of cleaning the suit, he could be sure that he and his children would always find a place in the municipal lodging-house for widowers and their dependents, while his wife was being buried in the municipal cemetery.

In any event, Glasgow's municipal socialism was an internationally known phenomenon and, indeed, was all the rage in progressive circles in the United States where it spawned dozens of books and articles.[15] For North American reformers, Glasgow was The Good City. The historian of this phenomenon, Bernard Aspinwall, could only find one article on contemporary Birmingham and one on contemporary Nottingham. Given the reputation of Birmingham for progressive municipalism under the Chamberlains, this is all the more remarkable. Chisholm and his fellow Councillors wanted to turn Glasgow into a model municipality with, of course, model citizens. As Aspinwall puts it:

> Humanitarianism, or welfare capital operating at municipal level, sought to enable the deserving to help themselves: the undeserving could be taken in hand and given suitable treatment and assistance. Liberalism with a large injection of Christian duty forced the consideration of urban problems.[16]

What is intriguing about Glasgow's municipal socialism is that it had nothing whatsoever to do with socialism as commonly understood in either the Labourist or revolutionary tradition. Socialists in Glasgow had no political representation worth talking about before 1890. As David Whitham puts it:

> Municipal socialism...was born in town halls, of liberal and even conservative administrations with hardly a socialist in sight, and being an '-ism' described a philosophy or at least an idea rather than an activity. To add to the paradox, the heroic period of this socialism without socialists was between 1885 and 1905, just before labour gained a real foothold in the town halls and with the advent of labour power municipal socialism seemed to decline.[17]

It would have been more accurate to say 'ideology' here rather than 'idea'. Be that as it may, these large-scale enterprises inspired a series of articles in the *Times* at the beginning of this century, not to mention a letter from a Glasgow Councillor attacking Chisholm for spending over £10,000 in one year on 'banquets, receptions, *conversaziones*, and entertainment'.[18] The problem with municipal socialism, wrote the *Times'* correspondent, was that, logically, there was no end to its expansion. When in Feburary 1901 the Corporation of Glasgow proposed to borrow £750,000 and impose a penny rate for the purposes of building municipal waterworks and council housing, the *Glasgow Herald* felt that enough was enough:

> We are to pledge the credit of the city in order to borrow £750,000 for this vague and indefinite purpose, and we are to burden the rates with interest and sinking fund on the debt. Where is this kind of thing to end? It is the curse of municipalities that they are able to borrow far too easily. The Municipality of Glasgow has far too many irons in the fire – too many faddists in its council chamber. The municipal debt is growing at a portentous rate, and in the name of economy and common sense a protest must be made against the addition proposed on it by the Improvements Committee. [19]

(It is not difficult to see that what the *Herald* was really saying was that it did not want middle-class ratepayers' money spent on building council houses for workers, the City Improvements Committee being responsible for such development.)

The main newspaper in the *other* Scottish city camouflaged its envy with sarcasm:

> Glasgow has the most sublime Corporation in the world. It would be rash to call this in question, for the Corporation itself has said it. Again and again the world has heard of the greatness of the Glasgow municipal body. It has gone into fields into which other Corporations have not ventured. It has carried out schemes which other Corporations have looked at askance. It has never lost an opportunity of setting itself above all other municipal bodies and even above the ordinary law of the land.[20]

Chisholm himself had a long letter published in the *Times* on 24 October 1902, rebutting the allegations made about Glasgow's municipal socialism and, written by a man who plainly had more enthusiasm than natural political skill, it was an effective defence of the city's operations. Lord Provost Chisholm deserves to be remembered well.

Thomas Lipton was born in Crown Street in the Gorbals in 1850, of an immigrant, teetotal Presbyterian family from Clones in County Monaghan.[21] His childhood was a happy if impoverished one, informed by that cheerless Christianity in which Ulster Presbyterians specialise. At the age of fifteen he went to the United States and had an adventurous four years in which he was variously a tobacco plantation labourer, plantation book-keeper, stowaway, tram-man and latterly a grocer's assistant in a New York multiple store, so sharing the same trade as Chisholm. In New York he learned the art of marketing. He came back to Glasgow with some capital and within a year had opened his first grocer's shop in Stobcross Street. In less than five years he had twenty shops and was a brilliant advertiser of his goods. In one stunt he had advertisements painted live on pigs. In another he had sovereigns hidden in huge cheeses! His success was based on cutting out middlemen and getting produce direct from Irish farmers. At the age of forty, and against all predictions, he successfully broke into the tea trade and became a multi-millionaire. He again used clever sales gimmicks like blending tea to suit local drinking water in the different regions of Britain.

Although a Liberal by disposition, Lipton does not seem to have been involved in party politics in Glasgow: his politics was making money, at which he was superbly talented. He was, however, very proud of being a Glaswegian, and supported a number of local charities. In 1931, for example, he gave £10,000 for the widows and their children in the city. But what Lipton is best remembered for is his obsession with sailing, and his financing of a string of famous yachts in a series of unsuccessful attempts at the America's Cup. Lipton hob-nobbed with the rich and famous and lunched with Theodore Roosevelt, President of the United States. He was created a Baronet and a Knight Commander of the Royal Victorian Order. Lipton and Chisholm both rose from humble beginnings and through hard work achieved commercial success. What they both exemplify is a pride in a city in which the route to the top was wide open, a city with such self-confidence that it municipalised everything in sight for the ultimate benefit of its citizens – citizens like themselves, that is, morally scrupulous, hard-working, hard-headed, teetotal exemplars of the Protestant ethic. The immoral, the undeserving, the drinkers – the Catholic Irish, that is – were there to be controlled and disciplined, for their own good. The benefits of Glasgow's municipal socialism were not really for them: they were for the city's middle class and 'respectable' working class.

The central problem with the politics of Glasgow's Liberals was the old problem with Liberalism: it did genuinely believe in reform, but that reform was to be moral, not social. The evils of turn-of-the-century Glasgow were defined as personal or racial, rather than social. And as people like Chisholm and Lipton governed that society they were unlikely to give it away. Furthermore they had little understanding of or sympathy for those at the bottom. Beatrice and Sidney Webb encountered that when they visited Glasgow in 1890:

> In the evening S.W. [Sidney Webb] and I wandered through the Glasgow streets. A critical twenty-four hours, followed by another long walk by glorious sunset through the crowded streets, knocking up against drunken Scots. With glory in the sky and hideous bestiality on the earth, two socialists came to a working compromise.[22]

It is time to turn to the local socialists.

The ILP and the Red Clyde

Socialism in Glasgow in the first two or three decades of the twentieth century was extraordinary in scope and unequalled in Britain. The Red Clyde was a real and very important phenomenon. Let us deal right away with the standard view of the romantic left. Neither during the war years nor in 1919 was Glasgow in something called a 'revolutionary situation'. The mass of working people were not Bolsheviks, nor were the vast majority of their leaders. But Glasgow in 1919 was the nearest thing to a revolutionary situation seen in twentieth-century Britain. One major mistake by the government *could* have led to an insurrection: a few strategic moves by the Red Clydeside leaders *could* have led to a local seizure of power by workers. But these mistakes and moves did not occur. With one or two exceptions, like John Maclean, the Red Clyde leaders were not revolutionaries; Scots Calvinists and Irish Catholics make poor Lenins and Trotskys. So what were the politics of the Red Clyde?

The origins of Glasgow's socialism lie squarely in the radical politics of its nineteenth-century working class, as described in the previous chapter. There was an evident continuity between the radical democracy of the Lowlanders, the anti-landlordism of the Highlanders and the Irish, the nationalist aspirations of the latter and the socialism of the 1920s. In the huge 1884 Great Reform demonstration in the city the links were explicit:

> ...the french polishers carried a miniature wardrobe they had carried in 1832, the Glasgow upholsterers carried their 1832 sofa, and the Boot and Shoemakers carried their Chartist flag. There were large numbers of working models throughout the demonstration, cutting off lords' heads, the House of Lords as a flywheel, kilns to smoke them in, dyes for them, exploding boilers and saws. Every trade had their own particular solution to the abolition of the House of Lords. [23]

As the nineteenth century drew to a close the links between these two groups became increasingly close. Until the mid-1880s the Irish Catholic vote went 'conditionally' to whoever supported Home Rule.[24] The Glasgow branch of the Home Rule movement, the Irish National League, was the biggest and most active in these islands, not excluding Dublin, Belfast and London. It was very well organised in West Central Scotland, in parallel with church parishes, in its efforts to get all eligible members onto the voters' roll. The Glasgow Irish were regularly addressed by such leaders as Parnell, Redmond, O'Connor and Michael Davitt of the Irish Land League. The Irish League had close connections with the Highland Land Law Reformation Association and with such Scottish radicals as John Ferguson, Keir Hardie and Cunninghame Graham.[25] In the 1880s the Highland Land League came into existence to mirror its Irish sister, and throughout this decade Irish rallies in Glasgow contributed funds and support to help Scottish crofters fight eviction.[26] In 1892 Michael Davitt spoke at a series of meetings in Glasgow attacking Scottish landlords and evictions, while John Ferguson of the Irish National League, a town councillor from 1893, was pressing home attacks on urban land speculators and property-owners. Ferguson became a co-founder of the Scottish Labour Party in 1888 with Keir Hardie, before returning to the Liberal fold. From about 1885 the first Irish electors were voting for Labour candidates against the instructions of the machine.[27] By the end of the century the Highlanders and the Irish could not have been co-operating more closely, as Tom Gallagher documents.[28] The rise of socialism was to take advantage of this natural alliance.

The Scottish Labour Party was founded in 1888, and merged into the Independent Labour Party (ILP) in 1894. The ILP dominated working-class politics in Glasgow until the Second World War. It won ten out of 75 council seats in 1898 and became known for its committed stand for the 'municipalisation of housing under equitable conditions of labour'.[29] At this time not one ILP leader was a Catholic. By the end of the nineteenth century, however, the Irish Catholics were actively backing Trades Council-endorsed candidates for the Corporation and the United Irish League (which linked the various strands in the Catholic community) and the ILP were now endorsing each other's candidates.[30] This development took place in spite of the fact that the Catholic

Church was formally very much opposed to socialism, as the important 1891 papal encyclical *Rerum Novarum* had made clear.[31] Social justice was one thing, the socialisation of the means of production quite another. But John Wheatley, previously in the United Irish League and now in the ILP, founded the Catholic Socialist Society in 1906 to show that Catholicism and socialism were not incompatible, that the radical Labourism of Glasgow was not the revolutionary socialism of Russia or Germany. After trouncing an ecclesiastical watchdog set upon him in a debate in the local Catholic newspaper, the *Glasgow Observer*, Wheatley had cleared the ground for Catholics openly to support Labour candidates. The Catholic vote for Labour at municipal elections increased steadily between 1910 and 1914, at least tacitly endorsed by the Church.[32]

There were two critical reasons for the ILP's dramatic success in capturing the allegiance of the Glasgow working class and (at least electorally) healing the splits within it caused by skill, gender and religion. The first was its ideological and organisational structure, and the second was its adoption of housing as *the* political issue on Clydeside.

Although it had branches, and women's sections within these branches, the Glasgow ILP was essentially a federal organisation loosely linked with a wide range of other socialist and radical groupings. Its newspaper *Forward* (founded in 1906) was open to all groupings of the left, including the considerable anarchist presence in Glasgow and the Scottish nationalists. The articles and advertisements in *Forward* give the clue to its politics. Its socialism was a moral one, which believed passionately that human beings, women and children as well as men, were entitled to spiritual as well as material well-being. Nowadays we might call it a rich quality of life. As well as arguing for the *peaceful* socialisation of the means of production (in a manner never made totally clear, but essentially through radical parliamentary reform), the Clydeside ILP also believed that the working people were entitled to seek artistic and cultural fulfilment. They were entitled to enjoy the wonders of nature and the countryside, and *Forward* contained many articles which anticipate Green politics.

Thus the advertisements in this weekly paper during, say, the first three decades of this century, carried announcements for socialist choirs, socialist drama groups, socialist Sunday Schools, socialist reading groups, socialist debating groups, socialist evening classes, socialist cycling clubs and socialist rambling clubs, amongst others, all evidence of a thriving political counter-culture. It was highly involved in the grass roots at the neighbourhood level through organisations like Ward Committees, the Co-operative movement, the Co-operative Women's Guilds and the Labour Representation Committees, aimed at getting all eligible supporters onto the electoral roll. It was closely tied in with Highland and Irish societies, and could easily make tactical alliances with Celts of a more Marxist disposition. To take but three of the better-known Red Clyde leaders, it is not by accident that John Maclean's parents were both Highlanders and victims of the Clearances, his father from Mull and his mother from Corpach; Maclean was brought up on stories of the bitter injustice of the Highland Clearances.[33] Harry McShane's father was from a Catholic family from County Tyrone in Ulster,[34] and Willie Gallacher's father was Irish, his mother a Highlander.[35]

The Glasgow ILP, then, came from the grass roots and organised among the grass roots, although it probably appealed most to skilled workers. It was a *collectivist* party whose loose structure was the despair of harder-headed revolutionaries and trade unionists, but whose responsiveness to currents among the people, ability to articulate their demands and facility at political mobilisation is the dream of many present-day socialists. Its politics sprang from and mirrored the rural, Celtic origins of so many of its constituents, and its passion for radical reform was the urban analogue of their desire for change. Its inspired quest to educate working people, in the broadest sense of the term, sprang from the best traditions of Scots Presbyterianism. Quite simply, there was nothing like the Glasgow ILP anywhere else in the country.

A scan of the *Young Socialist*, the Glasgow-produced magazine of the National Council of British Socialist Sunday Schools, an ILP creation, gives us an insight into this kind of socialism – always remembering that it was for children. The issue for January 1909 contains the following news item:

> An interesting ceremony took place on the 29th at Kinning Park Socialist Sunday School, when the youngest child of our Superintendent, Comrade Hopkins, was named. Comrade Charles Scott took up the duties of Superintendent for the day, and right ably he performed that duty. Comrade Lizzy Glasier, who had a grand reception, gave an eloquent address suitable to the occasion and traced the ceremony of baptism from its origin. Taking the baby in her arms, and holding her up in full view of the audience, she named her Agnes Moreland Hopkins, and expressed the hope that she would grow up to be a good and pure woman... The singing of 'The Red Flag' brought one of the most interesting and impressive ceremonies that had been seen by the large audience who were present to a close.[36]

The editorial in another issue reads:

> ... the gospel of Socialism is aflame with a *reasoned* idealism that flashes from soul to soul with a non-consuming fire. It glows with a vivifying and transforming influence within the mind and heart of every man, woman, and child it touches...Into the darkest dens of squalor, poverty and ignorance its illuminating rays are carrying the light of a great promise. A promise that all life there shall be cleansed, purified, uplifted and the homes of the people made places of sweet and wholesome habitation out of which a new life will rise.[37]

The passionate moralism and the sheer commitment and enthusiasm which the Glasgow ILP inspired in its members continued well into the interwar years. In a chapter in his memoir tellingly entitled 'The Gutters Will Run With Tea', veteran Glasgow journalist and writer Cliff Hanley makes a couple of typically incisive comments. About the local ILP in the 1930s he wrote:

> The ILP meant a lot in Glasgow because it kept its hands clean and stood by its principles even when they had become unpopular and there is nothing laughable about the brotherhood of man.[38]

And about the commitment of members:

> Sometimes I used to walk home with another member, who lived two miles beyond my home, to continue the argument. We walked slowly in case he reached home before the thing was properly thrashed out.[39]

Yet some academics have dismissed the Clydeside ILP as little more than a socialist club or debating society; Middlemas, for example, argued that:

> It did not make for dynamic activity, and the ILP remained a party of almost personal exchanges, lacking the necessary roughness of a political organisation.[40]

The staggering inaccuracy of this judgement becomes clear if we look at the remarkable political success of the ILP in the area of housing and rents. Moreover the formidable political skills of ILP leaders like John Wheatley and Paddy Dollan were admitted even by their most bitter enemies.

Before, say, 1885 the Glasgow working class did not perceive housing as a top political priority. As Patrick Dollan puts it:

> Housing reform was never even mentioned as everybody thought it was in accordance with the wishes of Divine Providence that miners, iron and steel and other workers, should be obliged to rear their families in single-apartment dwellings.[41]

But after the 1885 Royal Commission on Housing, the housing question was to become the single biggest and most persistent political issue on Clydeside for the next century. It temporarily ceded first place to unemployment in the interwar years but was, of course, closely related to that problem. The ILP orchestrated a brilliant campaign around this issue.[42] Wheatley and Kirkwood reduced meetings of the Corporation to chaos on several occasions by admitting delegations of protesting housewives to the chamber. The issues of year-long leases, warrant sales, the profits factors made out of slums and the urgent necessity of building council houses were debated daily, and were the subject of myriad public demonstrations and meetings. Everybody lived in a house, after all, and the fact of the matter in Glasgow was that the majority of the houses workers lived in were grossly over-crowded. To repeat the figures, the 1911 Census showed that 66.3 per cent of the population of the city lived in houses of one or two rooms, while half of all couples lived in single-ends. In the same year a Liverpool docker or seaman could expect to live in a four-room terraced house with a small backyard containing a toilet. The people most affected by bad housing were, of course, the women of Glasgow, whose domain it was. It is hardly surprising that many of the most talented and committed ILP campaigners on the housing issue were women: Helen Crawfurd, Agnes Dollan, Mary Barbour are only the best known names. Paddy Dollan himself learned fast from his mother:

> It was my mother who prompted me to agitate for better housing. I remember her saying that it was a queer Christianity which compelled a mining couple and ten children to live in a single apartment while clergymen occupied the best mansions in the village.[43]

It was the rotten conditions of the miners' housing and their resulting agitation which had been instrumental in the establishment of the Royal Commission on the Housing of the Working Classes of Scotland in 1912. This was to report in 1917, unequivocally stating for the first time in British history that the state had a *duty* to build housing for the working class.[44] In case there had been any equivocation on the part of the Commissioners, the dramatic events of the 1915 Rent Strike in Glasgow made the case perfectly plain. In an act of incredible stupidity, the factors and property-owners of Glasgow quite opportunistically put up house rents in a situation of wartime monopoly, as many English munitions workers were moved into the city.[45] With their men away in the trenches fighting for King and Country, the women of Glasgow were quite rightly livid. The ILP cleverly organised the grass-roots anger and a massive rent strike was declared. When some rent strikers were taken to court the size and anger of the ensuing demonstration left the government in no doubt that there would be a general strike on Clydeside if the rent strikers were convicted. Helen Crawfurd describes the scene in her autobiography:

> I will never forget the sight and sound of those marching men with black faces. Thousands of them marched through the principal streets down to the Sheriff Court and the surrounding streets were packed. John Maclean, MA, afterwards imprisoned for his anti-war activity, and first consul for the USSR in Glasgow, was one of the speakers, who from barrels and upturned boxes, addressed the crowds.[46]

A Rent Restriction Act which froze rent at the pre-war level and, even more importantly, established the principle of government intervention in setting rent levels, was rushed through parliament.

The ILP's close connection with the housing question continued unabated after the First World War, concentrating on the rapid building of council housing and the rents restriction issue. It was this latter issue which led to the large-scale, protracted 1920s Rent Strike in Clydebank, and to a lesser extent in Glasgow, which was the launching pad for the ILP's sensational successes in the 1922 General Election and the return of ten Red Clyde MPs from the city to Parliament.[47] It was the style of the ILP's politics and its sustained political concentration on the housing issue which lay at the heart of the phenomenon of the Red Clyde rather than the more dramatic events of the 40-hour strike, which we shall examine in a moment. The housing issue always had the potential for mass mobilisation of both men and women of all backgrounds, while the engineers' agitation affected only men, and skilled men at that. And the ILP as a political party was organically involved with its supporters at a neighbourhood level in a way that the ASE never was, nor could be.

Before turning to the engineers, two other groups important in the city's socialist politics must not be forgotten. The first is the Jews. Refugees from Tsarist pogroms, the Jews poured into the Gorbals at the turn of the century, just as the Irish had done a half century before them and the Pakistanis were to do a half century later. In this sense, Glasgow was the only truly cosmopolitan city in Scotland. Many of these refugees were intensely political people, and not a few had been anarchist and socialist revolutionaries in Russia and Poland. In his memoir of the Gorbals Ralph Glasser describes the premises of the Workers' Circle in Oxford Street:

> In bookshelves fixed to one wall were rows of revered source books – Mill, Spencer, Marx, Engels, Keir Hardie, Lenin, Kropotkin, de Leon, Kautsky. Heaps of socialist and anarchist papers and pamphlets, dog-eared and tea-stained, lay on a table nearby. On the walls, in frames of slender gilt, hung faded sepia pictures of Kropotkin, Marx and Proudhon and one of frock-coated men brandishing guns and sabres at a Paris Commune barricade.[48]

Glasser also provides an interesting description of one of the countryside socialist camps common for Clydesiders in these years.[49] The Jews provided their own distinctive input to the crucible of Glasgow socialism, as can be seen from the pages of *Forward*.

The second section is the Glasgow anarchists. The first anarchist group in the city was set up in 1903 with a membership of 50 who had come from the old Socialist League of William Morris.[50] They established the

Glasgow Communist Propaganda Group, which spoke at all the numerous public speaking places in Glasgow. They were noteworthy for their principled stand against the First World War, and many of their number were imprisoned as Conscientious Objectors and brutally treated. Four Glasgow COs, one of them Jewish, died in military captivity. Guy Aldred, an Englishman who was to become postwar 'leader' of the Glasgow anarchists, served the first of many periods in prison during the war years as a Conscientious Objector. He moved to Glasgow on his release in 1919, helped found the Glasgow Communist Group which took over from the pre-war Propaganda Group, and was soon a familiar figure at political meetings, particularly on Glasgow Green. The anarchists' headquarters in Glasgow's West End was called Bakunin House. Aldred and his comrades were most noteworthy for their struggle to preserve the right of free speech on Glasgow Green. This important traditional right had been removed by a Corporation by-law in 1916 and put into operation in 1922. In spite of all the anarchists' efforts, including a fine performance by Aldred at a Sheriff's hearing and a High Court appeal, the law upheld the Corporation's decision. The anarchist grouping made an important contribution to the Glasgow left and, together with John Maclean's group, constituted the revolutionary critique of the reformism of both the ILP and, later, the Communist Party.

The Engineers and Syndicalism

The contribution of Glasgow's engineers to the socialism of the Red Clyde was also vital. But that input is much more complicated than is generally allowed. As we have seen from the testimony of people like Harry McShane – without a doubt *the* contemporary commentator – the engineers perceived themselves as labour aristocrats. Their trade union, the ASE, was originally far from militant; indeed, until the last decade of the nineteenth century it was more of an exclusive club and friendly society than a fighting union.[51] It signalled its social and political difference from the semi- and unskilled workers by refusing to support their numerous strikes during the 1880s and 1890s, but the events of these two decades were to change that.[52] International competition forced a series of trade crises on the engineering industries and the employers went on the offensive, their Liberal principles seeming to evaporate when their profits slumped. There was a series of bitter strikes and lock-outs as the engineers fought to preserve their jobs – and their status. This is the period when the first conflicts about 'dilution' appear. The term refers to the employers' increasing practice of introducing new technology which could be operated by a semi-skilled worker, or a boy, thus deskilling the engineers. Not surprisingly, the previously elitist engineers learned their trade union politics very fast.

That politics was dominated by revolutionary syndicalism, which is not to say that the majority of engineers were revolutionaries. Indeed, the majority of engineers were in the ILP, but their leadership contained many members of the Marxist Socialist Labour Party and Social Democratic Federation. Syndicalism was a movement containing various tendencies, not all of which were in accord. Holton provides a useful definition:

> What this group had in common was first of all the objective of emancipating the working class from capitalist society through revolutionary industrial confrontation (direct action and the General Strike) rather than political means, that is, the agency of a revolutionary party or parliamentary politics. Such objectives are further linked to the notion of workers' control over post-capitalist society through industrial rather than political organisation, namely, by the direct producers themselves rather than some kind of state.[53]

The syndicalists were, therefore, socialists of a deeper shade of pink than the ILPers, whom they frequently ridiculed as mere 'reformists'. But the two groups shared one political inspiration, the dream of a socialist future.

While that of the ILPers was somewhat arcadian and was to come about through some kind of parliamentary osmosis, the syndicalists at least had a strategy for getting there. Their numbers were relatively small, but not only were they immensely talented politically, they also had an influence out of all proportion to their numbers in the emerging shop stewards' movement.[54] As we have seen earlier, many of the Glasgow engineering works and shipyards were huge undertakings, containing numerous shops which were very difficult to organise politically. Trade union and other political meetings had to be held at lunchtime, off the premises, and were frequently addressed by John Maclean. These Glasgow engineers learned their politics in a hard school.[55]

While the engineers may have perceived themselves as the aristocrats of labour, they were still emphatically working-class, employees who had no hope of ever gaining a stake in the ownership of their works. In one crucial sense – their housing – they were practically indistinguishable from their less skilled brothers. The engineers lived in the same kind of tenement neighbourhoods as less skilled workers. Joan Smith, in her seminal comparative analysis of the Liverpool and Glasgow working classes, puts it thus:

> Skilled workers were more likely to inhabit the areas of new tenements and immigrants more likely to inhabit the decaying inner city. But the housing market in Glasgow was not one which exacerbated the status differences between skilled and unskilled workers. Although there was a vast difference between a single-end, a two-room apartment and a three-room apartment the Glasgow housing market was not one which allowed for the beginnings of owner-occupation, or for the large differences in degree that occurred in London and elsewhere between the living conditions of skilled workers and others. In times of bad trade all workers could move down the housing market, which was extremely fluid.[56]

So the social and political location of Glasgow's engineers in the Red Clyde was a much more ambiguous phenomenon than some of the more 'heroic' accounts would suggest.[57] There were several thoroughly reactionary strands in their culture, the main one of which was Freemasonry. Harry McShane paints the picture:

> Many engineering places had a strong freemason element in them, particularly among the foremen and managers. They were a closed clique with their own code of honour and their own secret meetings; they were all Tories and anti-Catholic. Freemasonry was probably stronger in Glasgow than the Orange Order. The Orange Order attracted Protestants of Northern Irish extraction, specially in the shipyards; freemasonry was more common among skilled engineers. All the freemasons were Tories because they believed in their right to be privileged workers and had great disdain for the Irish and the labourers. When I worked at Weir's I was approached to become a freemason: I am sure they hadn't realised I was an ex-Catholic.[58]

Another important point is that unions like the ASE and organisations like the Freemasons were exclusive *male* preserves and this in a city which, in the Scottish Labour Party had seen the first all-women socialist party branch in Britain. As Joan Smith says: 'The exclusion of women from "respectable" working-class society in this period was complete.'[59]

Thus at the start of the First World War, while there was the potential for political co-operation between skilled male industrial workers, unskilled workers and women in the community, the classic division between skill and lack of skill and between workplace and home prevented sustained large-scale political mobilisation. The events of the war were to change all that. Traditionally an introverted city, Glasgow's working class became more homogeneous as the introduction of dilution in the munitions industries eroded wage differentials between skilled and unskilled workers. People in the tenement communities were also bonded more closely together:

> Class sentiments and allegiances were also reinforced by the

war's impact upon working-class communities. The locally rooted character of working-class culture in Britain has often been noted, but seldom have those roots been more in evidence or more important than in 1914-1918. Not only did men join the forces with their workmates and fight and die as such, but those left behind were also forced to rely upon each other to an unusual degree.[60]

The flashpoint came with the 1915 Rent Strike, which has already been described. It is hardly possible to over-estimate the importance of this struggle. In spite of attempts by academic sociology to hijack this strike as some kind of 'urban social movement' devoid of real politics, neither the Glasgow working class nor the state had any illusions about its strategic importance.[61] It represented precisely that near fusion of industrial muscle and grass-roots community organisation which any government dreads. As we have seen, the wartime government was forced to pass emergency legislation, the 1915 Rent and Mortgage Interest Restriction Act, in an unparalleled intervention in the hitherto sacred property market. The Rent Restriction Act *did* defuse the situation in Glasgow, and allow the government to isolate and prosecute the engineers' leaders, but that does not detract from the fact that it was a famous victory for the local working class.

The dramatic events in Glasgow during the First World War, the continuing unrest amongst the munitions workers, the Clyde Workers' Committee, the anti-war movement, the shirracking of Lloyd George in the St Andrew's Hall on Christmas Day 1915 and the sedition trials are all now well known and do not need repeating here. What does need repeating is the genius and courage of John Maclean who was everywhere, agitating, organising, educating. At times he seemed like a one-man revolutionary party. Historians like Iain McLean have found it convenient to dismiss him, but Glaswegians are not easily fooled and they turned out in their tens of thousands when he was released from jail in 1917. Hamish Henderson's fine song, 'The John Maclean

March', expresses local feelings perfectly:

> Argyle Street and London Road's the route that we're marchin',
>   The lads frae the Broomielaw are here – tae a man!
> Hi, Neil, whaur's your hadarums, ye big Hielan' teuchter?
>   Get your pipes, mate, and march at the heid o' the clan.
> Hullo, Pat Malone, sure I knew ye'd be here so:
>   The red and the green, lad, we'll wear side by side.
> Gorbals is his the day, and Glasgae belongs to him,
>   Ay, great John Maclean's comin' hame tae the Clyde,
> Great John Maclean's comin' hame tae the Clyde.[62]

The drama climaxed with the events of the engineers' 40-hour strike which started on 27 January 1919. This was organised by the Clyde Workers' Committee, a gathering of shop stewards from all the main local shops and yards. The Committee was autonomous; it had nothing to do with the local official organisation of the ASE, which was opposed to strike action. The strike was effectively a general strike of the engineering shops and shipbuilding yards on the Clyde. Even Willie Gallacher, who was notably prone to claim a central role in all matters to do with the Red Clyde, described it for what it was:

> But for those of us who were leading the strike, we were strike leaders, nothing more; we had forgotten we were revolutionary leaders of the working class and while we cheered the flying of our [red] flag, it had not for us the significant meaning it had for our enemies. They saw it as the symbol of an actual rising; we saw it as an incident in the prosecution of the strike. We were all agreed on the prosecution of the strike for the 40-hour week, but we had never discussed a general line against capitalism, and never could have agreed on it, even if we discussed it.[63]

This statement supports what has already been noted, that the engineers, both in their wartime political grouping, the Clyde Workers' Committee, and their peacetime trade union, the ASE, were more concerned with their own privileges and conditions of work than with social insurrection. But their enemies viewed things more seriously. The upshot was an unprovoked and doubtless pre-planned police riot in George Square on 'Bloody Friday', 31 January 1919. The police charged a peaceful demonstration supporting the strike and pitched fighting erupted, during which Davie Kirkwood and Willie Gallacher were batoned. Fighting raged round the inner city all night. The next day saw troops in the city, tanks in George Square and machine-gun posts on the roofs overlooking the square. There are many myths about the Red Clyde, but the fighting on Bloody Friday and the troops and tanks were for real; these incidents were filmed and the footage still exists. The strikers' leaders were systematically arrested, tried and jailed or 'deported' to other cities. The 'revolution' did not break out, but the engineers won a 47-hour week, a not insubstantial gain, as it meant starting work at 8 rather than 6 o'clock.

To all intents and purposes this ended the more dramatic aspects of the Red Clyde. What had been learned? Harry McShane supplies the answer:

> We regarded the 40-hour strike not as a revolution but as a beginning. Other things would follow: it was the first rank-and-file agitation to be led by socialists after the war. The working-class movement was bigger at the end of the war than before and the socialists themselves had hardened.[64]

They had also learned a very great deal about political organisation. Events in Glasgow now tended to centre in the Corporation where the Labour group under the lead of John Wheatley kept up the pressure about unemployment and housing. The 1919 Housing and Town Planning Act had been passed and housing and rents were still red-hot issues. Wheatley and his lieutenants campaigned for the Corporation of Glasgow to utilise the provisions of the legislation to the full and accelerate the building of council housing. They were known as the 'slum smashers'. This campaign received mass support. Elsewhere a revolutionary analysis was still preached by

Guy Aldred and John Maclean, Harry McShane and the other members of the inspired 'Tramp Trust Unlimited', who until the death of Maclean on 30 November 1923, at least, never gave up on agitation and propaganda. Although syndicalism was to all intents and purposes dead, some of the authorities still viewed Glasgow as the socialist epicentre of Britain, as the following state paper of 1921 indicates:

All outbreaks of Bolshevism should be dealt with rapidly by men in authority on the spot who know all the facts and who have power to act quickly. In Glasgow, the headquarters of the Bolshies [*sic*], the police are obviously either afraid of them or they have instructions to ignore the persistent preaching in public of sedition.[65]

What broke out in Glasgow in 1922 was the General Election. Thanks to endless work at getting supporters onto the electoral register, the housing and rents issues and a superb machine run by Paddy Dollan, the ILP won ten seats in the city.[66] It was perceived by both Glaswegians and the authorities as a red avalanche. The *Glasgow Herald*'s leader on the result must surely count as the most hypocritical in its history:

We cannot view without profound dissatisfaction the significant gains made by Labour in industrial Scotland and most conspicuously in the Glasgow constituencies... The lesson writ large over the electoral returns is that Labour, notwithstanding the incongruous elements it may include and the natural tendencies it would display to split under the strains and stresses of responsible administration, is for fighting purposes a united and formidably organised body skillfully addressing itself to class prejudice and to individual cupidity – emotions, passions and desires far more potent than those which the commonplaces of the ordinary politician can arouse...It is certainly easier in this country to create a mass of socialists by depressing the standards of morality than it is to keep the majority to sound ideas of citizenship.[67]

The London *Times* similarly was not amused:

> No one can make even a cursory investigation of the
> methods of propaganda pursued by the Labour Party on the
> Clyde without discovering in them the real foundation of
> victory. Year in and year out, the Clyde area has been
> saturated with socialist teaching... Socialist study circles,
> Socialist economic classes, Socialist musical festivals,
> Socialist athletic competitions, Socialist choirs, Socialist
> dramatic societies, Socialist plays – these are only a few of
> the devious ways in which they attempt to reach the
> unconverted. Then there are the Socialist Sunday schools –
> a far more potent agency than the 'proletarian' Sunday
> schools, with which they are not to be confused. Last, but not
> least, there are the Socialist newspapers, of which *Forward*
> is the most important. From time to time free distribution of
> thousands of copies has taken place.[68]

Parliament

When the new MPs left Glasgow on 21 November 1922,
thousands of well-wishers thronged the station. They
sang both 'The Red Flag' and the 124th Psalm – 'A
Grateful Song of Deliverance' – the old Covenanting
anthem. The combination perfectly encapsulates the
Glasgow ILP. Their public manifesto is still a stirring
document:

> The Labour Members of Parliament for the City of Glasgow
> and the West of Scotland, inspired by zeal for the welfare of
> humanity and the prosperity of all peoples and strengthened
> by the trust reposed on them by their fellow-citizens, have
> resolved to dedicate themselves to the reconciliation and
> unity of the nations of the world and the development and
> happiness of the people of these islands.
>
> They record their infinite gratitude to the pioneer minds
> who have opened up the path for the freedom of the people.
>
> They send to all peoples a message of good-will, and to the
> sister nations of the British Commonwealth fraternal
> greetings.
>
> They will not forget those who suffered in the War, and will

see that the widows and orphans shall be cherished by the nation.

They will urge without ceasing the need for houses suitable to enshrine the spirit of home.

They will bear in their hearts the sorrows of the aged, the widowed mother, and the poor, that their lives shall not be without comfort.

They will endeavour to purge industry of the curse of unhealthy workshops, restore wages to the level of adequate maintenance, and eradicate the corrupting effects of monopoly and avarice.

They will press for the provision of useful employment or reasonable maintenance.

They will have regard for the weak and those stricken by disease, for those who have fallen in the struggle of life and those who are in prison.

To this end they will endeavour to adjust the finances of the nation that the burden of public debt may be relieved and the maintenance of national administration be borne by those best able to bear it.

In all things they will abjure vanity and self-aggrandizement, recognizing that they are the honoured servants of the people, and that their only righteous purpose is to promote the welfare of their fellow-citizens and the well-being of mankind.[69]

Ordinary Glaswegians believed that the millenium had arrived. Extraordinary Glaswegians like John Maclean knew that it hadn't. Nonetheless, the Glasgow group of MPs – or to be more correct, George Buchanan, David Kirkwood, Jimmy Maxton, Campbell Stephen and John Wheatley – was to provide a left-wing critique of the parliamentary Labour Party and an inspiration to socialists all over the country. They *cared* about their people, unlike Ramsay MacDonald and his ilk. Their successes were the outcome of long political struggles in Scotland stretching away back into the nineteenth

century and earlier, as we have seen. These MPs constituted the most visionary socialist group ever seen in
Westminister. Helen Crawfurd, Agnes Dollan, Mary Barbour, Andrew McBride, Harry McShane, Willie Gallacher,
John Maclean, Willie Paul, Guy Aldred, Jimmy McDougall, Paddy Dollan and all the rest of the other Red
Clydesiders were the most talented group of socialists
ever seen in this country. No British city has ever produced such inspired organic intellectuals of the working
class in such quantities. Their achievements and many of
their names may have been substantially forgotten now,
but not in Glasgow, or elsewhere in Scotland, where
folk-memories of this extraordinary group are alive and
well.

References

1. Iain McLean, *The Legend of Red Clydeside*, Edinburgh, John
Donald, 1983, spends 296 pages in getting it comprehensively wrong.
See my review of this book in *History Workshop Journal*, No. 18, 1984
and McLean's reply in the following issue.
2. Calum Brown, *The Social History of Religion in Scotland Since
1730*, Methuen, 1987, p.173. This is a key reference for anyone
wishing to understand the Byzantine nature of ecclesiastical politics
in Scotland.
3. Ibid., pp.136ff. See also Henry Hunter, *Problems of Poverty:
Selections from the Economic and Social Writings of Thomas
Chalmers, DD*, Thomas Nelson, n.d.
4. Norma Denny, 'Self-Help, Abstinence and the Voluntary Principle:
The Independent Order of Rechabites, 1835-1912', *Scottish Labour
History Journal*, No.24, 1989, p.26.
5. Ibid., p.44, footnote 56.
6. Ibid., p.30.
7. See T.C. Smout, *A History of the Scottish People, 1560-1830*,
Fontana, 1974, Ch.XVII for an important discussion of education in
Scotland. The discussion is continued for the modern period in the
same author's *A Century of the Scottish People, 1830-1950*, Fontana,
1987, Ch.IX.
8. Keith Burgess, 'The Political Economy of British Engineering
Workers During the First World War' in L. Hainson and C. Tilly
(eds.), *Strikes, Wars and Revolutions: An International Perspective*,
Cambridge University Press, 1989, p.303.
9. See Damer, 1989, op. cit., pp.67ff., for a discussion of the abuse of
these 'lines'.

10. Joan Smith, 'Labour Tradition in Glasgow and Liverpool', *History Workshop Journal*, No. 17, Spring, 1984.

11. These and subsequent biographical data on Samuel Chisholm were kindly made available to me by Irene Sweeney, research student in the Department of History, University of Strathclyde, from material collected for her PhD. I am most grateful to the author for her generosity.

12. R.K. Middlemas, *The Clydesiders: A Left Wing Struggle for Parliamentary Power*, Hutchinson, 1965, p.17.

13. Smout, 1987, op. cit., Ch.II.

14. R.E.C. Lond, *Fortnightly Review*, January 1903, quoted in ibid., p.45.

15. Bernard Aspinwall, *Portable Utopias: Glasgow and the United States, 1820-1920*, Aberdeen University Press, 1984, pp.240-1.

16. Ibid., p.155.

17. David Whitham, *Municipal Socialism*, unpublished MA dissertation, Middlesex Polytechnic, 1989, p.22. I am grateful to the author for making his dissertation available to me.

18. Quoted in *Times*, 6 October 1902.

19. Ibid.

20. *Scotsman*, 2 July 1902.

21. Biographical material about Lipton comes from the *Scots Magazine*, N.S., Vol.63, No.2, May 1955, and Sir Thomas Lipton, *Leaves from the Lipton Logs*, Hutchinson, n.d.

22. Beatrice Webb, *My Apprenticeship*, Longmans, 1926, p.410.

23. Joan Smith, 'Class, Skill and Sectarianism in Liverpool and Glasgow, 1880-1914' in R.J. Morris (ed.), *Class, Power, and Social Structure in British Nineteenth Century Towns*, Leicester University Press, 1986, p.186.

24. J. McCaffrey, 'Politics and the Catholic Community since 1878', in David McRoberts (ed.), *Modern Scottish Catholicism, 1878-1978*, Glasgow, Burns, 1979, p.146.

25. Anthony Ross, 'The Development of the Scottish Catholic Community, 1878-1978', in ibid., p.42. See also T.W. Moody,'Michael Davitt and the British Labour Movement', *Transactions of the Royal Historical Society*, Vol.3, 1953.

26. Ian Wood, 'Irish Immigrants and Scottish Radicalism, 1880-1906' in Ian MacDougall (ed.), *Essays in Scottish Labour History*, Edinburgh, John Donald, 1978, p.76.

27. McCaffrey, op. cit., p.148.

28. Gallagher, op. cit., p.29.

29. Middlemas, op. cit., p.24.

30. Wood, op. cit., pp.84ff.

31. Ibid.

32. Middlemas, op. cit., p.29.

33. Nan Milton, *John Maclean*, Pluto Press, 1973, p.15.

34. Harry McShane and Joan Smith, op. cit., p.3.

35. William Gallacher, *Revolt on the Clyde*, 4th edition, Lawrence & Wishart, 1978, p.1.

36. *Young Socialist*, Vol.IX, No.1, January 1909, p.383. I am most grateful to my collegue and friend Keith Burgess for sending me

photocopies of his collection of this magazine. 'Hopkins' is an unusual name in Glasgow and it is probable that the child being named was the daughter of ILPer Harry Hopkins, another well known Red Clyde leader. Lizzy Glasier was the sister of Bruce Glasier and was a well known activist in the Socialist Sunday School movement.

37. Ibid., Vol.IX. No.4, April 1909, p.436.
38. Hanley, op. cit., p.31.
39. Ibid., pp.100-1.
40. Middlemas, op. cit., p.31.
41. Sir Patrick Dollan, typescript autobiography, no title, n.d., Glasgow Collection, Mitchell Library, p.148.
42. Damer in Melling (ed.),op. cit.
43. Dollan, op. cit., p.171. It should be noted that as a boy, Dollan (b.1885, d.1963) worked in one of the sixteen pits in Baillieston on the eastern boundary of Glasgow. These pits employed 4,500 men who lived *in* the city, in Baillieston, Tollcross, Shettleston, Carmyle and Sandyhills.
44. *Royal Commission on the Housing of the Industrial Population of Scotland, Rural and Urban*, Cd.8371, pp.1917-8.
45. Damer in Melling (ed.), op. cit. See also Joseph Melling, *Rent Strikes: People's Struggle for Housing in West Scotland, 1890-1916*, Edinburgh, Polygon, 1983. See also the Sheffield Womens' Film Co-operative's film *Red Skirts on Clydeside*.
46. Helen Crawfurd, typescript autobiography, n.d., p.114, quoted in ibid., pp.98-9. This typescript is held in the Marx Memorial Library, London.
47. See Seán Damer, *State, Local State and Local Struggle: The Clydebank Rent Strike of the 1920s*, University of Glasgow Centre for Urban and Regional Research Discussion Paper No. 22, 1985.
48. Ralph Glasser, *Growing Up in the Gorbals*, Pan, 1986, pp.6-7.
49. Ibid., pp.90ff.
50. This and the subsequent information on Guy Aldred and the Glasgow anarchists comes from John Taylor Caldwell, *Come Dungeons Dark: The Life and Times of Guy Aldred, Glasgow Anarchist*, Barr, Ayrshire, Luath Books, 1988.
51. Smith, 1986, op. cit., p.190.
52. Keith Burgess, 'New Unionism for Old? The Amalgamated Society of Engineers in Britain' in W.J. Mommsen and H.G. Husung (eds.), *The Development of Trade Unionism in Great Britain and Germany, 1880-1914*, Allen and Unwin, 1985, p.174.
53. Robert Holton, 'Revolutionary Syndicalism and the British Labour Movement', in Mommsen and Husung (eds.), op. cit., pp.267-8.
54. Raymond Challinor, *The Origins of British Bolshevism*, Croom Helm, 1978.
55. W.F.H. Kendall, *The Revolutionary Movement in Britain, 1900-1921*, Weidenfeld and Nicholson, 1969.
56. Smith, 1986, op. cit., p.187.
57. e.g. Foster and Woolfson, op. cit. and W. Gallagher, op. cit.
58. McShane and Smith, op. cit., p.19.
59. Smith, 1986, op. cit., p.195.
60. James Cronin, 'The Crisis of State and Society in Britain, 1917-

1922' in Hainson and Tully (eds.), op. cit., p.467.

61. Manuel Castells, *The City and the Grassroots: A Cross-Cultural Theory of Urban Social Movements*, Edward Arnold, 1983.

62. The complete words of this song are in many collections of folk/political music and it has been recorded many times, notably by The Laggan in their *Scottish Folksongs* LP and also on their *UCS* LP.

63. Gallagher, op. cit., p.220.

64. McShane and Smith, op. cit., p.109.

65. PRO F/37/1/35, letter to the Prime Minister from Sir Alfred Mond enclosing an article on 'Bolshevism', n.d., c.December 1921. The note says that 'The Writer of this article is a man of wide experience and intimate knowledge of the conditions in the country, but Sir Alfred Mond does not entirely agree with him.' The writer is not named but the hysterical nature of the piece suggests one of the upper-class, freelance counter-revolutionaries common at the time.

66. The connection between the Clydebank Rent Strike and the 1922 election successes are discussed in Damer, 1985, op. cit.

67. *Glasgow Herald*, 17 November 1922, quoted in Damer, 1985, op. cit., p.20.

68. *Times*, 28 December 1922.

69. Kirkwood, op. cit., pp.192-3.

5 The Depression

The First World War had resulted in considerable social change in Glasgow, as elsewhere in Britain. As we have seen, one of these changes was a tightening of social ties, a kind of grim solidarity, in working-class neighbourhoods. This was cemented by anger at war-profiteering by house factors and others, and a genuine revulsion at the carnage whose horrific scale became increasingly visible as the war wore on. Several of these changes which were quite dramatic in Glasgow were to vanish abruptly with the Armistice. The first of these was youth employment, as a large number of eleven-year-old boys had become horse-drawn van-drivers. The history of Clydeside industry in the war years describes some of the consequences of this policy:

> The young hopefuls organised a race through the centre of the City, and as they whipped their ill-fed horses to a shambling canter, they were followed by a cascade of their freight behind them. Later in the war some boys were promoted to drive motor lorries. One of the features of Armistice Day was the behaviour of the lorries employed in bringing milk to the City. As the boy drivers got the news they ceased to deliver milk, and added to the prevailing noise by driving through the streets with all their cans rattling until their petrol was exhausted.[1]

The second was the employment of women in previously all-male trades. During the war this had led to a great deal of trade union anxiety about 'dilution'. In January 1916, according to the Ministry of Munitions, there were 18,500 women working in the metal trades in the Clyde district, some of them Gaelic-speakers recruited from the

Highlands and Islands.[2] Many of them were employed in the shipyards and their work included the following activities:

> ... attending plate-rolling and joggling machines; back-handing angle irons, flanging, fitting, upholstering, and polishing; drillers' and caulkers' assitants; platers' helpers; rivet-heaters; holders-on; crane driving; catch girls; firing plate furnace; general labouring (gathering scrap and cleaning up vessels in construction).[3]

But the Ministry of Munitions and the trade unions were in agreement that these women would be returned to the home immediately the war was ended, and that is exactly what happened, in a process which was to be repeated at the end of the Second World War.[4] Male control of the engineering trades on Clydeside was well-nigh absolute.

Because of near full employment, endless overtime, reasonable rates of pay and restricted pub opening hours there was a definite increase in the standard-of-living of most Glaswegians during the war. The statistics of the Glasgow Savings Bank make this plain:

> At the credit of the depositors there stood in the bank in 1914 £1,118,293; in 1918 the sum was £13,000,000; and in addition investments in Government Stock were made through the bank to the extent of more than £3,000,000. In this one savings institution alone ... the savings of the people amounted to over £17,000,000.[5]

When the economic crash came in 1921 it was all the more terrible for coming so suddenly after a period of relative prosperity.

The 1921 slump, which was to become the Great Depression, was in Glasgow due essentially to the Clyde's over-commitment to shipbuilding and heavy engineering. It was exacerbated by wartime over-production. There were simply too many nations building too many ships, particularly warships. During the war years 487 naval ships with a tonnage of 816,428 were built on the Clyde, with 44 vessels launched in the

Fairfield yard alone.[6] The manufacturing employers launched an offensive to cut costs. The resulting situation in Glasgow was catastrophic. By early 1922 there were some 90,000 workers officially registered as unemployed, with another 10,000 returned as under-employed.[7] And these were *male* workers only. A decade later, in 1932, the figure was 131,000, when one-third of the working population was unemployed *all* the time, and sometimes the figure was as high as 50 per cent.[8] Put at its simplest, the unemployment rate was never below 20 per cent in Glasgow from the early 1920s until the late 1930s, and was over 25 per cent from 1930 to 1935. Poverty was endemic in the city.

The Clyde Rent War

This poverty was exacerbated by the housing situation. We have already seen that there was a large number of empty houses in the years before the war, but by the end of 1915 there were hardly any, the incoming munitions workers having occupied all the previously unused housing. But the shortage of both labour and materials during the war, and the consequent lack of maintenance, meant that the existing stock deteriorated rapidly. If this were not bad enough, the 1920s saw protracted agitation on the rents issue. The rent restriction imposed by the 1915 Rent Act was meant to run for only six months after the war had ended. Immediately after the Armistice the Glasgow Property Owners' and Factors' Association demanded a large increase in rent which was promptly opposed by the city's tenants organised in the Scottish Labour Housing Association, a creation of John Wheatley and the ILP. The owners wanted a complete return to the market, but this was not an achievable or realistic objective. The Clydeside socialists were too well organised on the general housing problem, and were too well aware of the strategic importance of the rents restriction issue. A campaign against increases was immediately organised and, while vociferous in Glasgow, its most effective base was to be seven miles downriver in Clydebank.[9]

In 1920 the government passed a Rent Restriction Act, which was intended to be a compromise. It awarded the property-owners an immediate 15 per cent increase in the rent of the controlled houses, with a further 25 per cent if essential repairs were done. The tenants' movement promptly pointed out that *no* repairs had been done since 1914, and precious few before then. A 24-hour general strike was called for 23 August 1920. The response in Glasgow was impressive, as an aerial photograph of the large demonstration on Glasgow Green printed in the local newspapers testifies. At this meeting the 'Notices of Increase' in rent which the factors had delivered to the city's tenants were piled up and set alight, and resolutions against paying the increase passed. In the event, however, there was little resistance in Glasgow when the factors came round to collect the increased rent.

But the matter was far from over. ILP lawyers found an important technical flaw in the 'Notice of Increase' of rent and argued that the increase was therefore illegal. Again tenants were urged not to pay the increases and this time more responded. Glasgow saw renewed mass agitation and the property-owners responded by taking out eviction orders in the courts against tenants who refused to pay the increase. The Labour Housing Association pointed out that the cases could be continued in the Sheriff Court, which was hardly likely to grant thousands of decrees for the eviction of unemployed tenants. Indeed, the Glasgow Sheriffs appear to have been not unsympathetic towards the plight of poor tenants. But the property-owners persisted in taking out actions. The *Glasgow Herald*, a newspaper not normally noted for its sympathy for ordinary people, reported in 1921 on the human consequences of this endless litigation against poor people:

> The court-room was crowded, and the passages were thronged with people who were waiting for their cases to be called. Their appearance gave a somewhat vivid impression of the distress prevailing in the city. Most of them were

poorly clad, and not a few showed traces of the pinch of poverty. There were women wearing shawls and carrying children in their arms, and bent old men who seemed to find the climb up the stairs to the court-room a tax on their strength. Here and there could be seen disabled men on crutches, and a large proportion of the crowd were [sic] unemployed, as the subsequent proceedings in the court showed ... About 300 decrees for ejection were granted.[10]

The ILP made great political capital out of all this, aided by the almost mindless rapacity of the local property-owners and factors. The prospect of wholesale evictions was something guaranteed to raise the ire of Glasgwegians descended from Highlanders and Irish forcibly put off their land. The campaign was orchestrated by Wheatley, and centred upon contesting the legality of 'Notices of Increase' in rent and 'Notices to Quit', i.e. eviction notices, in the courts. Neither Wheatley nor his lieutenants Paddy Dollan and Davie Kirkwood wanted fighting on the streets. If there was to be resistance to evictions, it was to be done peacefully, by blocking the stair with local women when the Sheriff Officers arrived to put the tenants out. Even then, this tactic was seldom used in Glasgow, although it was to become commonplace in Clydebank. A further dimension was added by a local theatre group, the Shettleston Players, touring a play called *The Fear of the Factor*. (Shettleston in the East End of Glasgow was the district where John Wheatley lived and which he represented on the council, and was to be his parliamentary constituency.)

The ILP seized upon another technical but real flaw in the factors' 'Notice to Quit' and fought a test-case for a Clydebank tenant in the Sheriff Court. This was to become famous as Kerr v Bryde. The Sheriff found in favour of the tenant: the Notice was illegal. The property-owners were outraged and immediately appealed against the decision in the Court of Session (the Scottish High Court for civil affairs). They could hardly believe their ears when the Law Lords upheld the

Sheriff's decision. They appealed again, to the ultimate court, the House of Lords. This time they were completely shattered; on 3 November 1922 the Lords again upheld the decision of the lower court!

The Scottish Labour Housing Association immediately issued a statement that tenants could now claim back from their landlords a sum equivalent to twelve months' rent and rates. Simultaneously the ILP cashed in on the situation by saying that in the forthcoming General Election a vote for the Liberals or the Tories was a vote for the landlords. We have already seen the result. Ten ILP members were elected for Glasgow city alone, while Davie Kirkwood ran away with Dumbarton Burghs, which contained Clydebank. Without a doubt it was the rents issue which catapulted these men into Parliament. It is equally certain that it was this issue which politicised so many working-class women in the city, and produced socialist and Communist leaders of the calibre of Agnes Dollan, Mary Barbour and Helen Crawfurd. This was to be the Red Clydesiders' greatest triumph. Ironically, it was also the beginning of the end of the Red Clyde, although the housing issue was to run and run.

Unemployment

The mass unemployment which started shortly after the end of the First World War resulted in widespread but leaderless discontent. As Harry McShane commented: 'In the winter of 1920-21 it had become obvious that the official trade union movement was going to do nothing about unemployment.'[11]

Two militant tactics emerged from the working-class movement on Clydeside to fill the gap. The first was action on the parish council, the body responsible for setting the rate of Poor Relief – the dole – which was all that was available when unemployment benefit ran out. The second was action through the National Unemployed Workers' Movement (NUWM).

Until the First World War parish councillors were

automatically middle-class people and the scales of Poor Relief they set were minimal; they did not want to burden the rates which they paid. Harry McShane had been instrumental in forming a Glasgow Unemployed Committee, with local committees all over the city.[12] These committees put up candidates for election to the parish councils. Those who were successful tried to get the dole increased. (This campaign was particularly successful in the industrial villages in the Vale of Leven, outside Glasgow, where the political complexion of the council was such that the area was known as 'Little Moscow'.[13]) Committee members also fought individual cases and, when results were not forthcoming, McShane and his comrades organised imaginative demonstrations, including marching columns of the unemployed into the City Chambers. The unemployed committees also fought evictions. In 1922 McShane was again at the centre of resistance to the eviction of a family in South York Street in the Gorbals, which resulted in mass meetings in the street, the intervention of a local Bailie and the local MP – and the subsequent trial of McShane for sedition. After seven weeks in jail he was tried, and the verdict was 'Not Proven'. McShane came out of jail and promptly joined the Communist Party, which was by then beginning to make its presence felt in Glasgow.

The NUWM was exceptionally well organised in Glasgow, particularly from 1930 onwards. It had numerous local branches, eight flute bands, and held many huge rallies and demonstrations in the city in those years.[14] Some, like the Glasgow Green meetings of October 1931, turned into police riots when the marchers were attacked without provocation. The Communist Party was centrally involved in the NUWM and the organisation of these demonstrations, and there was a Russian representative of the Communist International, George Borodin, in Glasgow assessing events. According to McShane's memoirs, there was hesitation in the party leadership as to whether or not the unemployed demonstrators should be 'armed' with walking sticks.

With McShane in jail again, it was decided not to equip marchers in this way, with the result that many of these defenceless men were batoned severely by the police.[15] Glasgow also sent large contingents on the 1922, 1930, 1932 and 1934 Hunger Marches to London. It would be safe to say that Glasgow was the most militant city in Britain on the unemployment issue, but the demonstrations were not organised by the ILP who viewed with horror the frequent clashes with the police. Indeed, the Labour and Communist Parties were at daggers drawn in Glasgow throughout this period.

One outcome of unemployment in Glasgow was unexpected. As the Depression ground on with no sign of relief, thousands of workers began to turn to the outdoors for cheap recreation. As we have seen, there had been a socialist counter-culture of cycling and rambling clubs in the city since the turn of the century, but this was a quantitatively new phenomenon. The unemployed discovered hill-walking, cycle-touring and climbing – and the beauty of their own country. The famous climbing club, the Craig Dhu, was formed by unemployed workers. Bob Grieve describes meeting them:

> I was serving an apprenticeship and when it expired which was early '32, the Depression was coming to its peak and I was dismissed because the office I was in was only keeping married men – quite rightly so but very tough on me. And therefore I was on the dole for a period. About nine months. And I spent quite a lot of time moving about on hills and I met some curious and interesting people, living on very little. Chaps from the shipyards, engineering shops of Glasgow, not many but I knew them. I got to know them all and it was during that period that the first democratic or proletarian climbing clubs were formed, like the Craig Dhu, the Lomonds and so on ... [16]

Tom Weir has also written of his experiences as a young man during this period, and his books subsequently inspired many young Scots people to head for the hills.[17] This invasion of the hills was not at all to the taste of the landowners and the lairds, and there were frequent clashes between gamekeepers and unemployed walkers and climbers, especially as the latter were quite prone to take the odd grouse, rabbit or trout for the pot! These confrontations with gamekeepers were sufficiently widespread that they found their way into fiction; Compton Mackenzie's novel *The Monarch of the Glen* gives a humorous account of such encounters.[18]

But the dominant memory of the Depression among Glaswegians is one of a never-ending, slow-motion horror show, where the battle for survival took many casualties. Everyday life had a bleakness which the elderly now recall with a shudder. The leitmotif of this period for many Glaswegians is the career of Benny Lynch the boxer. A Gorbals boy, he became British, European and World Flyweight champion in a spectacular series of fights in the 1930s. The punters say that he was the best fighter his country has ever produced. But Benny had a drink problem, hit the skids and wound up drinking cheap fortified wine and all sorts of poison. He drank himself to death in 1946 at the age of 33, but is remembered throughout Glasgow with nothing but affection on the 'there but for the grace of God' principle.[19]

For outsiders, the 1920s and 30s were the period when Glasgow became synonymous with squalor and violence. Hugh MacDiarmid, who cordially loathed Glasgow, summed it up thus:

> I'd rather cease from singing,
> Than make by singing wrong
> An ultimate Cowcaddens,
> Or Gorbals of a song.[20]

The ultimate insult, you might say. But then MacDiarmid never understood Glasgow; he simply didn't have the wit for that.

The Gangs and the Hardmen

There have been gangs in Glasgow for at least a hundred years. One early gang was the Penny Mob in Townhead around 1880, which was a sectarian group with some 300 members, each paying a penny per week against fines. The early twentieth century saw the Hi-Hi in the north of the city, the Ping-Pong in the east, and the San Toy, the Tim Malloy and the Village Boys in the south. The 1920s and 30s saw the appearance of the Redskins, the Norman Conks (a Catholic gang) and the Billy Boys (a Protestant gang), the Dempsey (Catholic), the Breezy (Protestant), the Bee Hive – and the deadly Tripe Supper Boys in Govan.[21] The Baltic Fleet from Baltic Street led to one of Glasgow's best ever graffiti: 'The Baltic Fleet Sails, OK'. It is important to get these gangs in perspective, which *No Mean City* signally fails to do.

The Glasgow gangs were creations of poverty and unemployment; in this sense, there have always been gangs in large British cities, not just in Glasgow. The intentional inter-gang violence was real, even if sensationalised by both the press and books like *No Mean City*. These gangs seldom contained more that a couple of dozen core members, although there were many more aspirants and hangers-on. Cut-throat razors were used, although it is certain that more young men carried them than used them. Glasgow's Chief Constable from 1931, Percy Sillitoe, who served his apprenticeship in the British South African Police in Rhodesia, states in his memoirs that beer bottles were more commonly used as weapons than razors.[22] It is hardly surprising that, given the sectarian tensions in the city, the miseries of the Depression should see them expressed violently.

But the biggest and most successful gang in Glasgow was always the city's police force. Organised professional crime on any scale was impossible in the city under such an efficient and tough force. So one aspect of local crime was sporadic and highly ritualised gang fights. There was no monetary gain in this gang warfare, only status for the 'leaders-aff'. The police prevented a great many fights, and broke up many more. The very lack of large-scale crime gave them the time to do this. Sillitoe, who had come to Glasgow from Sheffield where he had made his reputation busting the local razor gangs, boasts quite openly in his memoirs that from time to time the police used the tactic of the pre-emptive strike. For example, he organised an attack by mounted and foot police on the Billy Boys' flute band when 'Only one of their number ... escaped injury.'[23] A more common tactic was to let the gangs knock lumps out of each other and then wade in when they were exhausted. In fact Sillitoe formed a gang-busting squad out of the toughest cops on the force, and they acted as a sort of dirty dozen. Further, in an arrangement which might have been merely tacit, the surgeons in the Glasgow Royal Infirmary were none too gentle in stitching the wounds of gang members. An elderly Blackhill man who was a gang member in these years told me:

> They took us to the Royal and they stitched our heads and they didn't give a damn how they stitched it and it was sore. I was more sick with that than what I was with the prison.[24]

The gangs were obviously made up of 'hardmen', a phrase which is redolent with meaning in Glasgow, but again, it is a notion which is widely misunderstood. There was in fact a continuum of hardmen in the city. To begin with, every street had its own hardmen who were well known. These were ordinary workers who would unhesitatingly go out the back-court, take their jackets off and have a 'square-go' with whoever had offended them. (A 'square-go' means a man-to-man unarmed fight.) This was – and still is – a normal practice in Glasgow. But such men were not professional hardmen; they did not earn their living by these fights which were neither organised nor the dominant factor in their lives. It was but one aspect, albeit an important one, of their masculinity, and all too often their fights were inspired by drink.

Then there were the hardmen who dished out violence on a semi-professional basis, frequently with weapons. They were the 'stick-men' or enforcers or collectors or leg-breakers who worked for themselves or other

employers of greater or lesser criminality. Glasgow's illegal street-bookies were the biggest employer of this
category. At the present time in Glasgow they are heavily
involved in the money-lending racket. They were and are
loathed and feared by ordinary people. The ordinary kind
of street hardman would see one of these types off nine
times out of ten in a square-go, but what is significant is
that they were, and are, organised. If a man got one of them
in a square-go, he would have to watch his back – or his
wife's or children's backs. This type of hardman is universally seen for what he really is – a despicable parasite.

The next type of hardman was the professional
criminal, one who made his living from crime. This was –
and again still is – a highly competitive and merciless
business, and one had to be tough to survive to protect
one's business. But these men, in their own way, had a
code of behaviour, if not exactly of honour. The Glasgow
gangsters in William McIlvanney's novels are of this ilk.
They are qualitatively different from the second
category, and one difference is that they have greater
cunning. Even then, in Glasgow, there were very few
villains with enough intelligence to be involved in what is
now called organised crime.

A passage from Ralph Glasser's autobiography about
the Gorbals makes clear the distinction between these
three types of hardmen. Glasser's friend Meyer, a
promising young boxer, had flattened two hoods of the
second variety: they were loan sharks who had been
beating up an elderly man in their debt. The boys knew
that reprisal was certain:

> Two evenings later I again went to collect Meyer at the
> workshop. As we walked along Bedford Street towards the
> Baths a large black car drove past us and stopped at the
> kerb a few yards ahead. Private cars were a rare sight in the
> Gorbals then, especially large and expensive-looking ones.
> We looked at it with interest. There were five men in it, two
> in front and three in the back; the one in the front passenger
> seat was expensively dressed – it must have been the first
> time I saw cuff-links worn – and that might have been
> enough to give him an air of authority. In his eyes there was

an expectation of obedience, but above all a cold, implacable will. He beckoned to us. As we came up to the car the other four, in a well-drilled movement, got out and surrounded us – large, silent, menacing. At a signal from the leader, two of them pinioned my arms and lifted me like a sack and set me down a few feet away. Then the four of them closed in on Meyer and pushed him close to the open passenger window so that he stood before the leader like a prisoner awaiting sentence.[25]

Meyer, no matter how hard he was at street level, was powerless against this kind of thug. The leader suggested that Meyer's fingers might get caught in a door or under a sledgehammer if he interfered in his business again. He also made Meyer an offer the boy could not refuse: a job working for him. Meyer got himself out of the predicament by joining the army.

A final category of hardman is known in Glasgow as 'mental', or a 'bampot', a psychopath who inflicts pain and injury on people for the pleasure it brings him. These men are deranged and unpredictable, but often very cunning; nobody trusts them and everybody avoids them. Not infrequently they kill each other. They do not subscribe to the code which the 'businessmen' share, and tend to be used on one-off contracts. In reality, these different categories of hardmen are not mutually exclusive, they tend to shade into each other. And there are others who refuse easy categorisation. For example, it is not unheard of in some neighbourhoods for a man insulted in a pub to go home and come back with a mash hammer and split his rival's skull open. The Glasgow gangs of the interwar years included all categories except the 'businessmen' type. The problem for the city's image in this period was that it became nationally if not internationally crystallised as full of murderously violent gangs locked in permanent warfare. It was all very useful as a moral panic for deflecting attention from the roots of the problem. While the real violence in Glasgow was without a doubt the violence of poverty, the romanticisation of the hardmen also ignored their innocent victims, the passers-by, the elderly, who were injured as a gang fight swept past or when two hoodlums went for each other in a pub.

At this juncture, we should note something about the national image of Glasgow which had been established during these Depression years. It was a relentlessly *male* one. All the notions of hardmen, razor gangs, square-gos, heavy bevvy, sectarianism, football, shipbuilding and socialist politics were essentially masculine. Women were absent from the image although they were far from absent from, say, the day-to-day reality of local socialist politics. During the grim years of the Depression it was the women who bore the cost of supporting their families in both tenement and council houses. The true nature of that cost is revealed only in plays like Ena Lamont Stewart's aptly-named *Men Should Weep*, originally produced by Unity Theatre and recently revived by the 7: 84 Theatre Company Scotland, or Aileen Ritchie's *Can Ye Sew Cushions?*, an explicit attack on the sexism of *No Mean City*.

Catholics and Communists

1918 saw the Representation of the People Act which enfranchised the male population over 21, and the female over 30. This had particular significance in Glasgow, for it meant the inclusion of the bulk of the Glasgow Irish for the first time. Prior to this they had been excluded under the property-owning qualification; very few Glasgow Irish owned their homes prior to 1914.

The Easter Rising of 1916, the executions of the leaders including Edinburgh-born James Connolly (well known in Glasgow) and the ensuing War of Independence provoked a strong reaction amongst locals of Irish descent. After 1916 streams of volunteers, cash, small arms and dynamite (stolen from mines and quarries) crossed the Irish Sea. Local units of the IRA, including many ex-servicemen, were raised. The Treaty of 1922 which established the Irish Free State split the

Glasgow Irish, and the community was in turmoil, but the bloody sectarian conflict of Belfast did not erupt in Glasgow. Instead the Irish political machine, now known locally as the Murphia, took its people into the Labour Party. This machine was oiled by Wheatley's hand-reared boy, Paddy Dollan, by now an ILP councillor and local politician of consummate skill – although many students of the period sense that it was his wife Agnes, also an ILP councillor, who was the more powerful. The ten seats won by the ILP in Glasgow at the end of 1922 depended in no small way upon the Irish vote.

Another piece of 1918 legislation also accelerated the move of the Irish behind Labour: the Education (Scotland) Act by which the state accepted financial responsibility for Catholic education. Both primary and secondary Catholic schools moved into the public sector, and Catholic parents no longer had to pay out of their own pockets for the education of their children. ILP leaders in Glasgow had long supported such legislation, but the most important reason for the move to the left was that, even before the war, prominent ILPers like John Wheatley had shown that what they were campaigning for was social reform, not social revolution. Charles Diamond, the proprietor of the local Catholic newspaper, and an important opinion-leader, put it like this:

> In our view at least, the Labour Party is not a party of revolution, of Bolshevism, or social destruction. And thousands of Roman Catholics in every part of the country have recorded their votes for Labour candidates because they believe that the party stands for *fairness all round*. That is the workers' demand and that is the plain and invariable demand of the Roman Catholic Church.[26]

In short, the Glasgow Irish were voting for a party which was going to deliver the kind of goods they wanted: council houses and safe jobs, preferably with the Council.

The irony is that the very move of the Catholic voters behind the ILP in Glasgow – and the ILP *was* Labour in Glasgow until the Second World War – sounded the death-knell of the Red Clyde. While the leaders of the Glasgow Irish contained many radical socialists of outstanding calibre, and while Irishmen and women were to be found in every progressive campaign, the majority of the community was solidly locked into reactionary parish-pump politics. Their politics were the politics of the Catholic Church, and the latter did its level best to ensure that matters remained that way. These politics were predominantly introverted and sectarian in the interwar years, and in no way socialist in the sense of the term understood by the Red Clydesiders. Harry McShane, as always, points his finger unerringly at the heart of the matter. Here he describes the effects of the post-war opening up of the Labour Party to individual membership, as opposed to trade union and socialist affiliation:

> The system of individual membership affected the Labour group on the town council almost immediately. Catholics were elected who never pretended to be socialists, like old John Storie. He was an utterly honest man but tied up with the Catholic Church. Every morning on his way to the corporation he stopped at the building site of the new Lourdes chapel and school to check that the men were doing the work properly. As fewer ILPers and more men like this were elected, it became possible for Pat Dollan and others to do as they liked.[27]

Councillor Storie actually ran his constituency in Govan in the 1930s from the Irish Club in Neptune Street, known locally as the 'Irish Channel'.[28]

Theology aside, there was good reason for the Catholics of Glasgow to be introverted in the interwar years. As the Depression began to bite, anti-Irish sectarianism became more bitter. In these days of ecumenism, it is salutory to remember that the General Assembly of the Church of Scotland commissioned a report on the 'Irish Problem' in 1923. It was entitled *The Menace of the Irish Race to Our Scottish Nationality*. It says, *inter alia:*

They cannot be assimilated and absorbed into the Scottish race. They remain a people by themselves, segregated by reason of their race, their customs, their traditions, and, above all, by their loyalty to their Church, and gradually and inevitably dividing Scotland, racially, socially, and ecclesiastically.[29]

This kind of racist nonsense is all the more incredible in that the report notes on the very next page that Scottish industrialists had been actively *recruiting* labour in Ireland for more than half a century. It must also have sounded odd to the thousands upon thousands of Irishmen and men of Irish descent who had fought with the British forces during the First World War when, as Tom Gallagher notes, six Victoria Crosses were awarded to the Glasgow Irish.[30] In any event, there can be little doubt that a consequence of this orchestrated sectarianism was that a siege mentality developed among the local Catholics. They were hardly good candidates for red-hot socialism.

There was another issue amongst the Glasgow Irish which militated against such conversion – the protracted and bitter struggle between the local Catholic Church and the fledgling Communist Party. The latter was very well organised on Clydeside and contained members of the calibre of Harry McShane, Arthur MacManus, Helen Crawfurd and Willie Gallagher, all of whom visited the Soviet Union during the 1920s or 30s. One of the reasons for the bitter enmity was that not a few of the Clydeside Communists were ex-Catholics like McShane. A great deal of energy was spent in constructing Catholic 'fronts' to combat those of the Communist Party. Indeed, both organisations, sharing hegemonic ambitions, systematically trained their cadres to dismantle the arguments of the other, and to this day Glasgow is coming down with people who can prove or disprove the existence of God in elaborate detail! Maynooth and Moscow had much in common, and both were expert at producing blinkered dogmatists. The Spanish Civil War produced particularly bitter antagonisms, as Catholics and Communists accused each other of systematic atrocities. The Catholic Church's endorsement of fascist dictators like Franco merely because they were Catholics hardly endeared it to local socialists.

In the late 1920s and early 30s the Communist Party in Glasgow helped in digging the grave of the Red Clyde by slavishly adhering to the Moscow line that the Labour Party was 'social fascist' – in other words that it stood between true socialists and the revolution. The ILP therefore had to fight on two fronts: against the 'Moderates' (Tories) for control of the council, and against the Communists; as a result the Glasgow ILP's machine and *its* party line became more important than socialism. So although its ten MPs had gone to Westminster in 1922, it was not until 1933 that Labour finally captured the city's council. In a bitter irony, the local Communists' adherence to the dictates of Moscow resulted in relentless sectarian attacks on the ILP, blunted its radical Labourism and forced it to adopt a stance not a million miles from Stalinism. If that was not apparent in 1939, it certainly became clear after the Second World War.

The Communist Party's effect on Clydeside left-wing politics in the interwar years has been greatly exaggerated, particularly in its bible, the memoirs of Willie Gallagher. Its organisational strength lay in two spheres, the trade union movement and the struggles of the unemployed. The former area was not of great importance until the late 1930s because of the defeat of the General Strike of 1926 and the widespread victimisation of left-wing militants which followed. This isolation from the world of work was made worse because, during the Depression, only a tiny minority of industrial workers were in regular employment. But in 1937 the apprentices' strike on the Clyde was to involve 13,000 young engineers who elected a committee of 160 led by a member of the Young Communist League. This well organised strike forced the employers to make concessions after the boys had been out for a month.[31]

The party's involvement in and leadership of the unemployed struggles was, however, both real and heroic. It played no small part in enabling the unemployed and their families to survive those grim years.

Catholics and Communists apart, it was perhaps inevitable that the radicalism of the Red Clyde would be eroded as Labour won power at both the local authority and parliamentary levels. The organisation of the ILP had to be centralised to maintain a professional fighting machine, and this was the antithesis of its very essence in Glasgow. As the ILP itself fell apart and the Labour Party took over, the bureaucracy, with an inevitably centralising tendency, became greater, the paid full-time officials more numerous. The democracy, the communality, the grass-roots organisation of the ILP, its almost-literal broad church, its spontaneous affiliation with numerous cultural organisations all became atrophied. Organic association gave way to electoral machines geared to the needs of individual politicians.

There was a resurgence of strong socialist feeling in Glasgow with the rise of the Nazis and the outbreak of the Spanish Civil War. There were large numbers of Scots in the 2nd (British/Irish) Battalion of the XVth Brigade, including many Glaswegians, both Communists and ILPers. Many of these volunteers had been active in the NUWM.[32] The contingent of local Communists produced such notable leaders as Jock Cunningham, Peter Kerrigan and George Aitken. There is a memorial banner in the People's Palace Museum to those Glaswegians who fell in Spain; it contains 64 names, many of them plainly of Highland and Irish origin, and Glasgow also has its statue of 'Pasionaria', Dolores Ibarruri, on the Clydeside Walkway.

Just as important for ordinary Glaswegians was the Aid Spain campaign, which involved both fund-raising and political solidarity. This mobilised far more people than those who actually went to Spain to fight – and, most importantly, it was an area in which women could be politically active. There were twelve separate local committees in Glasgow, strongly based upon the NUWM, and they were able to hold rallies big enough to fill both the City Hall and the St Andrew's Hall on several occasions.[33] The Glasgow Workers' Theatre Group produced *On Guard for Spain* in many venues in 1937 and 1938.[34] The ILP raised money in support of the POUM, in whose militia George Orwell served, while Glasgow anarchists Jane Patrick and Ethel MacDonald were working in Barcelona with the CNT, the anarchist trade union. The Glasgow Jewish community and university staff and students were also prominent in their suppport for Republican Spain.[35] The Scottish Trades Union Congress sent a ship loaded with food, clothing and blankets and this was organised by the Glasgow Trades Council.[36] In 1938 some 150,000 people took part in a May Day rally for Spain.[37] In short, many Glaswegians recognised only too well the reality of the threat of fascism.

But Catholic fears of Communism ran so deep that Catholic Labour Party councillors obstructed attempts by tramway workers to make collections in their workplace for Republican Spain and voted in favour of allowing a meeting of the pro-Franco Friends of Nationalist Spain in the City Halls. They were expelled from both the Labour group on the council and the Labour Party itself.[38] It should also be remembered that the only group of genuine volunteers from anywhere in Europe who went to fight on Franco's side were General O'Duffy's Blueshirts from Catholic Ireland who did precious little fighting except amongst themselves, and ironically were shot up by fellow fascists![39] The Blueshirts' role in defending Catholic Spain against the red hordes was praised from Glasgow's pulpits as much as it was in Ireland.

The Corporation, Council Housing and Corruption

If unemployment and poverty were important political issues in interwar Glasgow, housing absolutely dominated municipal politics. They were, of course, closely related issues. In 1918 a conservative estimate was that the city needed 57,000 new houses immediately. The Corporation's Question Books show that hardly a meeting of the council passed without many questions on housing being tabled. A series of Housing Acts in 1919, 1923, 1924, 1930 and 1935, and a parallel series of Rent Restriction Acts had committed the state to permanent intervention in the property market. There is no doubt that the initiation of this legislation had come about principally as a result of the agitation of the Red Clydesiders. Local councils were now required to build housing schemes ('estates' in England) for the 'general needs' of working-class tenants. In Glasgow the resulting schemes were to refract the class structure of the city more clearly than anywhere else in Scotland. The three categories of interwar housing scheme tended to reflect in bricks and mortar the perceived divisions within the working class of the Victorian years.

Before discussing these schemes, it is important to understand clearly the contemporary nature of the housing problem and who needed rehousing in the city. Firstly, it should not be forgotten that all slums were tenements but not all tenements were slums. There were, as we have seen, well proportioned and structurally sound tenements for both the upper and lower middle class, and also respectable working-class tenements containing small houses. Finally, there were structurally unsound and thoroughly insanitary tenements jam-packed with small houses. The latter, incapable of improvement or repair, were the true slums and were so designated by the Medical Officer of Health. But 'slums' were also to be found, for example, in the first category where an old Georgian or early Victorian town house had been 'made-down' into numerous single apartments. Secondly, in the years after the First World War, all these categories of tenements, with the exception of the first, were bulging at the seams. There were therefore many lesser professional and white-collar tenants who were overcrowded, as well as a much larger number of perfectly respectable manual workers of varying degrees of skill. This latter category always contained the largest number of tenants needing rehousing in the interwar years. It is impossible to state accurately the proportion of tenants living in the slums, but it was smaller than those living in the stucturally adequate but small and therefore overcrowded tenement houses. An estimate of the proportion of tenement dwellers living in slums in this period would be between 10 and 15 per cent. Thirdly, the rents issue in all controlled properties was of great political importance in this period. The owners demanded the immediate relaxing of controls; the tenants, through the ILP, demanded the continuation of rent control and fair rents tribunals. The point is that whatever the supply of council housing in the two interwar decades, there would still have been an insatiable demand.

The housing schemes built under the 1919 Housing Act were supposed to be for the 'general needs' of the working class, and in Glasgow this category was called 'Ordinary', a misnomer if ever there was one. These were élite schemes like Mosspark, Knightwood and Riddrie, four-in-block cottage-type houses laid out as garden suburbs at the low density of nine houses per acre. Each house had three, four or five bedrooms, a living-room, bathroom and scullery, the latter equipped with a gas cooker, gas boiler, washing tub and larder. To this day they are leafy and well-ordered schemes with manicured gardens guarded by the ubiquitous gnomes.

The tenants in these prestige schemes were very rarely working-class families. The Mosspark scheme was built in 1924 and was without a doubt the élite scheme in interwar Glasgow, and continued to hold that position for many years after the Second World War. In terms of occupational structure, 16.2 per cent of the first tenants to move in to the new scheme were 'professionals', 30.7 per cent were 'intermediate' and 27.5 per cent were 'skilled non-manual'. Only 18 per cent were 'skilled manual' while a miniscule 0.3 per cent were 'unskilled'.[40]

This came about for two main reasons. Firstly, although these houses were subject to a generous subsidy, post-war rents were kept high by the local Scottish Office's insistence on 'economic rents': £28 a year for a three-bedroom house (the smallest) in Mosspark. An original tenant commented:

> This place was full of professionals – teachers, government officers, and Corporation workers. Everybody knew that you had to be earning £5 per week to get a house.[41]

Secondly, the contemporary housing allocation policy, although formally based upon a points system favouring the families of ex-servicemen long resident in the city, was actually operated informally on a 'common-sense' basis of what constituted 'desirable' tenants. The result was suspiciously similar to that which would have occurred had Corporation officials had a free hand in allocating houses: respectable, professional or white-collar workers, nearly all of them Protestant, acquired these desirable tenancies. Catholics were conspicuous by their absence from Mosspark. An elderly tenant, a former Tory councillor, put it to me quite bluntly:

> Well, there was a religious bias – it didn't exist only in Mosspark despite its proximity to Ibrox Park, but I think that's dying out in Mosspark – there's not the same religious bias in Mosspark because there's not the same religious-minded people in Mosspark as there used to be ... there was bias against Roman Catholics.[42]

One of the few tenants of manual working-class origins explained how her family had obtained a house in Mosspark:

> Dad came out of the war with an artificial leg, and they had four children and then they had Jean after. And that was like five girls and my father and mother in a room-and-kitchen. And there was no possibility of getting a house.
> My mother was a fighter, and my mother went up to the Housing Department *every* day, *every single* day. And finally they got so disgusted with her that they gave her a house,

but she didnae take just *any* house. She took the house that *she* wanted. She said, 'My husband lost a leg fighting for this war and we have five children and we want a decent house in a decent place to live. That was what he went and fought for.'[43]

Freemasonry seems to have been actively involved in the social life of Mosspark, if not also in the allocation of houses there. The *Glasgow Herald* describes the ceremony at the laying of the foundation stone of the new Presbyterian church in 1925:

> The Masons marched in procession from the temporary church in Arran Drive to the site of the new building at Balloch Gardens, and there the full ritual of applying the tools of the craft, laying the stone, and placing the casket containing memorial documents and coins in the cavity, and the symbolic use of the cornucopia and the pouring of wine and oil on the stone was performed.[44]

The *Herald* notes that the Earl of Stair, as Immediate Past Grand Master of Scotland, presided, while six kirk ministers were involved in the Masonic rites before a large crowd of spectators. The paper also noted that it poured with rain! These Masonic rituals emphasised the religious as well as class characteristics of this kind of housing scheme, underlining that this was no place for the unskilled manual worker who was, almost by definition in contemporary Glasgow, Irish and Catholic.

Needless to say, the Labour councillors cottoned on to the fixing very quickly, and began pressing the 'Moderates' or 'Progressives' (Tories) on the issue. Rosslyn Mitchell tables the following question to the Convenor of the Special Committee on Housing and General Town Improvement as early as 1922:

> Will the Convenor state how many of the houses erected by the Housing Department since 1918 are occupied by ex-soldiers, and how many by persons who are not ex-soldiers?[45]

Another councillor asked in 1924:

> Is it the case that a house in Corkerhill Road, Mosspark, has been let to a member of the Medical Profession, who (a) is the proprietor and occupier of a house of a rental of £75, at Ladybank Drive, Craigton, and (b) who was the proprietor up till Whitsuntide of this year, of another house, at a rental of £75, at Dargavel Avenue, Dumbreck?[46]

In spite of their councillors' effort, it is plain that the ordinary people of Glasgow in the overcrowded slum tenements were being actively excluded from Arcadia.

A second category of schemes was built, principally under the provision of the 1924 Housing Act designed by John Wheatley as Minister of Health in the Labour government. These were known as 'Intermediate' schemes, because the houses in them were to be let at 'intermediate' rents. They were less generous both in their internal dimensions and external layout than the houses in the 'Ordinary' schemes; the majority were tenemental in design and so had front- and back-courts rather than individual gardens. But they did have separate kitchens and bathrooms, although the internal electricity provision consisted of only one 5-amp plug. It is plain from a reading of the Corporation minutes and the contemporary press that the ILP did not want tenement-type houses built in these new housing schemes; they were seen as representing everything that was bad about the 'good old days'. There was a heated argument in 1930, for example, about the West Drumoyne scheme, the prototype of the Intermediate category. The ILP, led by Councillor Mary Barbour, argued that there should be a mix of house styles in the scheme to include both cottage and flatted (four-in-a-block) houses, but the Tories controlled the council and, pressed by cost constraints, tenement housing was constructed.[47]

The Intermediate schemes housed the workers excluded from the first category – skilled and semi-skilled manual workers from Glasgow's shipyards and engineering firms, and similar Corporation manual workers. In West Drumoyne, to the south of Govan, built in 1933 and containing 836 houses, 88 per cent of the original tenants came from the neighbouring shipbuilding and engineering areas of Govan, Plantation, Kinning Park, Partick and Whiteinch. 43 per cent were skilled or semi-skilled manual workers in shipbuilding, engineering or the metal trades, while transport, food and labouring each accounted for a further 10 per cent.[48] While West Drumoyne did not have the élite status of Mosspark, it was still an eminently respectable and well-ordered housing scheme, as pioneer tenants recall:

> Oh yes, it was a lovely scheme – it was for toffs, all church-going and refined.[49]

And:

> When I came it was beautiful with lovely back courts just like lawns and trees and thick hedges and the front gardens kept lovely.[50]

And:

> It was a lovely scheme – do you know that the kids couldnae even take a leaf off a tree, the neighbours above would be shouting at their neck.[51]

As late as the 1970s, a century after the term was first coined, a senior Housing Department official described the Intermediate schemes to me as being intended for the 'respectable poor'. The corollary of this statement is that they were *not* intended for the 'disreputable poor' – the slum-dwellers, in short. Most of the tenants in the Intermediate schemes came from tenements which were in reasonably good structural condition but overcrowded due to the small size of the houses in them. These schemes were until relatively recently popular in Glasgow although they never manifested the élite characteristics of a Mosspark. Before the Second World

War allocation policies – not to mention rent levels – ensured that in Intermediate schemes the slum dwellers were conspicious by their absence.

The slum problem remained. Exposé after exposé – not to mention *No Mean City* – had described the horrifying conditions in which the poor were compelled to live. Glasgow's slums became emblematic of the ills of the nation, were toured by all sorts of intrepid slumologists and inspired a local series of 'social realist' novels which almost desperately tried to evoke the bleakness of life in them.[52] King Edward VIII even made a visit to the slums of Anderston, and was photographed doing so.[53] The Corporation of Glasgow used the 1930 and 1935 Housing Acts to erect a series of 'Slum Clearance' or 'Rehousing' schemes, the third category. These schemes were typically quite small, not more than 1,000 houses, and more usually half that size. The houses in them were similar to those in Intermediate schemes in terms of design, dimensions and external layout. They too had a small but separate kitchen and bathroom, water was heated in a tank behind the sitting-room and the official electricity provision in houses of all sizes was again one 5-amp plug. The kitchen contained one cold-water tap, a sink and a bunker, nothing else. Like the Intermediate schemes, the houses in the Slum Clearance schemes had front- and back-courts, but those in the latter tended to be smaller.

At this juncture, it has to be emphasised that Glasgow Corporation was highly innovative in the technical, the constructional, aspects of council-house building in the interwar years. As Nicholas Morgan has shown, these experiments began as early as 1918.[54] The use of concrete blocks in place of brick was of particular importance. The earlier rehousing schemes were constructed of these undressed concrete blocks. By the late 1930s the Corporation had developed its own unique process for pre-casting 'foam-slag' concrete blocks and these were used widely in later rehousing schemes where the external walls were pebble-dashed. These innovations were due in no small way to the energy and enthusiasm of the Corporation's first Director of Housing, Peter Fyfe, an engineer by trade. Creative innovations in council housing remained at the technical level, however, and design innovations were minimal.[55] Further, when the Housing Department was formed in 1919, it was immediately faced with the massive problems described earlier. Housing management and allocation were the responsibility of a separate department, the City Improvements Department, a lineal descendent of the Victorian City Improvement Trust. This department's management policies were adopted wholesale from the only model available which was, of course, in the private sector: the Glasgow Property Owners' and Factors' Association. We have already seen that they were a singularly tough bunch of operators. Thus the City Improvement Department's professional ideology never evinced the creativity and innovation of its sister Housing Department, which displayed a typically Glaswegian willingness to confront any problem, no matter what size.[56] (The two departments were eventually to merge into the Housing Management Department in 1967.)

To return to the rehousing schemes: one immediately apparent aspect is that many of them are tucked away out of sight on small, environmentally disadvantaged sites where the land was cheap; the subsidies available for these schemes were slight. Moorepark, for example, had a railway running down the back of it and a noisy wire press at another corner. Blackhill was bounded by a canal and the Corporation Provan gas works, with a railway siding running into it and a distillery and chemical works in the immediate vicinity. In addition to their other disadvantages these schemes therefore were subject to atrocious pollution in the appropriate weather conditions. Another aspect of these schemes is the meanness of their design and layout, and the drab aspect they present to the surrounding world. These are relentlessly cheerless barracks for the poor. This is intimately tied up with the ugly monochrome of the concrete blocks mentioned above, whether or not they were faced with pebble-dash. I recently took on a tour of these schemes a Polish film-maker brought up on a Warsaw housing scheme and familiar with the Stalinist monstrosities of Nowa Huta. She reacted with horror to what she saw; they were, she said, the worst housing schemes she had ever seen. It is plain that if the slum-dwellers of Glasgow were going to be rehoused by their council it was going to be in accommodation which complied with the absolute minimum standards of the appropriate legislation. It is interesting that housing built under this legislation in England is not so systematically ugly as it is in Scotland. It is hard to escape the conclusion that a Calvinistic mean-mindedness about the poor underlay the niggardly design of these schemes.

The pioneer tenants of these schemes reacted with delight to their new houses despite all their aesthetic deficiencies. An original tenant of the Blackhill scheme who had come from a slum in the Garngad said:

> It had two rooms, a toilet, a thing we didn't have down the road – a bathroom! The toilet in the Garngad was in the close.[57]

The near-rural setting of Blackhill was also much appreciated:

> ... the Blackhill that I remember was beautifully set – I only realise that by looking back – the canal banks were gorgeous, they had locks at the canal, they had the white houses that belonged to the railway, dotted as if they had been beautifully placed ... with wee plots.[58]

The sense of community was striking:

> I found that people were really very sociable, very neighbourly, very seldom you got a cross neighbour so that you could chap the neighbour's door and walk in.[59]

> Well it was a very close family atmosphere, everybody

knew everybody else, there was none of this snobbery, nobody would pass you by on the stair.[60]

No contemporary seems to have noticed that the seeds of the physical decline of this category of scheme were sown among the very first tenants. Many of the families which came out of the slums were very large. In one such scheme, Moorepark in Govan, with 516 houses, 60.1 per cent of the original population of 2,478 were children under the age of fifteen. One close of six houses contained 81 such children.[61]

The antagonism toward slum-dwellers and the Irish ensured that the tenants of this kind of scheme were stigmatised before they even set foot inside their new houses. They were subjected to an intense form of policing – by resident factors and 'Green Ladies' ('nurse inspectresses') from the Housing Department, health visitors, public health inspectors and, of course, the police proper. The whole process of rehousing from the slums was seen as 'of great sociological importance'.[62] If this were not bad enough, sometimes factors of an entirely local nature conspired to amplify the stigma of these schemes. Thus Moorepark in Govan rapidly became known as the 'Wine Alley', one end of Possilpark became known as the 'Jungle', while Blackhill gained city-wide notoriety due to a terrible accident at New Year 1949 when eleven tenants died of drinking methyl alcohol stolen from the nearby chemical works.[63]

Thus by 1939 the 'Ordinary' schemes contained predominantly white-collar workers and 'labour aristocrats', and not a few professionals; the 'Intermediate' schemes contained predominantly blue-collar workers, skilled and semi-skilled manual workers, the 'respectable poor'; while the 'Slum Clearance' schemes contained the unskilled workers, the 'disreputable poor'. In reality it was much more complicated than that. For example, the slum clearance schemes contained many skilled workers since, as we have seen, many of them were constrained to live in the slums for want of

anything better. But this three-tier system was certainly
the public perception of the Glasgow schemes, and was
even more certainly the way they were managed; the
Corporation Housing Department was a prisoner of its
own offensive ideology. To this day the distinctions
between them are obvious to the professional who with
one glance can normally tell under which Act a scheme
was built. Mosspark is still a leafy paradise to which
many tenants in lower status schemes aspire, while
Blackhill is a barren gulag where only the most
demoralised of tenants would accept a house.

All this council house development during the interwar
years was a political hot potato. Before gaining office in
l933 Labour put insistent pressure on the Moderates to
build more council housing, preferably with direct
labour. The national 'Crusade Against the Slums' had
struck a powerful chord in Glasgow. When Labour finally
gained control of the council it accelerated the building of
houses under the 1930 and 1935 Acts to house the slum-
dwellers. Under both the Tories and Labour there were
always whiffs of scandal about graft and corruption to do
with council-house building and allocation. In his memoirs
Chief Constable Sillitoe wrote:

> Graft and dishonesty haunted Glasgow Corporation like a
> spectre that nobody would swear to having actually seen but
> everybody felt sure existed. The newspapers conjectured
> about it, and the ranks of the police were full of rumours.[64]

In 1932 there were so many complaints about rigging
in the allocation of council houses that the council had to
set up a special sub-committee to investigate them.[65] In
1933 two employees of the City Improvements Department, which dealt with the allocation of houses, were
charged under the Prevention of Corruption Acts in the
High Court, found guilty and imprisoned.[66] Sillitoe then
secured the conviction of a city Bailie (magistrate),
obliging the Secretary of State for Scotland to institute
an official enquiry into the whole affair in 1933.[67] Its
report was singularly mealy-mouthed and discussed at

length the difficulty of finding conclusive proof of the numerous allegations that both councillors and officials took bribes from would-be council-house tenants.

It would have been surprising had there not been corruption within the Corporation in the awarding of contracts to build council housing schemes, and in the allocation of the houses themselves. In the first instance, huge sums of money were involved and, secondly, there were still thousands of desperate slum-dwellers more than willing to grease a palm for a prized tenancy in one of the new schemes. Getting one of these new houses was a major event in the lives of ordinary people in those years. A third consideration as far as corruption is concerned was that, as the Second World War approached, the Corporation of Glasgow was itself a vast bureaucracy employing 44,069 people, by far the biggest local authority in Britain.[68] It was the ambition of many to get a job with the council for it meant security of employment – and a pension among other perks. It is readily understandable that many clerks and other officials used their 'pull' to get their relatives preferential treatment on the housing list. It is even more understandable that an honest worker living in a slum, without such 'pull' in the Housing Department, should believe that the whole thing was a conspiracy. The rumours intensified after Labour gained control of the council for it became evident that, in terms of both jobs and houses, the Murphia was doing a good job for its people.

By the time of the Second World War stories about corruption were commonplace. Naomi Mitchison, visiting Glasgow in 1941, wrote:

> When I asked about corruption, everyone laughed; it seems to be too well known. No good socialist I know in Glasgow has much use for the 'Labour' councillors.[69]

The stories were to persist to the present day.

Once it dominated the council, Labour showed a philistine disregard for any considerations of good design and layout in its council housing schemes. The housing problem became a numbers game in which the only thing that mattered was how many slum houses had been demolished or new houses built in each successive year Labour had been in power. This obsession was to persist into the post-war decades. The poor standard of much of the housing was explicitly recognised in a 1935 Scottish Department of Health Report, the Highton Report, which noted that in comparison with council housing in Holland, Germany, France, Czechoslovakia and Austria, Scotland's was unimaginative to a degree. The report was perfectly plain:

> The deficiencies which exist in our Scottish schemes are on the aesthetic and social side of our housing activities rather than on the purely material side. These deficiencies will be supplied more by constructive thought and by a more sensitive attitude towards the educative and cultural implications of housing than by the mere expenditure of money.[70]

While this was undoubtedly true, it also has to be said that the Highton Report should not be taken at face value. It is possible that it was also intended to justify the subsidies for building *tenement* council houses under the 1935 Housing Act, which was aimed specifically at 'de-crowding' congested old housing. In this sense, the report was taking a side-swipe at the Labour Party. As a matter of fact, the European tenement-form council housing developments were of a lower constructional standard than those in Scotland and were subject to infinitely more draconian forms of management and supervision.

As far as the Murphiosi running Glasgow were concerned, their technical skills were always light-years ahead of their 'constructive thought' and 'sensitive attitudes' on the 'aesthetic and social side' of council housing. Such design innovations as did occur were too little and too late. The moral inspiration of the ILP and John Wheatley's dream of '£8 Cottages for Glasgow Citizens' had been translated into a slick machine particularly adapted to getting the vote in and getting its people jobs in the Corporation – 'in out of the rain', as one uncorrupt retired official put it to me. But it had its successes in the numbers game. Between 1920 and 1939 no less than 50,277 council houses were built in Glasgow, proportionately more than in any other British city: Glasgow had achieved its 1919 target.[71] The irony was that this figure was nowhere near high enough. The Corporation Housing Department, operating the new criteria for overcrowding laid down by the 1935 Housing Act, found that a colossal building programme was necessary if the whole of Glasgow's working population was to be satisfactorily housed. The numbers of additional houses required were as follows:

To replace unfit houses	15,000
To abate overcrowding	50,000
For general needs, i.e. houseless families, persons about to be married, etc.	35,000
Total:	100,000[72]

The arrival of the Second World War ruled out the implementation, let alone achievement, of such a programme.

The Empire Exhibition

The event which made a neatly symbolic end to the Depression for Glasgow was the Empire Exhibition in 1938. This was not the first large-scale exhibition held in the city; there had been successful events in 1888, 1901 and 1911. The 1938 exhibition was a huge extravaganza in Bellahouston Park. Initially the ruling ILP group on Glasgow council objected to the imperialist connotations of the event and wanted to stress international solidarity, but this opposition was over-ruled by the Scottish Office, and the event went ahead. The official guide to the exhibition laid out its objects:

1. To illustrate the progress of the British Empire at home and overseas.
2. To show the resources and potentialities of the United Kingdom and the Empire overseas to the new generations.
3. To stimulate Scottish work and production and to direct attention to Scotland's historical and scenic attractions.
4. To foster Empire trade and a closer friendship among the peoples of the British Commonwealth of Nations.
5. To emphasise to the world the peaceful aspirations of the peoples of the British Empire.[73]

Not surprisingly, Glaswegians' attention was not drawn to the fact that at the very moment the exhibition was on, a battalion of the locally recruited Highland Light Infantry was involved in an attempt to subdue the restless natives of the North-West Frontier.[74]

No effort was spared to make the exhibition a success. The official catalogue contains eight pages of the names of General Committee members, a veritable Who's Who of Scotland. The total budget was £10 million.[75] The architect with overall responsibility was Thomas Smith Tait who had a talented supporting team including Glasgow architect Jack Coia. The two biggest buildings were the Palaces of Industry and Engineering, connected by Dominions and Colonial Avenues. There were national pavilions from the UK, Scotland, Canada, Australia, New Zealand, South Africa, Burma, Southern Rhodesia, East Africa, West African Colonies and 'Composite Colonies'. The Scottish Pavilion included a reconstructed Highland village complete with Chief's Castle, a burn flowing into a painted backdrop and clanspeople spinning, weaving and singing in Gaelic. There was also a physical fitness pavilion, fountains, cascades lit up below in different colours, an amusement park provided by Billy Butlin, bandstands, a cinema, a Women's Pavilion, cafés, restaurants and milk-bars, model council housing, four churches and the 300 feet high 'Tower of Empire'. Glaswegians promptly called it 'Tait's Tower'. Tait oversaw the design of everything down to the last detail – colour schemes and the design of the dustbins – and the most up-to-date construction techniques were utilised. At its peak, 3,000 men were employed in the construction of the exhibition.

The exhibition was opened on 3 May 1938 by King George VI and Queen Elizabeth. When it closed on 29 October the total attendance was 12,593,232.[76] Whatever its imperialist pretentions, it was massively popular with Glaswegians who flocked in again and again, paying their 1 shilling entrance fee (children sixpence) to hear entertainers like Paul Robeson and Joe Loss's Band. It was plainly a diversion from the grim reality of the Depression and the grimmer reality of the impending war. That the war *was* impending was signified by the stress on vigorous youth throughout the exhibition. The celebration of empire was unashamed; the official guide contained the following remarks under its entry for New Zealand:

Maori and *pakeha* (the native name for the white man) are today equal partners in New Zealand, enjoying the same rights of citizenship and opportunity, hearing the same benefits of education and social services, united in devotion to the Empire and loyalty to the British throne. There is no distinction whatever between the races.[77]

The official guide also unwittingly struck a thoroughly Glaswegian note in its advertisement for VP Red Point Rich Ruby wine at 2 shillings a bottle – a favoured vino collapso of the period!

There can be no doubting the symbolic value of the Empire Exhibition for Glaswegians – it was not sited in the no mean city for nothing. At the end of the exhibition, Paddy Dollan went on record as saying:

I feel that the Exhibition has taught all of us a finer and more colourful way of living and that it is possible in Glasgow to educate and enjoy ourselves without drabness and greyness.[78]

Of the exhibition's last day Alastair Borthwick said:

> A quarter of a million people stood in the downpour to say
> goodbye to it, and they would not have done that if they had
> not had an affection for it. It had put colour in their lives,
> and they were grateful.[79]

The truly pathetic tone adopted by Captain Graham,
the General Manager of the exhibition, in his confidential
final report indicates the depth to which the city was felt
to have fallen:

> The mere building of the Exhibition had drawn attention to
> the skill of the men of Clydeside and its very incidence has, if
> nothing else, reminded the world of Glasgow's existence.[80]

References

1. W.R. Scott and J, Cunnison, *The Industries of the Clyde Valley
During the War*, Oxford, Clarendon Press, 1924, p.178.
2. Ibid., pp.3,98.
3. Ibid., p.86.
4. Government films at the end of the Second World War stressed that
as their men were on their way home, women workers should now
return to their homes and devote their energies to their families.
5. Scott and Cunnison, op. cit., p.173.
6. Ibid., pp.77-8.
7. Ibid., p.183.
8. W. Glen, *The Glasgow Council for Community Service in
Unemployment: A Brief History*, typescript, 1951, p.1. This book is
held in the Glasgow Collection of the Mitchell Library.
9. The important but little-known story of the 1920s Clydebank Rent
Strike is told in Seán Damer, *Rent Strike! The Clydebank Rent Strike of
the 1920s*, Clydebank District Library, 1982 and *State, Local State.
and Local Struggle: The Clydebank Rent Strike of the 1920s*,
University of Glasgow Centre for Urban and Regional Research
Discussion Paper No.22, 1985. The following discussion of the rents
campaign is derived from these sources. 'The Clyde Rent War!' was
the title of a 1925 ILP pamphlet by Paddy Dollan on the rents
campaign.
10. *Glasgow Herald*, 2 July 1921, quoted in Damer (1985), op. cit.,
pp.14-5.
11. McShane and Smith, op. cit., p.128.
12. Ibid., Chaps. 11, 14 and 15 for details.
13. Stuart Macintyre, *Little Moscows*, Croom Helm, 1980.
14. McShane and Smith, op. cit., p.185.
15. Ibid., pp.174 ff.

16. Quoted in 'Mountain Men' in Billy Kay, *Odyssey*, Edinburgh, Polygon Press, 1980, p.82.

17. Tom Weir, *Highland Days*, G. Wright Publications, 1984.

18. Compton Mackenzie, *The Monarch of the Glen*, 1983, Penguin.

19. John Burrowes, *Benny: The Life and Times of a Fighting Legend*, Fontana, 1982.

20. From Hugh MacDiarmid, 'In Glasgow' in Hamish Whyte (ed.), *Noise and Smoky Breath: An Illustrated Anthology of Glasgow Poems 1900–1983*, Glasgow, Third Eye Centre and Glasgow District Libraries Publications Board, 1983, p.33. I enthusiastically recommend this lovely book to anyone wishing further insights into how this city can inspire artistic tributes.

21. Douglas Grant, op. cit., pp.51ff.

22. Percy Sillitoe, *Cloak Without Dagger*, Cassell, 1955, p.125.

23. Ibid., p.131.

24. Taped interview with Mr M. of Blackhill.

25. Glasser, op. cit., p.66.

26. Quoted in T. Gallagher, op. cit., p.105.

27. McShane and Smith, op. cit., p.110.

28. Damer (1989), op. cit., p.105.

29. *The Menace of the Irish Race to Our Scottish Nationality: The Report to the General Assembly of the Church of Scotland on the Irish Question in Scotland*, Edinburgh, 1923. Some historians have claimed that this was not a General Assembly report, but one produced by the Scottish Protestant Association, a fundamentalist body, and that therefore it is not representative of Kirk opinion. I have given the title here exactly as it is printed on the copy held in the Mitchell Library. There were many such anti-Irish pamphlets – and even more scurrilous cartoons – printed during this period. For an example, see the one printed with my review article of Gallagher in *Cencrastus*, No.32, New Year, 1989.

30. T. Gallagher, op. cit., p.86.

31. Noreen Branson, *History of the Communist Party of Great Britain 1927–1941*, Lawrence and Wishart, 1985, p.180. See also Sandy Hobbs, 'Clyde Apprentices' Strikes' in Farquhar McLay (ed.), op. cit., pp.38–41.

32. Jim Fyrth, *The Signal was Spain: The Aid Spain Movement in Britain*, Lawrence and Wishart, 1986, p.209.

33. Ibid., pp.203, 210–1.

34. Ibid., p.128.

35. Ibid., p.210.

36. Ibid., p.260.

37. Ibid., p.286.

38. Ibid., pp.282–3.

39. c.f. Hugh Thomas, *The Spanish Civil War*, Penguin, 1965, pp.490-1.

40. All of the following data on interwar housing schemes are derived from my current research project 'A Social History of Glasgow Council Housing, 1919-1961', ESRC Project No. R000231241. The particular data presented here are from the Interim Report on this research: Seán Damer and Ann McGuckin, *'The Good and the Bad': A Tale of Two Schemes*, University of Glasgow Centre for Housing Research, 1989. All initials and names are pseudonyms.

41. Ibid., p.22.
42. Ibid., p.25. A word for non-Scottish readers: Ibrox Park is the home of Rangers Football Club, notorious for never playing a Catholic until 1989.
43. Ibid., p.22.
44. Quoted in ibid., p.25.
45. Corporation of Glasgow, *Question Book No. 3*, 5 January 1922.
46. Councillor Newman to the Convenor of the Housing Committee, Corporation of Glasgow, *Question Book No. 4*, 30 July 1924.
47. Corporation of Glasgow, *Minutes*, Print No. 12, p.166, 5 April 1929, Print No.13, pp.1178–9, 18 April 1929, and Print No.20, p.2104, 6 August 1929.
48. See footnote 30: unpublished data.
49. Ibid., taped interview with Mr N.
50. Ibid., taped interview with Mrs McL.
51. Ibid., taped interview with Mrs D.
52. See Section VII in Burgess (1986), op. cit.
53. c.f. Sir Alexander MacGregor, *Public Health in Glasgow*, Edinburgh and London, Livingstone, 1967.
54. Nicholas Morgan, ' "£8 Cottages for Glasgow Citizens": Innovations in Municipal House-Building in Glasgow in the Inter-War Years' in Richard Rodger (ed.), *Scottish Housing in the Twentieth Century*, Leicester University Press, 1989, pp.125–54. I have benefited greatly from numerous discussions with Nick about Glasgow's early council housing.
55. Nick Morgan and I are in amicable dispute about the extent of these design innovations. He thinks that they were fairly extensive in the late 1930s. I am unrepentant, and maintain that they remained at the cosmetic level. Happily, the reader can still judge for him or herself by visiting the different kinds of rehousing scheme!
56. See the discussion in Damer (1989), op. cit., and Nicholas Morgan, *People or Property? The Objectives of Housing Management Policies in the United Kingdom, 1880–1939*, paper presented to the Social Science Historical Association Annual Conference, Chicago, 1989.
57. Damer and McGuckin, op. cit., p.52.
58. Ibid., p.49.
59. Ibid., taped interview with Mr D of Blackhill.
60. Ibid., taped interview with Mrs O'M.
61. See Damer (1989), op. cit., Chapter 4 for details.
62. Ibid., p.82.
63. Damer and McGuckin, op. cit., pp.93ff.
64. Sillitoe, op. cit., p.114.
65. See Corporation of Glasgow, *Minutes*, Print No. 27, 5 October 1932, p.2796, para. 1.
66. Ibid., Print No. 22, p.2290, para. 6, 5 July 1933 and Print No. 25, p.2558, para. 3, 20 September 1933. See also the contemporary newspapers.
67. *Glasgow Tribunal of Enquiry (Allegations of Bribery and Corruption): Report*, Cmd. 4361, 1933.
68. George Montagu Harris, *Municipal Self-Government in Britain*, King & Son, 1939, p.86.

69. Dorothy Sheridan (ed.), *Among You Taking Notes: The Wartime Diaries of Naomi Mitchison 1939–1945*, Oxford University Press, 1986, p.214.

70. Department of Health for Scotland, *Working Class Housing on the Continent: Report* (the 'Highton Report'), Edinburgh, HMSO, 1935, p.25. Again, I have benefited from discussing this Report with Nick Morgan.

71. Computed from table on p.66 of Corporation of Glasgow Housing Department, *Review of Operations 1919–1947*, Glasgow,1947.

72. Ibid., p.32.

73. *Empire Exhibition : Scotland – 1938 : Official Guide*, 1938, p.66.

74. See the photograph in J. Hume and M. Moss, *Glasgow at War, Vol.1*, Nelson, Lancashire, Hendon Publishing Co., 1977.

75. Perilla Kinchin and Juliet Kinchin, *Glasgow Great Exhibitions: 1888, 1901, 1911, 1938, 1988*, White Cockade, n.d., p.130. The following details of the exhibition also come from this source.

76. Ibid., p.15.

77. *Official Guide*, op. cit., p.137.

78. Bob Crampsey, *The Empire Exhibition of 1938: The Last Durbar*, Mainstream, 1988, p.153. Crampsey's sub-title is most apt.

79. Alastair Borthwick, *The Empire Exhibition: Fifty Years On: A Personal Reminiscence*, BBC and Mainstream, 1988, p.31.

80. *Empire Exhibition 1938: Capt. S. Graham's Report to the Administrative Committee*, 11 January 1939, p.164. This Report is marked 'Private and Confidential' and is held in the Glasgow Collection of the Mitchell Library.

81. *Empire Exhibition: Scotland – 1938: Souvenir Handbook*, 1938, p.15.

6 War and Aftermath

The start of the Second World War saw renewed prosperity for Glasgow and the Clyde. The engineering shops and shipyards once more swung into full production, and the River Clyde became a vital port for Atlantic, Mediterranean, and later Russian convoys. The shipping was protected from U-boats by a steel boom floated across the river from the Cloch lighthouse to Dunoon. In 1940 Hitler personally ordered U-33 into the Clyde but it was picked up by HMS *Gleaner*'s Asdic, depth-charged and forced to the surface to scuttle itself.[1] The boom defences were never penetrated. During the war the Clyde and the Mersey between them handled 80 per cent of all shipping coming to Britain. From September 1940 to August 1945 the Clyde Emergency Port discharged and loaded 1,185 ships and 108 million tons of cargo.[2] A staggering 2.1 million service personnel were embarked and 2.4 million disembarked on the Clyde, many of them travelling on the liners *Queen Mary* and *Queen Elizabeth*.[3] The 37 yards lining the Clyde built 1,903 merchant and naval ships including two battleships, four aircraft carriers and ten cruisers. 637 vessels were converted for war use and no less than 25,000 repaired.[4] The North British Locomotive Company in Springburn turned out tanks as well as steam engines.[5] The huge Rolls-Royce plant was constructed from scratch at Hillington, and employed 27,600 workers by the end of the war.[6] The Clyde was also the base for the raids on the Lofoten Islands and Spitzbergen, the attack on the *Tirpitz*, the North African landings and the construction of the Mulberry Harbours for use after

D-Day. It was also the place where the survivors of torpedoed ships were brought ashore, and unfortunately they became an all too familiar sight during the war.[7]

In the city air-raid precautions were taken. Sandbagged baffle walls were constructed at the tenements' close-mouth, the entrance to the common-stair, and these developed a disconcerting habit of ambushing drunks! Shelters were built in back-courts and gardens. As elsewhere, children were evacuated to safe rural areas on the declaration of war, but three-quarters of them had returned home by the first winter of the war.[8] The city was flooded with troops, many of them foreign. In his affectionate memoir of the period, Bob Crampsey recalls the French and the Poles, especially the national anthem of the latter in translation:

> We particularly liked the 'March, March, Dombrowski' bit and felt very fierce and martial as we sang it. We noticed also that the Poles were better uniformed and smarter than our own troops and wondered why this should be so. Our chief interest at the moment remained the Alpine Shassoors [Chasseurs] and we went down to look at them – talking to them was out of the question – every night. One of our number claimed to be able to talk to them and earned great kudos from the casual way he delivered the phrase 'Ally zongferr, restiley skwee' which he maintained meant 'Go to Hell and Stay There'.[9]

So much for the Auld Alliance! Crampsey also notes the growing awareness of and support for the heroic endeavours of the Red Army in Glasgow as the war wore on:

> There was a real pro-Russian feeling...and the names of their generals, Budyenny, Voroshilov, Zhukov and Timoshenko were as well known as those of film stars or international footballers. My father insisted that the great Timoshenko was really an Irishman in exile but we did not believe him as we would have done three years earlier.[10]

Glaswegians put up with air raids with the same phlegmatic and humorous spirit found elsewhere in the country. Mrs Georgie Farish recalls her job as a young girl on the South Side:

> I also had a very important job during the War. I was the Entertainments Officer for our local Air Raid shelter, which ten families occupied. One of our neighbours had a small harmonium which he would bring with him, and it was my job to make up a list of songs, which was pinned on the door. Solo artists were also included if I could persuade them. We would all sit there, singing away and sipping from flasks which Mothers had prepared ... The reason we would be singing, apart from entertaining ourselves and passing the hours away till the All Clear sounded, was mainly to drown out the noise outside. Sometimes, I was allowed to look out the door and up at the sky to watch the Spitfires desperately trying to shoot down the German planes, the enemy who were trying to kill us with their bomb loads.[11]

A member of the Govan Reminiscence Group, Mr Grant McGregor, also has reason to remember one air raid:

> We got into the shelter, there was my mother and father and us two. And Clydebank was getting a right roasting at the time ... Quite near us, maybe within about a quarter of a mile, there was a gun site, and it was doing its damnedest too to knock off as many planes as it could ... But after a while my mother would say, 'I wonder how that dumpling's getting on.' And someone had to make a breenge when there was a wee lull, up, down the garden and in the door, see if the dumpling was all right and if it needed hot water ... This went on all night till at six o'clock in the morning the all-clear went. And the first thing that we did was to make a dive into the kitchenette to see if the dumpling was all right! But it was a very good dumpling, I can tell you that, maybe because it was boiled so long, or perhaps because nobody was hurt, everybody was alright.[12]

Glasgow was badly bombed on a number of occasions, but was fortunate not to have to face the sustained bombing which London had to endure. On 18 September 1940 a bomb dropped on George Square, sure evidence of the fact that Goering was trying to get the ILP councillors![13] The cruiser HMS *Sussex* took a direct hit while lying in the Yorkhill basin in the city on 18 September 1940, and was sunk at her moorings; she was not to sail again for two years.[14] But the big raids came on the nights of 13–14 and 14–15 March 1941, the same nights that Clydebank was blitzed. 647 people were killed in Glasgow, 1,680 were injured and 6,835 tenements were damaged all over the city. Three tenement blocks at Maryhill were destroyed and Yarrow's shipyard at Scotstoun and the surrounding tenements were also badly damaged.[15] A similar number of people in Clydebank were killed but that town was devastated. Glasgow was bombed again in April and May, with the last raid coming in May 1943, one which destroyed Alexander 'Greek' Thomson's church at Queen's Park.[16]

Apart from men and women in the armed forces, many young women were drafted into the Womens' Land Army with predictably hilarious results as they encountered farm animals for the first time. Here, in a taped life-history, a Govan woman describes her first attempt at milking cows:

> … an us comin from Glasgow, Govan especially, ah didn't know anything about a farm... So, we had tae learn tae milk the cows, the cow got its tail and it swished right round in ma face, and ah got the milk stool and hit the cow back with it, and ah got suspended for a month. Ah had tae work for a month without pay … Oh ah wanted tae run away but we were too far away and ah knew it was conscription, so ah couldn't run away and ah nearly broke my heart, ah was so far away from everybody.[17]

In spite of the gloom and grime of wartime Glasgow, the city could still offer a culinary surprise or two; Naomi Mitchison again:

> In Glasgow, Rogano's was full up so we dined at the Grosvenor, quite well, any amount of cream, probably made from pig's fat treated, but who cares? Odd to have a proper

dinner in Glasgow, after so many high teas there with my prolet and semi-prolet friends; one gets out of the habit. I begin to know Glasgow, to have emotional content about one place or another, as I had once for London. A nice, nice city, so friendly – so warm in its personal relations, so damned ugly.[18]

Chief Constable Sillitoe managed to pull another of his surprises. He uncovered another network of graft and corruption amongst councillors in 1941, and a total of six were jailed – including the Convenor of the Police Committee! Sillitoe's self-righteousness is striking as he describes these incidents in his memoirs, but the scandal was real enough:

> A a result of these disclosures, Glasgow came perilously close to being disgraced. The Secretary of State for Scotland, the Right Honourable Tom Johnston, warned me that if I got any more of that sort of thing and other people were convicted he would have to consider very seriously putting in a Commissioner to act in place of the Corporation.[19]

Industrial Restructuring

The war years had led to the temporary expansion of Glasgow's and the Clyde's heavy manufacturing base, and also to another radicalisation of labour force although neither to the same extent nor in the same direction as during the First World War. A new shop stewards' movement had emerged from the still-warm ashes of the old, largely under Communist leadership. There were renewed apprentices' strikes in 1940, the re-emergence of a Clyde Workers' Committee and a vigorous strike of women engineering workers in the Rolls Royce factory at Hillington.[20] In the immediate post-war years the situation for the traditional industries looked quite promising. There were still 26 yards working on the Clyde in 1946, and the following year, at 6 per cent, Scottish unemployment was low, and it was to sink to near 3 per cent in the next three or four years. Between 1945 and 1947 the Clyde yards still produced 25 per cent of the world's shipping and employed 47,000 workers.[21] However, optimism was misplaced as the high post-war production on the Clyde was only possible because most other European capacity had been knocked out, but would soon be back again.

Throughout the 1950s the manufacturing sector was to decline rapidly. Many commentators have attempted to explain this phenomenon, and they have all come up with much the same answer. The owners of Glasgow's heavy engineering and shipbuilding plant were, as we have seen, tantamount to a cartel which dominated West Central Scotland and which refused to innovate either in terms of capital investment or management structures. Their profits were invested not in their own businesses, but abroad. They did not follow up on the technological innovations which had mushroomed during the war, nor were they interested in research and development. The opportunities offered by light engineering, the major post-war boom sector, were ignored. They insisted upon retaining a patriarchal management grip on workers' lives. The result was a series of highly specialised, hierarchical businesses which were totally inflexible. It was inevitable that, sooner or later, they would go to the wall; the Second World War had merely postponed their execution.

Britain's post-war indebtedness to the USA ensured that the executioners were ruthless. North American financiers and industrialists flooded into Clydeside as they did elsewhere in Europe. As Foster and Woolfson put it:

> The American business men in charge of implementing post-war reconstruction policy drove extremely hard bargains with their British counterparts. In 1945 they demanded the end of all empire tariff protection and the immediate convertibility of sterling. In return they made cash available at a high rate of interest, to ease Britain's post-war crisis. When, within two years, these terms had precipitated a still greater crisis, a massive balance of payments deficit and a run on sterling, their next instalment of aid (the Marshall Plan) was tied to a package of controls

that enabled them to intervene almost at will in crucial areas of the economy.[22]

The requirement that recipients of aid under the Marshall Plan buy the surplus of liberty ships built in American yards during the war effectively meant the beginning of the end of large-scale Clydeside shipbuilding.[23] Clyde-built ships fell to a mere 4.5 per cent of world launchings in 1958.[24] Between 1954 and 1964 Glasgow lost 59,000 manufacturing jobs, an equivalent of 19 per cent of total manufacturing jobs.[25] But it was not just the accelerating loss of traditional manufacturing jobs which was the problem. What also needed to be taken into account was that the demographic, physical, political and cultural structures of Glasgow were intimately tied up with this heavy engineering, as we have seen in previous chapters. So, as the city's heavy industry went to the wall, its very fabric became obsolescent. Gerry Mooney has summed up admirably the situation facing both central and local government in Glasgow:

> If the Clydeside economy was to recover and prosper then the physical redevelopment of much of Glasgow, and of other major towns in the region, was an integral part of that process. In this respect, the proposals for the containment and redevelopment of Glasgow go hand in hand with proposals for industrial decentralisation and diversification.[26]

In other words, large-scale restructuring of both the housing and labour markets, as well as the physical and social environment, was necessary. How was this gargantuan task to be achieved?

The Clyde Valley Regional Plan

The housing and population characteristics of post-war Glasgow still beggared description. According to the 1951 census the city still contained 1,090,000 people, of whom 750,000 were living in some 1,800 acres at an average density of 400 persons to the acre. Some neighbourhoods still contained 700 persons per acre. No less than 50.8 per cent of the city's houses were of one or two rooms and 24.6 per cent of the population lived at a density of more than two persons per room; 44.2 per cent of houses were overcrowded. A staggering 29.2 per cent of houses lacked an inside toilet while 43 per cent had no bath.[27] The comparable figures for London were 5.5 and 1.7 per cent respectively. Glasgow was quite simply in a class of its own as far as bad and overcrowded housing in Britain was concerned. The destruction, damage and lack of maintenance during almost seven years of war had exacerbated the problem, but equally serious was the fact that the pre-war Scottish criteria for overcrowding, being less stringent than those in England, had camouflaged the reality in the tenements. Once they were made compatible the true scale of the problem began to be realised. Yet again, council housing dominated municipal politics.

The Scottish Office had established the Clyde Valley Regional Planning Advisory Committee in 1943 to look into the whole question of economic and physical restructuring of the Clydeside conurbation in the post-war years. Thus began what was to become the most celebrated and acrimonious of the many post-war arguments between the Scottish Office and the Corporation of Glasgow, in which the former was cast in the liberal, the latter in the reactionary, role.

The fundamental issue was whether or not the population of Glasgow could be rehoused within the existing city boundaries in a mix of high density modern housing. Glasgow's Master of Works and City Engineer, the patriotically named Robert Bruce, maintained that it could. Besides the city centre development, the Bruce Plan envisaged suburban redevelopment along the then fashionable 'neighbourhood unit' lines – nineteen community areas each containing five neighbourhood units with an average population of 10,000, grouped around the community school. Bruce maintained the same

massive contempt for architects' highfalutin design ideas
shown by his interwar predecessor, Thomas Somers.[28]
The Labour-controlled Corporation backed the Bruce
Plan for two reasons: to maintain the city's rates income,
and secondly to preserve its own electoral base. In short,
at a time when the 'embourgeoisement' of the working
class was being noised abroad, it wanted to consolidate
its power. The Bruce Plan said that 200,000 new houses
were required, many to be built at high density in
tenement-style blocks on the city's periphery. The
Murphiosi were prepared to build them, and to hell with
planning, whatever that was.

The Scottish Office-sponsored Clyde Valley Regional
Plan was designed by Patrick Abercrombie, assisted by
Robert Matthew. This plan, which in fact reflected
central government national strategy for restructuring
an obsolete economy and obsolete cities, involved
dramatically reducing Glasgow's population by moving
250,000 people to the New and Expanded Towns in the
nearby countryside – Cumbernauld, Linwood and East
Kilbride, and even Glenrothes in Fife. The 1960s saw
Irvine and Erskine join the list while Stonehouse was
added in 1972 (to be un-designated four years later.) This
plan, in short, required a drastic drop in the city's
population so that the people who remained could be
rehoused at reasonable densities. It is instructive that
this plan was enthusiastically backed by Bailie Jean
Mann, an ILPer of the interwar years, a member of the
Town and Country Planning Association and a municipal
housing expert. She and her colleagues in the city's
Labour Party made a simple equation between tenements and slums – an equation which, as we have seen,
was fallacious. The Abercrombie Plan wanted to preserve
Glasgow's green belt and obtain lower densities within
the city. To this end it proposed to rehouse 250,000
people – a quarter of the city's population – outside
Glasgow. The conflict between the Corporation and the
Scottish Office grew more and more bitter.

The Corporation was anxious to obtain a solution to

this conflict, for at the end of the war there were a staggering 100,000 families on the waiting list, of whom 40,000 were technically homeless.[29] A wartime report had already indicated how badly these tenants wanted to get off the waiting list and into a new house.[30] In the post-war years, with the dawning of the Welfare State and a Labour government, the Glasgow working class made it perfectly plain, through the machine, that it expected the city's Labour council to put into effect the interwar promise of the ILP that the people would all have good houses – and preferably not tenements – at low rents. That was a central plank of Clydeside socialism. The problem for the Corporation of Glasgow was how it was to be achieved. It is noteworthy that neither the Bruce nor the Abercrombie Plans said anything systematic about the economic regeneration of Glasgow. Bruce was vaguely optimistic that the traditional manufacturing industries would be maintained if the city's population base was kept up, Abercrombie relatively pessimistic. By the same token, neither plan said anything about what kind of *city* the new Glasgow was going to be. And nobody, of course, consulted ordinary Glaswegians about any of this.

In the event, Abercrombie's plan won the day and Bruce resigned in 1947, to vanish from history. But he left an important legacy to Glasgow which was incorporated within Abercrombie's plan: the notion of peripheral estates. It was simply impossible to move to New Towns *all* the people who needed rehousing – that was a quarter of the city's population. Thus the 'big four' estates were built from the late 1940s through the 1950s: Castlemilk, Pollok, Drumchapel and Easterhouse. They came to contain 10 per cent of the population of the city. Not only that, they came to be the litmus test of the Corporation's success or failure in rehousing its people. The Housing Department's slogan at this period – the late 1940s and early 1950s – was 'The Maximum Number of Houses in the Shortest Possible Time'. The numbers game had come to roost with a vengeance. The

Corporation put out a stream of propaganda about its effort: two films were made, progress reports were issued, a newsletter was circulated and press releases were ten-a-penny. The Housing Department accelerated its pre-war programme of holding Health and Housing Exhibitions. Its Reviews of Operations and Annual Reports were almost smug in their self-satisfaction.[31] The numbers of houses erected *were* impressive:

Table 3: Local Authority House Completions, Glasgow, 1945–57

1945	600	1952	3,929
1946	1,731	1953	5,690
1947	2,944	1954	6,460
1948	2,898	1955	5,340
1949	4,011	1956	5,038
1950	4,155	1957	5,579
1951	3,839	Total	52,214

Source: Corporation of Glasgow Housing Department, *Housing Centenary, 1966.*

What was erected was totally unimpressive. The four peripheral estates, housing some 130,000 people in 44,000 houses by 1969, were completely devoid of any services. There were no buses, pubs, shops, schools, community facilities, not even roads. In the early 1950s the Corporation was spending £30,000 per week transporting children from these schemes to and from school by bus.[32] The absence of pubs led to the spread of shebeens – illegal drinking dens and off-licenses where for years the price of a half-bottle of wine and a can of beer was £1, a 33 per cent mark-up. These schemes were abominations of desolation. Numerous contemporary experts had warned of this, including Jean Mann – it was precisely what had happened in the pre-war years, albeit on a much smaller scale. But the Murphiosi were now mesmerised by their own success in getting large numbers of houses up; the tenants were left to fend for themselves. The Labour machine in Glasgow was not interested in 'garden-suburb' or 'neighbourhood unit' principles for its constituents. It was above all totally uninterested in beauty, let alone notions of town planning. Yet again, it was the women of Glasgow who were left to carry the can in the windswept canyons of the huge peripheral schemes. Even the *Glasgow Herald* could recognise that:

> The great challenge to the tenants of many of the new Glasgow housing estates is that of remoteness. The men are aware of remoteness from their work; the women of remoteness from shops ... and perhaps also of remoteness from relatives and friends to whom they could formerly turn in times of trouble ... according to social workers problems in housing schemes conform to a plan. Honeymoon of the tenancy – six months ... first year – burden of rent and hire purchase; and in the second or third years tenants are forced – some the hard way – to learn principles of household budgeting.[33]

The patronising attitude of the social workers should not be allowed to obscure the fact that the grannies of these working-class women tenants had been obliged to learn the principles of household budgeting way back in the so-called good old days.

Nonetheless, just as in the interwar housing schemes, Glaswegians initially reacted with delight to their new houses in these outlying schemes. Gerry Mooney has collected pages of appreciative comments about the Pollok scheme in the south-west of the city, for example.[34] But the barrenness of their setting, the absence of local facilities and the lack of responsiveness of the Murphiosi meant that the tenants' movement was going to arise to fill the gap. The 1950s saw a wave of militant tenants' politics start in Glasgow's peripheral schemes, particularly in Pollok. There, tenants battled to create a more humane environment than the existing barren wasteland. They campaigned for shops, transport, schools, community-halls and for various forms of collective 'self-help' – youth clubs, socialist Sunday schools, socialist choirs and political organisations of different kinds. These campaigns have been curiously

under-studied, but militant action took place all over the
city, in places as far apart as Arden, Maryhill and
Merrilee, and most particularly in the Gorbals.[35]

What is important to understand about these tenants'
campaigns is that they were a qualitatively new
phenomenon; this is the period which saw the start of
what we would now call 'community politics' in Glasgow.
The potential for the stormy and sustained rent strikes of
the interwar period had been removed to all intents and
purposes by the rents rebate scheme. Therefore tenants
had to devise new forms of political action to get the
services which Labour had failed to provide. The anger
and innovation of the tenants' action took the Murphiosi
by surprise, for since 1933 they had come to take support
in the schemes for granted. Now, in a post-war era where
there was talk of 'affluent workers' and 'you've never had
it so good', it was plain that the Labour vote in the
peripheral schemes could *not* be taken for granted and
certainly not until the local political machine had been
established. The local Labour Party had to deliver at
least some goods if it was to retain and strengthen its
hold on the local state. In the meantime, it abused and
slandered the tenants for fighting for the services it
should have provided in the first place.

Elsewhere, redevelopment roared ahead. The Corporation's Development Plan of 1954 designated three areas
as suitable for immediate redevelopment. They were the
Gorbals, Govan and Royston, containing 15,666 houses.
The city's Medical Officer of Health reckoned that there
were another 17,000 houses in small pockets scattered
round the city which should also be demolished.[36]

It was no accident that the Gorbals was the first to go;
it was, after all, the locus of *No Mean City* and was
synonymous internationally with slums and violence.
The area had inspired a play, *The Gorbals Story*, and a
ballet, *Miracle in the Gorbals*. Both productions said
more about middle-class guilt than the reality of life in
the Gorbals. They certainly did not stop the total
devastation of the area. More than 100 acres containing

20,000 people were cleared at a cost of £13 million – but only 10,000 were to be allowed in the new houses.[37] There are only a handful of original buildings still standing in the Gorbals, the most important of which is the justly famous Citizens' Theatre. The new Gorbals was heralded by the rise of huge multi-storey blocks of flats towering over the south side.

In a curious footnote to the history of the Gorbals, Alexander MacArthur, the author of *No Mean City*, was found on the night of 4 September 1947 lying beside the Rutherglen Bridge, not far from the Gorbals. He was unconscious and had drunk a bottle of disinfectant; taken to hospital, he later died there. Apparently he had tried without success to get various short stories and plays published after *No Mean City*. Jack House, the doyen of Glasgow journalists, maintains that he was totally untalented and had wholly unrealistic perceptions of his own abilities.[38] MacArthur accused Robert Leishman, the author of *The Gorbals Story*, of plagiarising a play which he had submitted to both the Citizens' and Unity Theatres.[39] Linda McKenny, the historian of Scottish theatre, has studied both scripts and is sure that there is no evidence for plagiarism and that Unity Theatre's commitment to working-class drama would have ensured that something like *The Gorbals Story* have been performed in any event. She also feels that MacArthur's hand-written notes on his script suggest a mind under profound stress, for whatever reason.[40] It seems charitable to assume that McArthur's success with *No Mean City* had brought him no peace, and that he committed suicide when the balance of his mind was disturbed.[41] A final comment on this tragic affair is that the book has always been much more successful in England than in Scotland, where it is regarded with amused contempt.

The Gorbals treatment was aimed at the other 'Comprehensive Development Areas' in the city, and whole tenemental neighbourhoods vanished; Townhead, the Calton, most of Springburn, Govan and Partick were also scheduled to be razed, but by this time there was a popular outcry against the wholesale vandalism of Glasgow. Tenants' associations were formed and turned themselves into housing associations whose object was to modernise their tenements rather than demolish them. But for the initiative of organisations like the pioneering Partick Housing Association, it is highly likely that there would hardly be a working-class tenement block left in the city. The housing associations demonstrated that it was possible to preserve the shell of structurally sound tenements and completely renew the rest: roofs, windows, doors, plumbing, electricity and back-courts. The classic problem of how to fit a bathroom into the small tenement houses was solved by making two flats out of the normal three on every landing.

By the start of the 1960s the problems of the peripheral estates were evident and new building forms had to be found to rehouse those displaced by the mass demolition. Many, of course, went to the New Towns. The Corporation's answer for the rest was to move into systems building, and the 1960s saw the mushrooming of the multi-storey tower blocks which punctuate the city's skyline. The Corporation of Glasgow was nothing if not technologically innovative, but sensitivity to the requirements of its people was conspicuous by its absence. The Corporation was by now totally in thrall to the numbers game and its uncritical acceptance of whichever building system was then in vogue resulted in thousands of tenants' lives becoming a misery with endemic damp, huge heating bills, fire hazards, inadequate elevator systems and poor sound insulation – not to mention panels falling off external walls and crashing to the ground. 294 tower blocks were to be built in Glasgow before the programme was halted, leading to Adam MacNaughton's famous folk song, the 'Skyscraper Wean', whose chorus goes:

> Oh ye cannae fling pieces oot a twenty storey flat,
> Seven hundred hungry weans'll testify to that.
> If it's butter, cheese or jeely, if the breid is plain or pan,

The odds against it reaching earth are ninety-nine tae wan.[42]

Eventually in 1974, the then Labour leader of the council said:

> In Glasgow we will not be building any more high flats after this. It is just not worth the candle. We have had a large number of complaints from both young and old people. The planners should have told us about the difficulties before they were built – but they did not. We had to find out for ourselves ... They are socially undesirable.[43]

While the Red Road blocks, at 34 storeys reputedly the highest in Europe, dominate the eastern approaches to the city, the development which came to symbolise the stupidity of the Corporation and the inadequacies of systems-building was without a doubt the Hutchesontown 'E' complex in the Gorbals. Using a French system developed for the Algerian climate, a huge rectangular deck-block development was built. Even before it was open, there was a major problem, as the site was full of old mine workings. Hutchie E, as it was known, was a complete disaster from the day it was opened. Like many atrocious housing developments, it was riddled with damp, and a shipyard worker who was a tenant there assured me that the only way he could get his wallpaper to stay up was to rivet it to the walls! The tenants formed the Gorbals Anti-Damp Campaign and fought back against the Corporation and the contractors who blamed the damp on their heavy breathing and told them to sleep with the windows open.[44] But the tenants continued their campaign and eventually, twelve years after Hutchie E was opened, all 2,000 of them were rehoused.

This was another famous victory, for the Corporation, politicians and experts were forced to admit that the awful conditions in the development were nothing to do with the living habits of the tenants. The political campaign waged by the Gorbals tenants was successful in spite of the Labour Party, not because of it, and its lessons were exported to tenants' groups all round Britain. That it took twelve years to win is an indicator of the entrenched arrogance of the council, on the one hand, and of the determination and organisational skill of ordinary Glasgow tenants on the other. It was an absolute scandal that so many people should have had to endure such appalling conditions for so long – with the added indignity of being victims who were blamed for the Corporation's crass stupidity. And Hutchie E was only the most notorious instance of a widespread problem. A tenant appearing as a witness before the 1986 Grieve Inquiry into Housing in Glasgow said it all:

> We have suffered from experts in the past: it was experts who built the Titanic and the Tay Bridge and you know what happened to them.[45]

Stalinism and Labourism

The main reason for the failure of so much of Glasgow Corporation's rehousing policy was the failure of the socialism of the local Labour Party. A most curious phenomenon had come to pass in the post-war decades. The ILP as an *Independent* Labour Party had died. The city Labour Party claimed its mantle, but, with the exception of a few survivors like Jean Mann from the heyday of the interwar years, city councillors were singularly bereft of the moral honesty, passion and vision of their predecessors. They were wanting both imagination and talent. There were two reasons for this. The first was the control of the party machine by the Murphiosi; they were not interested in politics but in power – and profit. The most famous example of this transformation, sadly, was Paddy Dollan, who as Lord Provost had forgotten his roots to the extent that he accepted invitations to Masonic Burns Night suppers.[46] The massive demolition and construction contracts of the post-war years were constantly tainted with allegations of corruption, as was the process of housing allocation. This latter led to an enquiry and resignations in 1977. Similar allegations are heard to the present day.

The second reason for the bankruptcy of the Labour Party's socialism was the ease with which it accommodated itself to the Stalinism of the local Communists. It would be hard to find Communists more uncritical of the Moscow line throughout the late 1940s, 50s and 60s than Clydeside Communists. The local Communists had a powerful base in the local trade union movement, particularly in the engineering and shipbuilding trades. But, more generally in Glasgow, the predominance of the Murphiosi meant that the Communists never got a seat on the council. But for all their eschatological differences, the two groups shared a similar psychology: they were both obsessed with power, adept conspirators, authoritarian to a degree and profoundly sexist. The differences between the right wing of the local Labour Party – which meant most of it – and the local Communist Party were invisible to the naked eye. This is, of course, a paradox, for the two groups could have famous public feuds, such as the famous disputes over contraceptive and abortion legislation in which commitment to a kind of feminism led local Communists to adopt a much more principled position than the Catholic-inspired Murphiosi. The similarity was one of *mentality*. Although both groups had members who were strong supporters of tenants' associations, both saw power as residing ultimately with (male) workers organised in trade unions rather than in tenants' groups which have a tendency to be dominated by women. Their rhetoric was therefore well-nigh indistinguishable, with the exception that for the Communists the Soviet Union was the Good Society. In any event, the two groups could do business with each other and often did. The losers were the ordinary people of Glasgow who were faced with an increasingly unresponsive and uninterested political machine; they still are.

In the shipyards, however, the Communists' power base was real. From the beginning of the war they

dominated the shop stewards' yard production committees to the extent that Stephen's and Fairfield's would
not co-operate with them.[47] As Foster and Woolfson have
shown, the Communists dominated the convenorships in
the yards, and under their influence there were mass
discussions of strategic issues such as industrial
organisation. The shipbuilders won a major strike,
ostensibly about wage differentials but actually about
control of the job, in 1956. But the shipbuilding industry
was in international decline and the rate of closure of
smaller and marginal yards accelerated until in the
1960s Fairfield's was the only remaining shipyard within
the boundaries of Glasgow. Other employers were quite
happy to see it go to the wall in order to mop up skilled
labour, but to their dismay George Brown rescued the
yard in 1965. Fairfield was then incorporated in Upper
Clyde Shipbuilders. But the situation was not getting
any better and in June 1971 the yard was bankrupt. The
rest is history. Led by an exceptionally able bunch of shop
stewards, the UCS workforce opted for the ingenious
tactic of a 'work-in'. This immediately dispelled the
tabloid press's image of irresponsible workers striking for
no reason. It also circumvented what would have been
the illegal tactic of an occupation. The shop stewards'
committees also broadened the campaign by involving
the wider trade union movement, the churches and a
host of other organisations. In no time at all the whole of
Scotland was behind the UCS men's 'right to work' and
everybody who was anybody was trying to jump on the
bandwagon and get their photograph taken with Jimmy
Airlie, Sammy Gilmour, Jimmy Reid or Sam Barr.

As is well known, the campaign was ultimately
successful; Fairfield's was not closed down although
inevitably the workforce was slimmed down in subsequent years. It is hard to overestimate the importance of
the UCS work-in. Not only did it save hundreds of jobs, it
provided a definitive political experience for workers who
were already no political slouches. Moreover, because of
its brilliant organisation, it inspired workers elsewhere

in the country. It has provided the direct model for numerous other work-ins, of which the Lee Jeans work-in at Greenock, organised almost exclusively by women, and the Caterpillar campaign are probably the most celebrated.[48] It has also been vital in ensuring that the whole population of Scotland is kept posted about industrial struggles and involved in them because the success or failure of these campaigns affects whole towns.

A central problem with this strategy is, of course, that it gives predominance to *organised* workers, meaning male trade unionists in the main. While UCS and Caterpillar and Ravenscraig have to be defended, there are many other political struggles in which the trade union movement is conspicuous by its absence – like the tenants' campaigns mentioned above. In this sense, Clydeside Stalinism is profoundly sexist, as well as élitist. But as a local political phenomenon its power is declining rapidly. The proportion of male skilled manual workers in manufacturing industries in Glasgow's labour force, the Stalinists' power base, has contracted dramatically over the last couple of decades. Furthermore, the collapse of the Soviet satellite states in Central and Eastern Europe has almost certainly signed the death certificate of Glaswegian Stalinism. But the legacy of the UCS work-in is still powerful in Glasgow. It would be fair to say that Jimmy Reid, one of its leaders, is now one of the most loathed men on Clydeside. He is regarded as a self-seeking and vain turncoat, who, in sinking so low as to write a column for the *Sun*, is beneath Glaswegians' contempt.

Popular Culture

Relative post-war affluence meant that Glaswegians were able to enjoy all the traditional pursuits for which they didn't have the money during the Depression. Football, of course, raged in the city and was totally dominated by the 'Old Firm' of Celtic and Rangers, while the fortunes of smaller locally based clubs like Third

Lanark, Clyde, Queen's Park and Partick Thistle waxed and waned. All these teams have their own personalities; Queen's Park has an aura of the gentleman amateur while Thistle is a team which many support because they do not want to be drawn into the sectarianism which besets the Old Firm. Attendances at matches were colossal, particularly Scottish Cup Ties and Scotland-England games at Hampden Park when the attendance was routinely around 130,000. The biggest single crowd was, in fact, in 1937 when the official gate was a staggering 149,547 – not even the poverty of the Depression could keep the fans away from a match with the Auld Enemy![49] In Glasgow, and indeed in Scotland at large, football has deep meaning for its supporters and can attain almost the status of an alternative religion. The success of the Wildcat Theatre Company's *The Celtic Story* made that evident, in case anyone doubted it. For many Glasgow families, happiness or misery varies directly with the fortunes of the team – and that means the *man*'s team – for football is the sporting expression of the city's hard masculine edge, and contains all the ritual displays of skill, courage, competition and controlled violence which the local version of machismo demands.

Pubs were another important aspect of popular culture, but again demonstrated the overwhelming patriarchy within the city. While there were many handsome city centre pubs – the Horseshoe Bar, Sloan's, St Mungo Vintners – neighbourhood bars were often cheerless and functional dives. Women were not wanted in such pubs and indeed respectable working-class women would not enter them, by and large. Some Glasgow pubs barred women totally, like Tennant's in Byres Road in the West End. Others would not serve women in the public bar, but only in the lounge where they would not be served a pint. Even in the early 1970s it was possible to go into half a dozen pubs in some neighbourhoods before finding one which would admit a woman.

The 10 o'clock closing hour meant that on Fridays,

paynight, many working men would head straight into the pub and reel out steaming at 10 o'clock. There can be no doubt that horrific domestic violence was the result. Even in the discreetly charming West End, my local, the Rubaiyat, was so full on a Friday night during the 1970s and 1980s that there would be a queue waiting to get in by 8 o'clock, on the basis of one out, one in. To get and hold a table meant having someone right in the doors when they opened at 5 o'clock. While it may not have had any impact on alcohol abuse, there can be little doubt that the change in the licensing laws to permit all-day opening and late closing has made Glasgow pubs more civilised places in which to drink. It has also meant the end of the city's shebeens, some of which were very colourful places if you did not mind the odd hard man or two.

As has been noted earlier, Glasgow has always been a dancing mad city. Venues like the Dennistoun Palais, the Locarno and the Majestic – 'Magic Stick' locally! – were immensely popular and there is happily a lot of film footage of large crowds involved in some very classy ballroom dancing. But places like the Highlanders' Institute with its Saturday night ceilidhs were also very popular. And the city was full of small local halls where there were regular dances, some of them with popular Irish dancing classes reflecting the origins of Glasgow's population.

The dancing also attracted some violence. Throughout the late 1960s and early 1970s there was an ugly atmosphere of violence in the city. Part of this was media hype, part of it was real. The area which became associated with gang violence was no longer the Gorbals, but the peripheral estate of Easterhouse. Largely as a result of its remoteness from the bright lights of the city centre, its lack of facilities and its young population, groups of teenagers would wander around with nothing to do. Inevitably, they formed gangs and there were fights; after all, Easterhouse is in Glasgow. In no time at all the media had these fights blown up out of all proportion into something approaching the Third World War. It was a classic moral panic, as Gail Armstrong and Mary Wilson have persuasively demonstrated.[50] But moral panics have consequences however unintended they might be. Easterhouse rapidly gained national notoriety as the successor to the Gorbals, a squad of police known locally as the 'Untouchables' started busting young people much faster and harder than they could bust each other, and irresponsible speeches were made in the House of Commons in which it was said that '... the Clyde is foaming with blood'.[51] It was *No Mean City* all over again. In 1968 the singer Frankie Vaughan flew in to mediate among the warring gangs, thus sealing the reputational fate of Easterhouse whatever else he may have achieved. In a famous incident the gang members dumped their weapons publicly and the nation saw a stunning display of ironmongery including knives, swords and kukris. At the time I was told that some of the teenage boys had nicked their fathers' war souvenirs! The response to all this was the establishment of a voluntary body known as the Easterhouse Project Trust which involved local young people. The Easterhouse Project was effectively two large tin huts. If the youth of Easterhouse had any doubts about how they were valued, they had no excuses now. Some very dedicated and clued up people worked in the project including Graham Noble, Glasgow writer Archie Hinds and detached policeman John Nolan. In a 'World in Action' television programme about the project in 1969 Hinds made the astute observation that by its very coverage of local events, television was turning Easterhouse into a zoo.

Glasgow's image was further besmirched at this time by the publication of an awful book called *A Glasgow Gang Observed* in 1973.[52] Large extracts from the book were published in one of the allegedly serious Sunday newspapers with an illustration showing someone getting a 'jaggy bunnit' – a bottle wrapped round his head. This book was a classic of prurient voyeurism cloaked in obscurantist sociological jargon. It was based on no more than 120 hours on the street with some teenagers in Maryhill and talks with the inmates of the Approved School where the author worked. He plainly swallowed the teenage boys' grossly inflated stories of gang warfare chib, malkie and hatchet. But when the rumble was impending – or allegedly impending – he ran away.

In any event, there can be little doubt that there was an atmosphere of violence about during the 1970s. There would be running fights outside the Sauchiehall Street dance-halls every Saturday night, and innocent people as well as gang members would get hurt. Many young people from areas with tough reputations – Easterhouse, Blackhill, 'Wine Alley' – would camouflage where they lived for fear of provoking an attack inside the dance-hall. This decade saw the beginnings of the negative television coverage of Glasgow discussed in Chapter 1. The violence mirrored the way the city appeared to the outsider – as an ocean of dereliction, blackened tenements, public drunkenness, dozens of unlovely skyscrapers, featureless housing schemes. It was as if this was all that Glasgow deserved.

And yet the city still had a lot of bazazz. The dance-halls and bingo-halls were full, the singing pubs were bursting at the seams, the folk pubs like the Scotia and Victoria Bars were coming down with musicians, the concert halls and theatres were well attended, Green's Playhouse and the Apollo provided numerous concerts for local young people, self-entertainment still flourished in the remaining tenement neighbourhoods and in the schemes, the Patter was as funny as ever; ordinary Glaswegians, in short, were still full of confidence. This period also saw two fine books published which accurately reflected the life of the city: Archie Hind's novel *The Dear Green Place* and Alan Spence's collection of short stories *Its Colours They are Fine*.[53] The problem with this period was that the majority of Glaswegians quite simply deserved a much better urban environment in which to live than the one they had been given by the council.

Glasgow's Miles Better

The pace of change in Glasgow began to accelerate through the 1970s. There were two basic changes which were to alter fundamentally the nature of the city. The first was the rapid population decline, the second the associated equally rapid decline in manufacturing jobs. The post-war population figures are:

Table 4: Glasgow Population, 1951–1991

1951	1,090,000
1961	1,065,017
1971	898,848
1981	763,162
1991 (est.)	688,195

Source: Andrew Gibb, *Glasgow: The Making of a City*, Croom Helm, 1983, p. 160; 1981 and 1991: Strathclyde Regional Council Executive's Department. (1991 figure projected from a 1986 base.)

The proportions of jobs in the manufacturing and service sectors in the city changed as follows:

Table 5: Glasgow City Employment Sectors, 1971, 1981, 1983, percentages

	1971	1981	1983
Manufacturing	34.7	24.9	23.7
Services	64.8	74.7	75.9

Source: Glasgow District Council Planning Department, 1984.

These figures speak for themselves. There has been a population decline of just under 40 per cent over four decades and an 11 per cent decline in manufacturing jobs in twelve years, while service sector jobs have increased by 11 per cent in the same period. Glasgow will never be the same again. As its population and traditional employment structure declined, so did its image. The number of negative stories and documentaries accelerated through the 1970s; it was as if the media were trying to deal Glasgow the *coup de grace*.

From being a tough, cheery and working city, it was increasingly portrayed as a violent, grim and workless place. The nadir of Glasgow's fortunes was reached on 22 January 1978 when the *Observer* colour supplement did a major piece on Glasgow's East End. All the photographs were in black and white. The cover picture showed a woman standing in a rubble-strewn back-court, photographed through a close-window in which all but one pane of glass is smashed. The text reads:

HOME, ROTTEN HOME

What it's like in the worst corner of Britain.
This woman was photographed
from the block of Glasgow flats where she lives.

Inside there were thirteen photographs conveying an overwhelming sense of misery, poverty and violence. Sub-heads to the pictures included 'Ghetto City of the Poor'. Chaim Bermant, author of the article:

> Glaswegians are anything but docile, but a heritage of hardship has given them a genial stoicism bordering almost upon resignation. Expecting little from life, they have been content with little and have not infrequently received even less.

While this is absolutely true, the overall tenor of the piece – photos and text – was blatantly offensive to Glaswegians. Chaim Bermant, a native of Glasgow who has written a sensitive novel about his childhood, should be thoroughly ashamed of himself for the disservice he did his city.[54] It was in the attempt to correct this image and thus win more jobs in the service industries that the

'Glasgow's Miles Better' slogan was coined. It has to be said that in terms of Glasgow's external image, the efforts of the image-makers have been outstandingly successful. It was to be only ten years before the *Sunday Times* colour supplement referred to in Chapter 1 completely reversed the appalling imagery of its predecessor. Glasgow is now The Good City, if not exactly the City of God. The problem with the rosy image is that it constitutes a façade which conceals a complex and harsh reality. As we saw in Chapter 1, Glasgow is, quite simply, not miles better for many of its people.

References

1. Paul Harris, *Glasgow and the Clyde at War*, Archive Publications, 1986, p.5.
2. Ibid., p.6.
3. Glasgow Chamber of Commerce, *Glasgow Made it Through the Depression: How Glasgow Came Through the 1930s Depression* Glasgow, n.d. (c.1984), p.15.
4. Harris, op. cit., p.87.
5. Ibid.
6. Ibid., p.86.
7. Ibid., p.4.
8. Ibid., p.13.
9. Bob Crampsey, *The Young Civilian: A Glasgow Wartime Boyhood*, Headline, 1987, pp.33-4.
10. *Ibid., p.140.*
11. *Georgie Farish, 'What Did You Do During the War, Mummy?' in A Bagful of Scripts*, Ibrox Writers' Group, 1989, p.64.
12. Mr Grant McGregor, Govan Reminiscence Group. I am grateful to Dennis Gallagher, Area Community Education Officer, and members of the group for letting me listen to their tapes. 'Breenge' is a Scots word meaning a violent dash.
13. Harris, op. cit., p.10.
14. Ibid.
15. Ibid., p. 52.
16. Ibid.
17. Taped life-history of Mrs D of Govan.
18. Mitchison, op. cit., p.137.
19. Sillitoe, op. cit., p.115.
20. Cf. Richard Croucher, *Engineers at War, 1939-1945*, Merlin Press, 1982, pp.123-6 and Foster and Woolfson, op. cit., pp.95-6, 285-92.
21. Scottish Office, *Industry and Employment in Scotland*, Cmd. 7125, 1947.
22. Foster and Woolfson, op. cit., pp.97-8.
23. Ibid., p.98.

24. Slaven, op. cit., p.218.

25. Glasgow Corporation and the University of Glasgow, *The Springburn Study*, 1967, para.4.17.

26. See Gerry Mooney, *Living on the Periphery: Housing, Industrial Change and the State*, unpublished PhD thesis, University of Glasgow, 1988, pp.209ff, for a seminal discussion of these events. Dr Mooney's forthcoming book, *Living on the Periphery*, Routledge and Kegan Paul, will be the definitive account of post-war industrial and urban restructuring in Glasgow.

27. Census of Scotland, *City of Glasgow*, Vol.III, 1951.

28. Mooney, op. cit., p.280, footnote 60. It is more than feasible that Somers' philistine attitudes were responsible for the 'non-design' of the city's interwar rehousing schemes as discussed in the last chapter.

29. Corporation of Glasgow Housing Department, *Review of Operations 1919-1947*, Glasgow, 1947.

30. D. Chapman, *Wartime Social Survey: The Location of Dwellings in Scottish Towns*, Edinburgh, 1943.

31. See Mooney, op. cit., for a detailed discussion of this programme. The films in question are held in the Scottish Film Archive in Glasgow.

32. Tom Brennan, *Reshaping a City*, Grant, 1959, p.41.

33. *Glasgow Herald*, 26 December 1956, quoted in Mooney, op. cit., p.250.

34. Ibid., pp.239ff.

35. Maurice Broady and John Mack (both then of Glasgow University) *did* study this movement at the time and wrote an unpublished book about it. The book never appeared because the authors were apparently told that they would be sued for libel if it were published (personal communication, Professor Broady). An incomplete ms. is held in the Broady Collection in the library of the University of Glasgow. It is noteworthy for finding numerous reds under the beds in the Glasgow tenants' movement – perhaps a reflection of the intensity of the contemporary Cold War. I am pleased to say that Charlie Johnstone is completing a PhD on the tenants' movement in the University's Department of Sociology.

36. Brennan, op. cit., p. 61.

37. Ibid., p.61.

38. Jack House, personal communication.

39. c.f. *The Word*, March 1947.

40. Linda MacKennie, personal communication.

41. MacArthur's atory is a fascinating one which needs further research; I hope to publish on the subject shortly.

42. Adam MacNaughton, 'Skyscraper Wean' in Norman Buchan and Peter Hall, *The Scottish Folksinger*, Collins, 1973, p.23. This justly famous song appears in many collections and on many albums.

43. *Glasgow Herald*, 19 November 1974.

44. Phil McPhee, 'Hutchie E – A Monument to Corruption, Stupidity and Bad Planning' in Farquhar McLay (ed.), op. cit., pp.47-8.

45. Mr Robert Alexander, Braidcraft Federation of Tenants' Associations, *Grieve Inquiry into Housing in Glasgow*, 1986, p.31.

46. c.f. Dollan, n.d., op. cit.

47. Foster and Woolfson, op. cit., p. 154. This important book is the definitive study of the UCS work-in.

48. Charles Woolfson and John Forster, *Track Record: The Story of the Caterpillar Occupation*, Verso, 1989.

49. Andrew Ward, *Scotland the Team*, Derby, Breedon Books, 1987, p.128. I am grateful to Ian Russell, International Correspondent of *The Punter*, for this reference and for many informed discussions about the game.

50. Gail Armstrong and Mary Wilson, 'City Politics and Deviancy Amplification' in Ian Taylor and Laurie Taylor (eds.), *Politics and Deviance*, Penguin, 1973.

51. Quoted in Ibid., p.74.

52. James Patrick, *A Glasgow Gang Observed*, Eyre Methuen, 1973. See my review of this book in *Hibernia*, 30 March 1973, for a contemporary critique. The author used a pseudonym for this book saying that he feared for his life from gang members. This is hardly surprising given the way he misrepresented their lives. His real name is Frank Coffield.

53. Archie Hind, *The Dear Green Place*, Hutchinson, 1966; Alan Spence, *Its Colours They are Fine*, Collins, 1977.

54. Chaim Bermant, *Jericho Sleep Alone*, Chapman and Hall, 1964.

7 Conclusion

Glasgow is, of all British cities, *the* industrial, working-class city *par excellence*. It is one whose identity – not image – is secure because it is cemented by its history of tough living and working conditions. It is, as we have seen, a city which has known a ferocious racial and religious sectarianism and a dreadful sexual chauvinism but one, paradoxically, whose identity is secure not because of the great divides between its people but in spite of them. This bonding was ensured by a common poverty which in turn resulted in a common culture of survival. Glaswegians themselves define this identity as socialist. They have created a formidable complex of institutions to carry and express their socialism, a network much denser than that anywhere else in the United Kingdom. The underlying unity of Glasgow's people is reflected in the way they celebrate their language with a unique enthusiasm, for that language is the key vehicle for expressing their identity and their self-confidence.

What the council and the public relations people have forgotten is that the city's *image* is a mere reflection, whether it is shaped by forces internal or external to the city. It is not the reality; it can never reflect the city's identity, for that is carried in the hearts of people, not in walls or ships however beautiful and strong these may be. Nor can a mere image ever capture the sense of place of Glasgow. Historically, Glasgow's bad image was largely created south of the border and had a lot to do with punishing its people for their radicalism and diverting their attention from the appalling conditions in which they had to live. Nowadays, it is to do with marketing the place, in selling it as a good location for government offices and outlets for the Next fashion chain. Both images are false.

Glasgow's problem is that it is a workers' city whose rulers resolutely pretend that it is something else. As it goes into the 1990s there can be no doubt, however, that it is assuming a different appearance. The drop in the city's population by almost 50 per cent since the war has seen to that. The city has also changed in that there is no longer a trace – in the council – of the spirit of the Red Clyde. The Labour Party is presiding over a policy which has effectively abandoned the city to speculators and hustlers. The banks of the River Clyde are becoming lined with yuppie flats, some, like those at the Broomielaw, of an unsurpassed ugliness. The gaps between these flats are punctuated with huge overpriced hotels. Trendy wine bars, restaurants and discos open faster than the naked eye can follow, some in the most unlikely of places, like the Bridgegate. The official position is that there is now a 'surplus' of 20,000 council houses in the city and that the big peripheral estates need to be broken up into manageable units, while the multi-storey flats beside the motorway receive fancy cupolas on their roofs to make them look attractive to would-be investors speeding past in their BMWs. The cupolas also help to keep out the endemic penetrating damp, but the investors need not know about that. Meanwhile, despite the rhetoric of 'community regeneration' and the like, the small rehousing schemes like Blackhill and Teucharhill and the 'Wine Alley' have been quietly abandoned, and as they accumulate more and more empty houses the easier it will be to declare them surplus to requirements and either demolish them or sell them off to be refurbished for newly arrived financiers and civil servants.

The city will look nicer too, as the century wears to an end. It is already a handsome place with its rows of elegant sand-blasted tenements and fine parks. As the remaining ugliness in the inner city is removed, we can hope to see more of the urban landsacpe ventilated with small parks and green spaces. But an unforgiveable amount of architectural vandalism has already occurred in the regeneration of Glasgow. The Scottish Exhibition and Conference Centre, the Forum Hotel beside it on the Clyde and the new flats at Kingston are all of a stunning mediocrity. It is hard not to be pessimistic about what is going to be built on the riverside site of the Garden Festival. In early 1990 the developers were advertising flats there for sums approaching £200,000. Meanwhile, there is no sign of well designed council housing for the city's young people, or elderly people who have served a life-sentence in peripheral schemes. The new Sheriff Court complex right in the heart of the city looks exactly like what it really is, a fortress with a holding area for hundreds of people 'in case of emergency'. Hutchie E has been demolished, but there are no prizes for guessing what kind of housing is going up in its place. John Wheatley and his comrades must be revolving in their graves.

The council's short-sighted insistence on redefining its labour market as oriented towards the service industries has meant that recent inward investment in Scottish light engineering and electronics has passed Glasgow by. At no time has there been any attempt to think of alternative economic or manufacturing strategies. In March 1990 almost three-quarters of the city's economically active population is employed in services and less than one-fifth in manufacturing.[1] The council seems to see the future of Glasgow as a city of cocktail-makers, waitresses and boutique owners. It has capitulated so thoroughly to Thatcherite values that it is happy to collaborate with whatever Mickey Mouse scheme is proposed to make a quick profit – even if that includes selling off the council houses for which it is legally responsible. Yet no less than 53 per cent of Glaswegians are still housed by the council. The culture of the city's working class is now being repackaged as some kind of anodyne and quaint survival instead of the result of two centuries' struggle – first against the city's uncaring capitalists and then against the city's uncaring Corporation. Services are being provided for yuppies in the inner city for which council tenants in the peripheral schemes have been waiting for decades. The 31.4 per cent of Glasgow's population who are Income Support recipients, or dependants and partners of such recipients, will be bought off with money from the European Community.[2] The disorganised and demoralised class will be organised and remoralised into the recreational class of the future, and will have to content itself with 'self-help' schemes and 'community businesses'.

The local Labour Party has lost touch with its principles and with its roots to the extent that it is in collaboration with the administration of a Poll Tax which is rejected by the vast majority of its constituents. With the Labour Party having a stranglehold on power in both Strathclyde Region and Glasgow District, this is utterly incomprehensible. On 28 March 1990 Strathclyde Region issued 280,000 Summary Warrants, including some 145,000 in Glasgow, against citizens who cannot or will not pay the Poll Tax.[3] I do not envy the first Sheriff Officer who tries to hold a warrant sale in Blackhill or Pollok.

In spite of all this, Glasgow will continue to be an exciting city in which to live – providing one has a job, that is. Those responsible for governing Glasgow might be trying to sell it for a song, but they will never succeed, as too many Glaswegians are far too conscious about their town to let this happen. *They* celebrate it with their own songs, for there has never been a more poetic city in these islands, and poems and songs continue to flow from its citizens' pens and word-processors. Instructively, those about Glasgow being European City of culture in 1990 are the funniest – and most savage.

It is, of course, a truism to say that the future is in the hands of the young, but I think that this is genuinely the case in Glasgow where the young people are plainly so immensely talented – as their sheer numbers in the world of successful pop and rock music indicates. They show no signs of losing the political astuteness of their forebears, and remain justifiably cynical about the system under which they live. They may be fiercely proud of their home city, but that does not mean a slavish adherence to whatever is the Labour Party's line. There are far too many young people in Glasgow marooned without jobs in the city's 'hard-to-let' housing schemes for them to see local politics through rose-tinted spectacles. However good the city's image is and however good it actually looks, it is not in good economic shape and young people are one of the most vulnerable groups in both the labour and housing markets. If the local council, instead of protecting them from the ravages of Thatcherism, turns its back on them as it did on so many of their mothers and fathers, it should not be surprised if in turn the young people abandon it. The fact that Labour has lost control of the anti-Poll Tax campaign is nothing to do with Militant conspiracies or the gullibility of young people; it has everything to do with Labour's political bankruptcy.

Labour in Glasgow is going to have to face some political realities if it wishes to stay in power in the city. It has signally failed to come up with any inspired campaign against Thatcherism in a city where it quite clearly has a mandate to burn down the City Chambers if doing so would get rid of the Tories. National disgust in Scotland with Westminster's routine ignorance of Scotland is alive and well in Glasgow, and was clearly demonstrated when Jim Sillars of the SNP won the Govan by-election in November 1988. That election was an unmistakeably Glaswegian signal to the city's Labour Party that the politically sophisticated people of Govan had had enough. They are still socialists, but socialists who want to express the distinctly Glaswegian and Scottish dimensions of their political identity. They refuse to say 'my party right or wrong'.

When the big party to bid farewell to the Year of

Culture ends around dawn of New Year's Day 1991,
Glaswegians will look around their city with approval.
Then they will say, 'Aye, very good. What about us now?'
There had better be some answers, for Glasgow is not for
sale.

References

1. Grant Baird and Jim Walker, 'Greater Glasgow', *Glasgow Herald*, 8
March 1990.
2. Strathclyde Regional Council, *Poverty in Strathclyde: A Statistical
Analysis*, No. 2, December, 1989, Appendix 6, p.50. This Appendix
demonstrates that on the basis of six different indicators of poverty,
Glasgow is at the top of the Regional league-table.
3. *Evening Times*, 7 February 1990, provides the latter figure, which
represents 30 per cent of those supposed to pay the tax.

Bibliography

Gail Armstrong and Mary Wilson, 'City Politics and Deviancy Amplification' in Ian Taylor and Laurie Taylor (eds.), *Politics and Deviance*, Penguin, 1973.

Bernard Aspinwall, *Portable Utopia: Glasgow and the United States, 1820-1920*, Aberdeen University Press, 1984.

W.W. Barr, *Glaswegians*, Glasgow, Richard Drew, 1973.

George Barras, The Glasgow Building Regulations Act (1892), *Proceedings of the Philosophical Society of Glasgow*, Vol. XXV, 1893-94.

J.J. Bell, *I Remember*, Edinburgh, The Porpoise Press, 1932.

Chaim Bermant, *Jericho Sleep Alone*, Chapman and Hall, 1964.

S. Berry and H. Whyte (eds.), *Glasgow Observed*, Edinburgh, John Donald, 1987.

Alastair Borthwick, *The Empire Exhibition: Fifty Years On: A Personal Reminiscence*, BBC and Mainstream, 1988.

Noreen Branson, *History of the Communist Party of Great Britain 1927-1941*, Lawrence and Wishart, 1985.

Tom Brennan, *Reshaping a City*, Grant, 1959.

H.F. Brotherstown, *Observations on the Early Public Health Movement in Scotland*, H.K. Lewis, 1952.

Callum Brown, *The Social History of Religion in Scotland Since 1730*, Methuen, 1987.

A. Browning, *Clyde Built Ships*, 3 vols., Glasgow Museums and Art Galleries, 1979.

Norman Buchan and Peter Hall,*The Scottish Folksinger*, Collins, 1973.

Keith Burgess, 'New Unionism for Old? The Amalgamated Society of Engineers in Britain' in W.J. Mommsen and H.G. Husung (eds.), *The Development of Trade Unionism in Great Britain and Germany, 1880-1914*, Allen & Unwin, 1985.

Keith Burgess, 'The Political Economy of British Engineering Workers During the First World War' in L. Harrison and C. Tilly (eds.), *Strikes, Wars and Revolutions: An International Perspective*, Cambridge University Press, 1989.

Moira Burgess, *The Glasgow Novel*, 2nd edition, Glasgow, Scottish Library Association and Glasgow District Libraries, 1986.

John Burrowes, *Benny: The Life and Times of a Fighting Legend*, Fontana, 1982.

J. Butt, 'Working Class Housing in Glasgow, 1851-1914' in S.D. Chapman (ed.), *The History of Working Class Housing*, Newton Abbott, David & Charles, 1971.

John Caldwell, *Come Dungeons Dark: The Life and Times of Guy Aldred, Glasgow Anarchist*, Barr, Ayrshire, Luath Books, 1988.

Alan B. Campbell, *The Lanarkshire Miners: A Social History of Their Trade Unions*, Edinburgh, John Donald, 1979.

Calum Campbell, *The Making of a Clydeside Working Class: Shipbuilding and Working Class Organisation in Govan*, Our History Pamphlet No. 78, 1986.

John Carvel, *Stephen of Linthouse: A Record of 200 Years of Shipbuilding*, Glasgow, Alexander Stephen, 1950.

Raymond Challinor, *The Origins of British Bolshevism*, Croom Helm, 1978.

A.K. Chalmers (ed.), *Public Health Administration in Glasgow: A Memorial Volume of the Writings of James Burn Russell, BA, MD, LLD*, Glasgow, James Maclehose and Sons, 1905.

T. Chandler and G. Fox, *3000 Years of Urban Growth*, Academic Press, 1974.

D. Chapman, *Wartime Social Survey: The Location of Dwellings in Scottish Towns*, Edinburgh, 1943.

Olive Checkland, *Philanthropy in Victorian Scotland*, Edinburgh, John Donald, 1980.

S.G. Checkland, *The Upas Tree: Glasgow 1875-1975*, University of Glasgow Press, 1976.

James Clelland, *Statistical Facts Descriptive of the Former and Present State of Glasgow*, Glasgow, Bell and Bain, 1837.

Clydeside Cameos, Sketches of Prominent Clydeside Men, 1885.

Corporation of Glasgow, *Minutes.*

Corporation of Glasgow, *Question Books.*

Corporation of Glasgow Housing Department, *Review of Operations 1919-1927*, Glasgow, 1927.

Corporation of Glasgow Housing Department, *Review of Operations, 1919-1947*, Glasgow, 1947.

Archibald Craig, *The Elder Park, Govan: An Account of the Gift of the Elder Park and of the Erection and Unveiling of the Statue of John Elder*, Glasgow, James Maclehose, 1891.

Bob Crampsey, *The Empire Exhibition of 1938: The Last Durbar*, Edinburgh, Mainstream, 1988.

Bob Crampsey, *The Young Civilian: A Glasgow Wartime Boyhood*, Headline, 1987.

Richard Croucher, *Engineers at War*, Merlin Press, 1982.

J. Cunnison and J.B.S. Gilfillan, *The Third Statistical Account of Scotland: Glasgow*, Glasgow, Collins, 1984.

Seán Damer, *Property Relations and Class Relations in Victorian Glasgow*, University of Glasgow Discussion Papers in Social Research No. 16, 1976.

Seán Damer, 'State, Class, and Housing: Glasgow 1885-1919' in J. Melling (ed.), *Housing, Social Policy, and the State*, Croom Helm, 1980.

Seán Damer, *Rent Strike! The Clydebank Rent Struggles of the 1920s*, Clydebank District Library History Workshop Pamphlet, 1982.

Seán Damer, *State, Local State and Local Class Struggle: The Clydebank Rent Strike of the 1920s*, University of Glasgow Centre for Urban and Regional Research Discussion Paper No. 22, 1985.

Seán Damer, 'A Billy or a Dan?', *Cencrastus*, No. 32, New Year, 1989.

Seán Damer, *From Moorepark to 'Wine Alley': The Rise and Fall of a Glasgow Housing Scheme*, Edinburgh University Press, 1989.

Seán Damer and Ann McGuckin, *'The Good and the Bad': A Tale of Two Schemes*, ESRC Interim Report, University of Glasgow Centre for Housing Research, mimeo, 1989.

Margaret Thomson Davis, 'The Breadmakers Trilogy', (*The Breadwinners, A Baby Might be Crying, A Sort of Peace*), Panther, 1985.

Margaret Thomson Davis, *Rag Woman, Rich Woman*, Corgi, 1988.

Norma Denny, 'Self Help, Abstinence and the Voluntary Principal: The Ancient Order of Rechabites, 1835-1912', *Scottish Labour History Society Journal*, No. 24, 1989.

Department of Health for Scotland, *Working Class Housing on the Continent* (the 'Highton Report'), Edinburgh, HMSO, 1935.

T.M. Devine, *The Tobacco Lords*, Edinburgh, John Donald, 1975.

T.M. Devine and R. Mitchison (eds.), *People and Society in Scotland: Vol. 1, 1760-1830*, Edinburgh, John Donald, 1988.

Tony Dickson (ed.), *Scottish Capitalism: Class, State and Nation from before the Union to the Present*, Lawrence & Wishart, 1980.

P.J. Dollan, *Jubilee History of the Kinning Park Co-operative Society*, Kinning Park Co-operative Society, 1923.

Sir Patrick Dollan, typescript autobiography, n.d., Glasgow Collection, Mitchell Library.

Empire Exhibition: Scotland – 1938 : Official Guide, 1938.

Empire Exhibition 1938: Captain S. Graham's Report to the Administrative Committee, 11 January 1939.

Frederick Engels, *Condition of the Working Class in England*, Panther, 1969.

The Fairfield Shipbuilding and Engineering Works,

London, 1909.

Georgie Farish, 'What Did You Do During the War, Mummy?' in *A Bagful of Scripts*, Ibrox Writers' Group, 1989.

Peter Fife, *Housing of the Labouring Classes*, A Lecture Delivered Before the Glasgow and West of Scotland Architectural Craftsmen's Society, printed by order of the Corporation of Glasgow, Robert Anderson, 1899.

Gerry Finn, 'Multicultural Anti-Racism and Scottish Education', *Scottish Educational Review*, No. 19, 1987.

George Forbes and Paddy Meehan, *Such Bad Company*, Paul Harris, 1982.

John Foster and Charles Woolfson, *The Politics of the UCS Work-In*, Lawrence & Wishart, 1986.

Jim Fyrth, *The Signal was Spain: The Aid Spain Movement in Britain*, Lawrence & Wishart, 1986.

Tom Gallagher, *Glasgow: The Uneasy Peace*, Manchester University Press, 1987.

William Gallagher, *Revolt on the Clyde*, Lawrence & Wishart, 1978.

General Assembly of the Church of Scotland, *Annual Report*, 1928.

Andrew Gibb, *Glasgow: The Making of a City*, Croom Helm, 1983.

Glasgow, Burns Country. Dunoon. Rothesay. Arran, Ward, Lock and Coy, Illustrated Guide Book, n.d. (c. 1940).

Glasgow Chamber of Commerce Journal.

Glasgow Chamber of Commerce, *Glasgow Made it Through the Depression: How Glasgow Came Through the 1930s Depression*, Glasgow, n.d.

Glasgow Corporation and the University of Glasgow, *The Springburn Study*, 1967.

Glasgow Municipal Commission on the Housing of the Poor, Minutes of Evidence, Vol. 1, Glasgow, William Hodge, 1904.

Glasgow: Municipal Enterprises, Souvenir Handbook issued by the Corporation on the occasion of the 22nd Congress of the Sanitary Institute held in Glasgow

25-30 July 1904, Glasgow, Robert Anderson, 1904.

Glasgow Tribunal of Enquiry (Allegations of Bribery and Corruption): Report, Cmnd. 4361, 1933.

Glasgow Presbytery Commission on the Housing of the Poor, 1891.

Glasgow Sketches, 1889, book of newspaper cuttings in the Glasgow Room, Mitchell Library.

Ralph Glasser, *Growing Up In The Gorbals*, Pan, 1986.

W. Glen, *The Glasgow Council for Community Service in Unemployment: A Brief History*, typescript, 1951.

A. Gray and R. Currie, *Clyde Shipbuilding c.1900*, Strathclyde Department of Education, Dumbarton Division, 1987.

Cliff Hanley, *Dancing in the Streets*, White Lion, 1979.

James E. Handley, *The Irish in Scotland*, Glasgow, John Burns, 1945.

John Hannan, *The Life of John Wheatley*, Nottingham, Spokesman, 1988.

George Montagu Harris, *Municipal Self-Government in Britain*, King & Son, 1939.

Paul Harris, *Glasgow and the Clyde at War*, Archive Publications, 1986.

Christopher Harvie, *No Gods and Precious Few Heroes: Scotland since 1914*, Edward Arnold, 1981.

Archie Hind, *The Dear Green Place*, Hutchinson, 1966.

Robert Holton, 'Revolutionary Syndicalism and the British Labour Movement' in W. J. Mommsen and H.J. Husung (eds.), *The Development of Trade Unionism in Great Britain and Germany, 1880-1914*, Allen and Unwin, 1985.

Emrys Hughes (ed.), *Keir Hardie's Speeches and Writings*, Glasgow, Forward Publishing, n.d.

John R. Hume, *The Industrial Archaeology of Glasgow*, Blackie, 1974.

John R. Hume and M. Moss, *Beardmore: The History of a Scottish Industrial Giant*, Heinemann, 1979.

J. Hume and M. Moss, *Glasgow at War, Vol.1*, Nelson, Lancashire, Hendon Publishing Co., 1977.

H. Hunter, *Problems of Poverty: Selections from the*

Economic and Social Writings of Thomas Chalmers, DD, Nelson, n.d.

G. Hutchison and Mark O'Neill, *The Springburn Experience: An Oral History of Work in a Railway Community from 1840 to the Present Day*, Edinburgh, Polygon, 1989.

Tom Johnston, *A History of the Working Classes in Scotland*, Glasgow, Forward Publishing, 1929.

Gareth Stedman Jones, *Outcast London*, Penguin, 1975.

Billy Kay, *Odyssey*, Edinburgh, Polygon, 1980.

James G. Kellas, 'Highland Migration to Glasgow and the Origin of the Scottish Labour Movement', *Bulletin of the Society for the Study of Labour History*, No. 12, Spring 1966.

John R. Kellet, *Railways and Victorian Cities*, Routledge & Kegan Paul, 1979.

J.R. Kellet, 'Property Speculators and the Building of Glasgow', *Scottish Journal of Political Economy*, VIII, 1961.

W.F. Kendall, *The Revolutionary Movement in Britain, 1900-1921*, Weidenfeld and Nicolson, 1969.

Perilla Kinchin and Juliet Kinchin, *Glasgow Great Exhibitions: 1988, 1901, 1911, 1938, 1988*, White Cockade, n.d.

Elspeth King, *The Strike of the Calton Weavers, 1787*, Glasgow Museums and Art Galleries, 1987.

Elspeth King, *Scotland Sober and Free: The Temperance Movement 1829 – 1979*, Glasgow Museums and Art Galleries, 1979.

David Kirkwood, *My Life of Revolt*, Harrap, 1935.

John Kuusa and Anthony Slaven (eds.), *Development Problems in Historical Perspective*, Scottish and Scandinavian Shipbuilding Seminar, University of Glasgow, (mimeo) 1980.

Tony Lane, *Liverpool: Gateway to Empire*, Lawrence & Wishart, 1987.

D.E. Lindsay, *Report Upon a Study of the Diet of the Labouring Classes in the City of Glasgow, 1911-12*, University of Glasgow Physiology Department, 1913.

Sir Thomas Lipton, *Leaves from the Lipton Logs*, Hutchinson, n.d.

A.L. Lloyd, *Come All Ye Bold Miners: Ballads and Songs from the Coalfields*, Lawrence & Wishart, 1978.

Moira MacAskill, *Paddy's Market*, University of Glasgow Centre for Urban & Regional Research Discussion Paper No. 29, 1987.

Guy McCrone, *Wax Fruit*, Pan, 1984.

J. McCaffrey, 'Politics and the Catholic Community since 1878' in David McRoberts (ed.), *Modern Scottish Catholicism*, Glasgow, Burns, 1979.

Ian McDougall (ed.), *Essays in Scottish Labour History*, Edinburgh, John Donald, 1986.

Sir Alexander MacGregor, *Public Health in Glasgow*, Edinburgh and London, Livingstone, 1967.

William McIlvanney, *Laidlaw*, Coronet, 1977.

William McIlvanney, *The Papers of Tony Veitch*, 1983.

Stuart Macintyre, *Little Moscows*, Croom Helm, 1980.

Compton Mackenzie, *The Monarch of the Glen*, Penguin, 1983.

Peter Mackenzie, *Reminiscences of Glasgow and the West of Scotland*, 2 vols., Glasgow, John Tweed, 1867.

Farquhar McLay (ed.), *Workers City: The Real Glasgow Stands Up*, Glasgow, Clydeside Press, 1988.

Iain McLean, *The Legend of Red Clydeside*, Edinburgh, John Donald, 1983.

D. Maclennan and A. Gibb, *Glasgow: No Mean City to Miles Better*, University of Glasgow Centre for Housing Research Discusson Paper No. 18, 1988.

Iain MacPhaidein, *An T-Eileanach*, Glasgow, Alasdair Maclaren & Son, 1921.

Phil McPhee, 'Hutchie E – A Monument to Corruption, Stupidity and Bad Planning' in Farquhar McLay (ed.), op. cit.

David McRoberts (ed.), *Modern Scottish Catholicism 1878-1978*, Glasgow, Burns, 1979.

Harry McShane and Joan Smith, *No Mean Fighter*, Pluto Press, 1978.

Joseph Melling, *Rent Strikes: People's Struggles for Housing in West Scotland 1890-1916*, Edinburgh, Polygon, 1983.

Memorabilia of the City of Glasgow Selected from the Minute Books of the Burgh, MDLXXXVII – MDCCL, Glasgow, James Maclehose, 1868.

R.K. Middlemass, *The Clydesiders: A Left Wing Struggle for Parliamentary Power*, Hutchinson, 1965.

H. Miller, *Papers Relative to the State of Crime in Glasgow*, Glasgow, W. Lang, 1840.

Nan Milton, *John Maclean*, Pluto Press, 1973.

Minutes of the Hibernian Society of Glasgow, 1792-1824.

Gerry Mooney, *Living on the Periphery: Housing, Industrial Change and the State*, unpublished PhD thesis, University of Glasgow, 1988.

Nicholas Morgan, ' "£8 Cottages for Glasgow Citizens": Innovations in Municipal House-Building in Glasgow in the Inter-War Years' in Richard Rodger (ed.), *Scottish Housing in the Twentieth Century*, Leicester University Press,1989.

H.B. Morton, *Old Glasgow*, Glasgow: Richard Drew Publishing, 1987.

Michael Moss and John R. Hume, *Workshop of the British Empire: Engineering and Shipbuilding in the West of Scotland*, Heinemann, 1977.

J.H. Muir, *Glasgow in 1901*, Glasgow, William Hodge, 1901.

Patrick Mulvine, *32 Years in Prison*, n.d., c.1890.

William Naismith, *City Echoes; or Bitter Cries from Glasgow*, Paisley and London, Alexander Gardner, 1884.

Nothing But the Same Old Story: The Roots of Anti-Irish Racism, Information on Ireland, 1984.

C.A. Oakley, *The Second City*, Blackie, 1946.

John Ord, 'The Origins and History of the Glasgow Police Force', Paper No. 6 to the Old Glasgow Club, 1906, in *Old Glasgow Club: Transactions, Vol. 1, 1900-1908*, Glasgow, Aird & Coghill, 1908.

R. Page Arnot, *A History of the Scottish Miners*, Allen &

Unwin, 1955.

P.L. Payne (ed.), *Studies in Scottish Business History*, Cass, 1967.

Sydney Pollard and Paul Robertson, *The British Shipbuilding Industry, 1870-1914*, Harvard University Press, 1979.

William Power, *Pavement and Highway: Specimen Days in Strathclyde*, Glasgow, Archibald Sinclair, 1911.

W.J. McQuarrie Rankine, *A Memoir of John Elder, Engineer and Shipbuilder*, Blackwood, 1871.

Register of Police Officers in the Strathclyde Regional Archives.

Reports of the Sanitary Condition of the Labouring Population of Scotland, 1842.

Richard Rodger (ed.), *Scottish Housing in the Twentieth Century*, Leicester University Press, 1989.

Anthony Ross, 'The Development of the Scottish Catholic Community' in David McRoberts, *Modern Scottish Catholicism*, Glasgow, Burns, 1979.

Ellen Ross, 'Survival Networks: Women's Neighbourhood Sharing in London Before World War 1', *History Workshop Journal*, No. 15, 1983.

Royal Commission on the Housing of the Industrial Population of Scotland, Rural and Urban, Cmnd. 8371, 1917.

Sir Walter Scott, *Rob Roy*, Nelson, n.d.

W.R. Scott and J. Cunnison, *The Industries of the Clyde Valley During the War*, Oxford, Clarendon Press, 1924.

Scottish Council (Development and Industry), *Inquiry into the Scottish Economy, 1960-61*, Paisley, James Paton, 1961.

Scottish Office, *Industry and Employment in Scotland*, Cmnd. 7125, 1947.

Second Report from the Select Committee on Artisans and Machinery, Vol. V, 1824.

Senex (R. Reid), *Glasgow, Past and Present*, Glasgow, David Robertson, 1884.

'Shadow', *Midnight Scenes and Social Photographs, Being*

Sketches of Life in the Streets, Wynds, and Dens of the City, Glasgow, 1858, University of Glasgow Press reprint, 1976.

Dorothy Sheridan (ed.), *Among You Taking Notes: The Wartime Diaries of Naomi Mitchison 1939-1945*, Oxford University Press, 1986.

Edward Shields, *Gael Over Glasgow*, Sheed and Ward, 1957.

Percy Sillitoe, *Cloak Without Dagger*, Cassell, 1955.

A. Slaven, *The Development of the West of Scotland: 1750-1960*, Routledge & Kegan Paul, 1975.

A. Slaven and D. Aldcroft (eds.), *Banking, Business, and Urban History*, Edinburgh, John Donald, 1982.

A. Slaven and S. Checkland (eds.), *Dictionary of Scottish Business Biography*, Vol. 1, Aberdeen University Press, 1986.

William Smart, A Living Wage, *Proceedings of the Philosophical Society of Glasgow*, Vol. XXV, 1893-94.

Joan Smith, 'Class, Skill and Sectarianism in Glasgow and Liverpool, 1880 – 1914' in R.J. Morris (ed.), *Class, Power, and Social Structure in British Nineteenth Century Towns*, Leicester University Press, 1986.

Joan Smith, 'Labour Tradition in Glasgow and Liverpool', *History Workshop Journal*, No. 17, Spring 1984.

T.C. Smout, *A Century of the Scottish People, 1830-1950*, Fontana, 1987.

Alan Spence, *Its Colours They Are Fine*, Collins, 1977.

Strathclyde Regional Council, *Strathclyde Social Trends*, No. 2, Oct. 1989, A Report by the Chief Executive.

Hugh Thomas, *The Spanish Civil War*, Penguin, 1965.

Derrick Thomson, *An Introduction to Gaelic Poetry*, Victor Gollancz, 1977.

J. Treble, 'The Market for Unskilled Labour in Glasgow, 1891-1914' in Ian MacDougall (ed.), *Essays in Scottish Labour History*, Edinburgh, John Donald, 1986.

J. Treble, 'The Seasonal Demand for Adult Labour in Glasgow, 1890-1914', *Social History,* 3, 1, 1978.

Tweed's Guide to Glasgow, 1872, reprinted by the Molendinar Press, 1973.

Andrew Ward, *Scotland the Team*, Derby, Breedon Books, 1987.

Adna Ferrin Weber, *The Growth of Cities in the 19th Century: A Study in Statistics*, Ithaca, NY, 1967.

Beatrice Webb, *My Apprenticeship*, Longmans, 1926.

Tom Weir, *Highland Days*, G. Wright Publications, 1984.

Hamish Whyte (ed.), *Noise and Smokey Breath: An Illustrated Anthology of Glasgow Poems 1900-1983*, Glasgow Third Eye Centre and Glasgow District Libraries Publications Board, 1983.

David Witham, *Municipal Socialism*, unpublished MA dissertation, Middlesex Polytechnic, 1989.

C.W.J. Withers, *Gaelic in Scotland 1698-1981: The Geographical History of a Language*, Edinburgh, John Donald, 1984.

C.W.J. Withers, *A Glasgow Keek Show*, Glasgow, Richard Drew, 1981.

Ian Wood, 'Irish Immigrants and Scottish Radicalism, 1880-1906' in Ian MacDougall (ed.), op. cit.

Charles Woolfson and John Foster, *Track Record: The Story of the Caterpillar Occupation*, Verso, 1988.

Frank Worsdall, *The Tenement: A Way of Life*, Chambers, 1979.

James D. Young, *The Rousing of the Scottish Working Class*, Croom Helm, 1979.

Index

Lightning Source UK Ltd.
Milton Keynes UK
UKHW021355070919
349307UK00013B/1292/P